Commodore Moore and the Texas Navy

Commodore Edwin Ward Moore
Commander of the Navy of—
the Republic of Texas
Foster. RICHMOND, VA.

Courtesy Mr. Eugene Moore Cochran

Tom Henderson Wells
Commander, U.S.N.

COMMODORE MOORE
and the Texas Navy

 University of Texas Press, Austin

International Standard Book Number 0-292-71118-2
Library of Congress Catalog Card Number 60-7667
Copyright © 1960 by Tom Henderson Wells
All rights reserved
Printed in the United States of America

Second Paperback Printing, 1988

Requests for permission to reproduce material from
this work should be sent to Permissions, University
of Texas Press, Box 7819, Austin, Texas 78713-7819.

To my children

  Lucy
  Sally
  Tom
  Christopher
  Julia

Float on . . . Navy, whilst a foe
To Texas breathes in Mexico;
Till every tyrant on her shore
Shall tremble at the name of Moore . . .

Anonymous
The Daily Bulletin (Austin)
January 7, 1842

Foreword

As a Texan and a naval officer I wondered why the accomplishments of the Navy of the Republic of Texas have received so little appreciation. Now, after a lengthy search into the question, I have been forced to these conclusions: first, that General Sam Houston succeeded in his efforts to destroy the fame of the Navy, and, second, that sea power is but little understood.

The naval history of Texas from 1839 until annexation is a record of Edwin Ward Moore's struggle against envy, poverty, ineptness, and deceit, as well as against disease, storms, and enemy gunfire.

The young and gallant Commodore Moore is an appealing person. From the obscurity of a junior naval officer in the humdrum United States Navy of the 1830's, Edwin Ward Moore immediately came into the limelight as the Commander of the Navy of the infant Republic of Texas.

Moore had problems great enough to challenge his ability to meet them. Almost his first act upon coming to Texas at the age of twenty-nine involved him in conflict with the ruthless cunning, boundless ambition, and immense prestige of General Houston, victor of San Jacinto and former President of Texas.

The great problem which Commodore Moore faced was one which has dogged military men in crises ever since political authority became separated from military power: that is, what is a military commander to do when his political superior makes disastrous military decisions? Can the military man—or any citizen—permit his country to fall when by his own initiative he can save it? This has been a perplexing problem through the ages; down the centuries people have questioned the ultimate loyalty of their leaders, and tomorrow the question will still be pondered.

From a strictly professional point of view Commodore Moore had the formation of a genuine navy on his hands, and he alone in all of Texas had the background and training to form it. As the only really experienced officer, he was required by law to act as purchasing agent, comptroller, and technical advisor, while actively engaged in command of the little fleet. It is due to his remarkable abilities that he was able to keep command of the Gulf of Mexico for so long a period. Commodore Moore's naval strategy was sound, and his tactics were excellent.

Sail was giving way to steam, and the young commodore knew it. He pleaded for funds to repair his steamship; he bitterly assailed neglect of it and predicted disaster if without it he had to fight the two modern iron steamers of Mexico with their new-type guns. Yet, when he desperately took his sloop and brig into action against the steam warships, he was able, in the only successful naval action of its kind, to defeat them with his two sailing vessels. Without Commodore Moore's dogged determination, intrepid spirit, and great skill, Texas might well have fallen to Mexico in 1843, instead of joining with the United States in 1846.

Once his day of glory passed, Texas and the world lost sight of Moore. Few, indeed, are those who know he ever lived.

Contents

List of Illustrations

Commodore Moore and the Texas Navy

A New Commodore for a New Navy

The United States, determined to maintain the fifteen-year-old Monroe Doctrine, in 1838 sent a squadron of U.S. warships, including the sloop-of-war *Boston,* on a cruise around Gulf of Mexico ports. In May the *Boston* put into Galveston for a few days. This principal port of the new Republic of Texas, a muddy, snake-ridden hog wallow with a few wooden houses, which soon would have its first case of yellow fever, was the base for the two-ship Texas Navy:[1] one vessel a hulk on its side on the mud flats offshore, and the other, the *Potomac,* the only Texas vessel afloat, rotting alongside a pier. At Galveston also were a two-story house with a brick chimney, some warehouses, and a number of alcoholics in naval uniform passing command from one to the other before being cashiered or overtaken by death.

An interested observer was the *Boston*'s First Lieutenant, confident, enthusiastic, energetic Edwin Ward Moore. Considered un-

[1] Philip Tucker, "A History of Galveston" (Archives Collection, University of Texas, Austin), p. 102.

usually bright, Moore was described as a man of science and of un-
daunted gallantry.[2] He was five feet eight inches tall, with fair com-
plexion, blue eyes, and dark hair.[3] He was a charming and per-
suasive conversationalist, who could defend himself in both Spanish
and English. Moore was also a thorough seaman. When the *Boston*
left Galveston, Moore almost surely had been offered command of
the Texas Navy.

He had almost a year in which to make up his mind while the
situation in Texas clarified.

Texas, largely settled by people from the United States, had broken
free of Mexico in 1836. The United States had not intervened, but
Southerners had assisted with arms, money, and volunteers. Texas'
application to the United States in 1837 for annexation was rejected.
However, she was recognized as an independent nation by the
United States, and, later, by France, but not by Mexico. Though the
Mexican Army was unable to cross the desert in northern Mexico to
reconquer Texas, and the Mexican Navy as yet lacked the competency to launch a sea-borne expedition against Texas, and her political unrest protected Texas, Mexico still claimed Texas.

Such precarious independence gave Texas poor credit in a money
market already made tight by depression. When the Texas Congress
authorized the borrowing of $5,000,000, the loan commissioners were
not able to find lenders.

Texas was almost wholly dependent on the United States for munitions and reinforcements. Since her commerce was mostly water-
borne, she was forced to insure reliable sea communications with
the United States. The Texas Congress, seeing this need, passed on 4
November 1837 an act authorizing a rather sizeable navy, on the assumption that the loan would be made.[4]

There would be new sailors, new officers, and a new commander.
It was this new navy which interested Lieutenant Moore. He followed each step of its organization, watching to see whether Texas

[2] George P. Garrison (ed.), *Diplomatic Correspondence of the Republic of
Texas,* II, Part 1, 416.
[3] George F. Fuller, "Sketch of the Texas Navy," *The Quarterly of the Texas
State Historical Association,* VII, 223.
[4] George P. Garrison, *op. cit.,* II, Part 1, 354.

really wanted a navy, and to decide whether he wanted to be part of it.

President Houston appointed Samuel M. Williams naval commissioner with authorization to arrange the purchase of the new ships. Even though the Senate refused to confirm the appointment, Williams concluded contracts with Frederick Dawson of Baltimore during the fall after the *Boston*'s visit to Galveston.[5] The contract was brought before the 1838–1839 session of the Texas Congress for approval.

In December 1838 the Senate considered a resolution to reorganize the Navy, which would have resulted in its dissolution. The first of the new Navy's defenders, ardent Robert Wilson, thinking himself in the minority, and in need of powerful allies, called upon Almighty God to strike dead anyone who would be so unpatriotic as to try to abolish the Navy.[6] He was expelled, re-elected, and returned upon the shoulders of some of his constituents, one blowing a bugle.

The Congress not only kept the Navy and confirmed Samuel M. Williams' appointment and the contracts with Dawson, but even passed an act authorizing the purchase from France of the Mexican vessels she took after the Pastry War.

Lieutenant Moore must have felt that Texas was committed to having a navy, for when the *Boston* went in to Pensacola, he went on three weeks' leave to Texas in order to discuss command of the new navy.

Why should Moore consider leaving the United States Navy?

For one thing, promotion was dismally slow. Most of the great captains of the War of 1812 were still captains twenty-five years later, and some were to hold on until the 1860's. Those of Moore's contemporaries who remained in the U.S. service were not promoted to captain until the Civil War. Moore could be a captain and commander in chief of the Texas Navy immediately.

Also, in 1839 the United States Navy was reducing in size and was backward in technology. The Texas Navy, on the other hand, currently negotiating the purchase of a steamer, was expanding. The

[5] Fred Dawson to Samuel Williams, 24 November 1838, Williams Papers (Rosenberg Library, Galveston).

[6] *Telegraph and Texas Register,* 29 December 1838.

post captaincy of the Texas Navy carried with it command of her most powerful ship, a new sloop-of-war much better than the *Boston*. Moore could hope for a similar ship in the U.S. Navy within ten years, if he was lucky, and if he had the right congressman behind him. Meanwhile, he would have to struggle even to remain on active service.

There was yet another reason why Moore was willing to leave U.S. service. In the U.S. Navy of the 1830's the Secretary of the Navy assigned all officers' duties. Assignments depended upon service reputation, the desires of the captains, and the whim of the Secretary. Since there were more officers than there were jobs, officers spent much time on leave at half pay—some practicing law (as Raphael Semmes), others writing books (as Charles Wilkes), still others in merchant ships (as Franklin Buchanan), and some lucky few as gentlemen of means (as Robert Stockton). Moore had little personal means, and no profession outside the Navy. He could not hope for continuous naval employment in the United States. Yet, he wanted to be a naval officer.

Moore's enemies later accused him of having a "roaming and unsettled spirit."[7] He liked to go to sea; he endured the hardships for the joy of living the life. Yet he sought responsibility and relished the execution of difficult tasks. The organizing of a navy to fight in an area made for sea power was a challenge to his liking.

Not everything, however, argued for his entering the Texas Navy. If Texas lost to Mexico Moore could expect to be executed. If Texas became a part of the United States he could not expect his old messmates to receive him back in their midst with any enthusiasm. The decision which Moore must make was not an easy one, even for a man of his nature.

Edwin Ward Moore was born in Alexandria, then part of the District of Columbia, on 15 July 1810.[8] His grandfather, Cleon Moore, had come to Alexandria from Colchester, Virginia, to hold political

    [7] Edwin W. Moore, *Reply to Pamphlet by Commanders Buchanan, DuPont, and Magruder*.
    [8] Edwin W. Moore to the Secretary of the Navy, 19 March 1825, Letters Sent Conveying Appointments and Orders and Accepting Resignations, Navy Records (National Archives, Washington), p. 46.

appointments. The family apparently still held land at nearby Oc-coquan, and Moore spent parts of his boyhood and his leaves from the Navy there. His grandfather had been one of the petitioners for the Alexandria Academy, a boys' school for which George Washington was one of the trustees. Among the boys in Moore's class was Robert E. Lee.

Stories from his family heritage enriched Moore's boyhood. His Grandfather Moore had been a Revolutionary officer, proudly wound-ed at the Battle of Brandywine. His great uncle Cato had also been a Revolutionary officer. A Strother relative had been a midshipman in the Virginia Navy. His uncle, Alexander Moore, doubly but distantly related to George Washington by marriage, had fought the British before the White House in 1814. His father, Thomas Moore, was a vestryman at St. Paul's Church. Thomas and Alexander Moore were members, and occasionally officers, of the Masonic Lodge to which Washington belonged, and took part in the festivities of the visit of the Marquis de Lafayette in 1824. On all patriotic occasions the band played Cleon Moore's stirring "Washington March," a composition now forgotten.

On 19 March 1825, while still a boy of fourteen, Moore was sworn into the U.S. Navy.[9] The navy had not yet started an academy ashore, but clung to the idea of shipboard instruction except just before pro-motion examinations. Moore learned practical as well as theoretical seamanship, used his leave periods and time on the sick list to study, and once attended college in Charlestown, in present West Virginia. He always stood second highest in his group. Throughout his career Moore had a first-rate service reputation. Even his severest critics never found fault with his competency.

Apparently Moore acquired malaria in his first cruise and suffered from it frequently for the next twenty years.[10] Fever was so severe in the Gulf that every summer the fleet had to be withdrawn to cooler waters to avoid decimation, but even so, few sailors escaped the

[9] Edwin W. Moore to Levi Woodbury, 6 February 1833, Letters from Officers of Rank below that of Commander, Officers' Letters, 1834–1840, Navy Records (National Archives), p. 33.

[10] Navy Department to Passed Midshipman E. W. Moore, 4 September 1832, Letters Sent Conveying Appointments and Orders and Accepting Resignations, Navy Records (National Archives), p. 153a.

great epidemics. Once, in 1828, Moore had the good fortune to receive a Mediterranean assignment in the *Fairfield*. A year later he was returned to Norfolk in the *Delaware* for shore duty. Sick leave and college followed. In 1831 he returned to the *Fairfield,* this time as Sailing Master and Acting Lieutenant. After eleven months in the West Indies the fever hit him hard. Once more he went on sick leave.[11] Again and again he asked for assignments, received them, but had relapses which required cancellation of orders.[12] Finally, in 1835, he was well enough to receive advancement to lieutenant, again second highest in his promotion group. Soon he had the orders which brought him south in the *Boston*.

When the *Boston* left the Boston Navy Yard 10 July 1836, she had extra officers and men for the West Indian Squadron. Moore was the sixth senior of eight lieutenants aboard. On the eighteenth a West Indian hurricane swept away her quarterboat and its davits. She rolled and labored so heavily that her Captain, Master Commandant Bladen Dulaney, was afraid that she would capsize (she actually did founder at sea several years later). Dulaney asked his lieutenants for their recommendations for saving the ship. Moore wrote the reply which suggested jettisoning 150 of the 32-pound shot and scuttling the berth deck to drain the water from the cabin and spar and berth decks into the bilges, where it could be pumped overboard. This was done, and the *Boston* limped into St. Thomas two weeks later with ten or fifteen men on the sick list but only one missing—a seasick marine who had jumped overboard during the storm.[13]

In September the *Boston* captured the little Texas privateer *Terrible,* and took her in to Pensacola for investigation as a possible pirate. This seems to have been Moore's first naval contact with the Texas Republic.[14]

[11] Edwin W. Moore to John Boyle, Chief Clerk, Navy Department, 7 April 1833, Letters from Officers of Rank below that of Commander, Officers' Letters, 1834–1840, Navy Records (National Archives), p. 22.

[12] Bladen Dulaney to Secretary of the Navy, 29 July 1836, Master Commandants' Letters, Navy Records (National Archives), p. 20.

[13] Log of the U.S.S. *Boston,* Navy Records (National Archives), 20 September 1836.

[14] Edwin W. Moore, "Statement of Service Accepted by Office Adjudicating Claims for Pensions or Bounty Lands," Record Group No. 15A (National Archives).

In February 1837 the *Boston* was stationed off the southwest pass of the Mississippi with orders to convoy every American vessel cleared by customs and destined for Texas, Matamoros, Tampico, or Veracruz.

Much of the *Boston*'s service was involved in supporting the Army's Seminole campaign. Most of the time this required long, monotonous patrols between the Bahamas and Florida to prevent arms-smuggling. Once Moore, co-operating with the Army, led the *Boston*'s boats in a successful expedition against Indians at Mullet Key at the entrance to Tampa Bay. A body of Seminole Indians was captured.[15]

Moore's seagoing background in the U.S. Navy made him an ideal choice for the head of the Texas Navy. He was familiar with Mexican ports. He had dealt with consuls and foreign navies. A year in the Norfolk Navy Yard had taught him how to manage funds, repairs, and alterations problems. He had a thorough background of many years' service on the Gulf in small ships. He was young enough to be flexible, and mature enough to have solid judgment. In one thing only was Moore lacking: experience at the seat of government.

No correspondence between Moore and Texas about his entry into the Texas Navy can be found. However, there is little doubt that Moore made a tentative agreement during a hurried visit to Texas in March, 1839. Texas authorities began referring to him in private correspondence in April. Moore did not resign from the U.S. Navy, because he needed a job until the new Texas ships were ready. He knew that he would have no trouble in resigning when the time was ripe; too many midshipmen were awaiting promotion.

Returning from his leave in Texas, Moore missed ship when the *Boston* sailed from Pensacola. He reported in to the Navy Department in Washington, writing to Commodore William B. Shubrick an explanation, which apparently was accepted. Moore's letter could not be found when he asked for it in 1846; it is still missing.

No sooner had Moore got back to Washington after this leave than his name began to appear in the papers as the commanding officer of the Texas Navy. This surprised the Secretary of the U.S. Navy, who

[15] George Bancroft to Commodore Edwin W. Moore, 28 February 1846, General Letter Book XXXVI, Navy Records (National Archives), p. 94.

immediately wrote to Moore demanding an explanation.[16] Moore said that he didn't belong to the Texas Navy, that he was a member of the U.S. Navy only. Then rumors began to go around town that he was recruiting from the *Boston,* and, furthermore, that he had enlisted some eighty of the crew. It was also rumored that he talked as many as fifty junior officers in the U.S. Navy into resigning. These rumors made considerable publicity in the U.S. just then because the Washington *Globe* had recently completed a series of articles exposing the inefficiencies and inequalities in Navy personnel matters. Also, the United States was trying to recruit men for a cruise to the Mediterranean and was having to delay the ships because of a lack of sailors.

Secretary of the Navy James K. Paulding was attempting to tighten up the slack administration of his predecessor. He kept writing to the commandants in New York and Baltimore asking for information on Moore's status and his recruiting activity. Commodore Charles Ridgley in New York said that he had it on pretty good authority that Moore actually was recruiting. One of Ridgley's officers, a Commander Forrest, had heard from Moore's cousin, Alex Moore, that Alex himself was recruiting and was going to be an officer in the Texas Navy.

It is possible that Moore was actively recruiting; however, he seems to have tried to stay out of Texas' business until he entered its service. For instance, when Texas Secretary of the Navy Memucan Hunt sent him instructions to buy pistols, Moore waited until he had left the U.S. Navy before placing the order. But he was First Lieutenant of the *Boston,* had spent three years on the ship, and was well-known, admired, and respected. His brother James had married and gone to Texas in 1832.[17] Moore himself, having recently visited Texas, was informed on prospects there. The *Boston* sailors were being paid off after their long cruise, and were naturally interested in the new navy being formed. Moore must have been a first-rate recruiter, even if he never actually spoke a word for the Texas Navy.

[16] James K. Paulding to E. W. Moore, 29 April 1839, Letter No. 216, Letters to Officers, Ships of War, Navy Records (National Archives), p. 414.
[17] Certificate dated 1 February 1838, Texas General Land Office Records (General Land Office, Austin).

Moore denied recruiting, denied connection with the ships build-ing in Baltimore, and denied appointment in the Texas Navy until finally the Secretary of the Navy started gathering information and witnesses for a possible court-martial.[18] One of the people the Secre-tary was anxious to reach was a boy named Samuel Edgerton, who had served under Moore in the *Boston*.[19] The Secretary heard a rumor that Edgerton was going into the Texas Navy to be the Com-modore's steward. The Secretary tried to re-enlist Edgerton, but was not successful. Edgerton came into the Texas Navy, was the Commo-dore's steward, and died on board the *Austin* near Tabasco in 1840.

Moore submitted his resignation on 8 July 1839, merely stating that he wanted to resign from the naval service.[20] It was accepted in writing on the sixteenth. The next day the Secretary of the Navy at-tempted to rescind the approval of the resignation, but was too late. Moore was already out of the United States Navy, and was free to enter the Texas Navy.

Moore stayed in New York for a while watching a test of a gun whose shot had an explosive in it. He wanted to get this type of am-munition for Texas, because it was believed to be vastly superior to solid shot. Solid shot could be fired more accurately and was longer-ranged, and it did more damage to the hull than shell or fragmenting projectiles; but since most commanders in those days wanted to cap-ture the other vessel for prize money rather than to sink it, they pre-ferred to disable her or kill her men.[21]

Moore started his journey to Texas in late August, arriving in Gal-veston on 4 October 1839 aboard the SS *Columbia*. There in Galves-ton were the first units of the new navy: the steamer *Zavala* (origi-nally the *Charleston*) and the little schooners *San Jacinto* (originally the *Viper*), the *San Antonio* (originally the *Asp*), and the *San Bernard* (originally the *Scorpion*). There also was the ninety-five–ton schooner *Louisville* (often called the *Striped Pig*), a watering vessel

[18] J. K. Paulding to Commodore Charles G. Ridgley, 1 June 1839, Letters to Officers, Ships of War, XXVII, Navy Records (National Archives), p. 42.

[19] J. K. Paulding to Commodore Jacob Jones, 24 June 1839, Letters to Officers, Ships of War, XXVII, Navy Records (National Archives), p. 77.

[20] Edwin W. Moore to J. K. Paulding, 8 July 1839, Resignations of Officers of the U.S. Navy, 1834–1840, Navy Records (National Archives), p. 212.

[21] E. B. Potter (ed.), *The United States and World Sea Power*, p. 264.

which Navy Agent William Brannum bought complete with sails, rigging, and seven water casks for $4,000 on 25 September.[22]

The most controversial of the vessels was the side-wheel steamer *Zavala*. She was bought in Charleston, South Carolina, by General James Hamilton, former governor of South Carolina and now Texas consul to Charleston. He had bought the ship, then requested authorization. The *Zavala* had three boilers, horizontal steam reciprocating engines, and paddle wheels on both sides, as well as a full set of sails. In her best days she made the 392-mile cruise from New Orleans to Galveston in 42 hours, an average of over 9 knots.[23] She burned coal, cord wood, and furniture in that order of preference, and in a similar voyage used 290 barrels of coal and 60 cords of wood. She was in constant need of repairs. This is not surprising inasmuch as steam was still a highly controversial subject in naval circles in the United States. While England had 55 steamships in her navy and France had 37, the United States had fewer than Sardinia and Sweden, only a single steamer, and that one the Naval Board wished to withdraw from service.

The United States did not have the industrial capacity to support many steamships nor the engineers to run them. The great days of the clipper ships were still ten or fifteen years in the future; steam technology lagged.

Texas was in far worse shape, not having any shipyards experienced in steam and only a very small navy yard. Even in Galveston there was practically no one who could do mechanical work.

The three schooners were the first vessels to be delivered under the Dawson contract. These speedy little 130-ton vessels were only 66 feet long, with six 12-pound short-ranged broadside guns. One of the schooners was supposed to have a 12-pounder pivot gun in place of two of the broadside guns. Each gun was to have 25 rounds of powder and 25 rounds of shot, 13 canister, and 12 grapeshot. The schooners were supposed to carry 12 muskets, 8 pistols, and 15 cutlasses for a full complement of 13 officers and warrant officers and 69 sailors

[22] Nelson J. Maynard to William Brannum, 24 June 1840, Texas Navy Papers (Archives, Texas State Library, Austin).

[23] Log of the *San Bernard*, 6 March 1840, Navy Records (National Archives).

and marines.[24] They were good ships, fast enough to outrun anything they could not outfight, with shallow draft in order to come close inshore. However, they were as tricky as yachts and required an alert watch and hardy crews. These little fellows with their very tall masts raking aft, low freeboard, and saucy air, must have delighted the new Commodore's eyes.

[24] Harriet Smither (ed.), *Journals of the Fourth Congress, Republic of Texas,* III, 119.

Fitting Out

In early October 1839, Moore set out for Austin, probably accompanied by Captain A. C. Hinton of the *Zavala*, making the journey through muddy river bottoms on horseback. The hills across the Colorado River were blanketed with oak and cedar, and green winter grass, after September rains, covered the spots left bare by the summer's sun. In spite of its remoteness and the danger of Indian attacks, the city was booming. Several hundred people now lived in Austin; immigrants came daily. Building lots were selling for $700. Many people had moved into their cabins after camping out on the ground since the founding of the city the winter before. A hundred or more cabins had been built. The President's house was the best, being two-story with porticos front and rear. A large two-room cabin with center hall housed Congress. The Navy office fared less luxuriously, and was in confusion from moving.

Secretary of the Navy Louis P. Cooke was fretting about expenses. He needed money. Everywhere he turned requisitions faced him. Provisions for the ships cost 300 per cent to 400 per cent more if bought in Texas than if bought in the United States.

Secretary Cooke realized his shortcomings in details about the employment of seapower. He asked President Lamar for a full-time naval officer assistant for technical matters.[1] When his recommendation was not taken the Navy was crippled. Time and again the fleet suffered from mismanagement and lack of informed support in the capital.

Moore had to call on the Secretary of the Navy and on President Mirabeau B. Lamar. As the new operating head of the Navy he needed policy guidance from his superiors and the opportunity to tell them what was necessary to carry out the policy. Just now the policy was to build and train a navy of a size and composition already determined, so that it could fulfil whatever mission might later be assigned.

First of all the ships needed men. The *Zavala* was manned by engineers pirated off the steamer *Rochester* by Captain James Pennoyer,[2] but the Dawson contract ships were being delivered by contractors. General Richard G. Dunlap, the Texas minister to the United States, had earlier written recommending that recruiting be done in New York, since one small ship would pass practically unnoticed in that great harbor, and ex-USN sailors would be available.[3] Then, too, firearms, technical books, and instruments were readily available in the big Atlantic coast ports. Secretary Cooke gave Moore orders to prepare the *Wharton* (then known as the *Colorado*) for the recruiting voyage and to assume command. He was given $40,000 and the authority to draw on the naval agent, John G. Tod, if he needed more money. The *Wharton*, built in Baltimore, had been delivered by an American crew to Galveston about a week after Commodore Moore left for Austin.

The *Zavala* was ordered to New Orleans for alterations and repairs. While Moore was still in the U.S. Navy, the *Zavala's* captain, Commander Hinton, wrote the then Secretary of the Navy, Memucan Hunt, described the *Zavala,* and requested money and authority to

[1] Charles A. Gulick, Jr., and others (eds.), *The Papers of Mirabeau Buonaparte Lamar*, No. 1360.

[2] James Pennoyer to Samuel M. Williams, 23 October 1838, Williams Papers (Rosenberg Library, Galveston).

[3] George P. Garrison (ed.), *Diplomatic Correspondence of the Republic of Texas*, II, Part 1, 410.

take her to New York or Baltimore, where he thought alterations could be done best and at the least cost.[4] However, he was now ordered to New Orleans.

Hinton wrote that the *Zavala* had a long 18-pounder, a long 12-pounder pivot gun and four 18-pounder medium-range guns with a space to mount two more 18-pounders. He thought the *Zavala* needed strengthening to hold the guns, and that she should have protection for her exposed engines. He recommended sale of her passenger-ship furnishings, which he estimated would bring about $10,000 in frontier Texas and thus pay for her own alterations. Hinton's recommendations were sound; they should have been accepted.

Hinton was given $9,000 to make the repairs and alterations designated by Moore after he inspected the *Zavala*, and to recruit sailors and marines. Hinton thought his instructions indicated a lack of confidence in his abilities; he resented Moore's appointment over him, and the more liberal treatment of Moore by the Secretary.

Poor Hinton was in over his head. He had had a few years' experience as a junior officer in the United States Navy, had resigned, had gone to South America, then had come to Texas, where he worked a few months as a clerk, read law, and finally came into the Texas Navy in 1837. He went to New Orleans in the *Zavala*, his first command, knowing little about mechanics, finances, or diplomacy. The *Zavala* was probably the first steam man-of-war Hinton had seen.

Upon reaching New Orleans he had troubles immediately. He wrote to Secretary Cooke right away saying he needed three or four thousand dollars more for necessary additional repairs. In view of the thoroughness of Moore's inspection it is amazing that Hinton should have discovered the need of a new foremast and new berth deck once he got to New Orleans.[5] His request arouses the suspicion either that Hinton was padding his repair list in order to make a profit or that he was being duped by contractors.

Then he found that Navy Agent William T. Brannum had already spent for other things $1,500 of his $5,800 maintenance money. Next,

[4] Harriet Smither (ed.), *Journals of the Fourth Congress, Republic of Texas,* III, 334.

[5] Harriet Smither (ed.), *Journals of the Sixth Congress, Republic of Texas,* III, 334.

it developed that New Orleans yards wanted cash for work done as it progressed instead of making up estimates in advance and collecting upon completion. This situation resulted probably, in part, because Texas credit was so notoriously poor and inflation was growing, and partly because the New Orleans yard, Bailey and Massy, wanted to keep revising its estimates, locating new work and running up bills.[6]

The harassed Hinton wrote weekly reports to Secretary Cooke, who, lacking technical knowledge and facing difficulties of confirmation (he was finally confirmed for his job by a 7–6 vote of the Senate on 4 January 1840), simply did not reply. Hinton did not know how much his over-expenditure would be; he thought three or four thousand dollars on 29 November, seven thousand on 7 January. When the bills were finally received in February he had spent $14,000 more than had been authorized. The only word he got from Secretary Cooke was a reprimand received 20 January 1840 that merely told him to quit offering gratuitous advice, to remain within the $9,000 allotted, and to stop talking about *good* money. Cooke said, with great calmness, that he knew of only one kind of money, good Texas Dollars, which, he neglected to add, had dropped from 1:4 to 1:5 in the New Orleans market.[7]

Hinton wanted advice or orders; he received a reprimand, which only added confusion. His sailors became more and more of a problem. Instead of being a smart-looking, enthusiastic lot, the sailors were being starved and frozen into desertion, on one such occasion appropriating the captain's gig. At one time the doctor certified that the sailors would develop serious illness unless warmer clothing were given to them; many had never received their initial outfitting of winter uniforms. Storms and rain held up work; with the delay, wharfage and food bills climbed. Hinton drew $726 of his own pay, most of which he said he lent his officers. Lieutenant Francis B. Wright of the *San Antonio* came to New Orleans to take out the few recruits Hinton had shipped, and left in a confusion of bad debts, charges, and counter charges. There apparently had been bad blood

[6] *Ibid.*, II, 336.

[7] *Journals of the House of Representatives, Republic of Texas, Fifth Congress, First Session*, p. 238.

between Wright and Hinton for some time. It was unfortunate for Hinton that Wright got back to Texas before Hinton, because his relationship with Wright was just one more count against Hinton when Secretary Cooke finally decided to act.

The bad thing for Hinton was that by the time things had really got out of hand, it was too late for him to do anything. Had he turned right around the first week and returned to Galveston without the completion of any work, he would have stayed out of trouble, but he would have gained a reputation for not getting things done. So he tried, and, like the rest of Texas, hoped that money would come in from somewhere, and that the *Zavala* could be a fine steam warship with a full crew and tiptop engines, rigging, and hull, ready for the big battle which would once for all make Mexico recognize Texas independence, open Texas to foreign trade, investment, and settlement, and incidentally get Hinton off the hook. Unfortunately for Hinton, instead of money, all he got was a curt dismissal from the Navy on 6 February 1840 in New Orleans. He went home to Texas hurt, bewildered, and bitter.

Hinton wrote to the Secretary of the Navy, to the President, and finally memorialized Congress requesting reinstatement in the Navy. A year later, Congress, while considering Hinton's case, passed an act making it unlawful to deprive an officer of his commission without court-martial.[8] This act was later to become an important part of the defence of Commodore Moore.

Hinton's case should have taught the Texas government a number of lessons about naval administration, but the lessons were not learned. The faults remained to plague Moore throughout his service to the Texas Navy.

One was the need for experienced naval officers in the capital who could issue sensible orders, understand the problems of the forces afloat, and give advice on naval matters. Lieutenant P. W. Humphries was brought up to help the Secretary as a clerk, but he was soon supplanted.

Another lesson was that orders should clearly state what the recipient is to do if he is unable to carry out his instructions. A third

[8] Joint Resolution Approved 4 February 1841, H. P. N. Gammel, *Laws of Texas*, II, 609.

was that naval commanders must receive enough information about policy of the government to be able to make sound decisions in the absence of definite orders. A fourth lesson was that the Texas Navy needed an administrative procedure for the handling of funds.

Hinton's orders of 29 October 1839, although they appear clear enough, left no room for the contingencies which so regularly arise when ships are overhauled in foreign ports. A ship is a complicated affair that frequently has grave, even dangerous, faults, which must be corrected immediately; otherwise, the repairs will cost a great deal later on, or the vessel may be lost. Commanders either must have orders which give them latitude in the expenditure of funds, or else must have a rapid means of communication with their headquarters ashore. The headquarters must be able to make and transmit its decision in time to make sense. Either the ship must hold the purse strings, or her captain must have access to the person who does.

Hinton's troubles were very likely the final reason for the withdrawal of the names of the navy officers submitted to the Senate for confirmation 18 November 1839. There were many arguments about the list. The Houston faction was unhappy that any appointments at all had been made by President Lamar while Congress was not in session. There was bickering about the relative rank of various officers. Several from the old Texas Navy had their relative seniority changed and were unhappy about their new positions. Room somewhere had to be made for John G. Tod, whom Memucan Hunt had promised the second rank in the Navy when Hunt was Secretary of the Navy. Unconfirmed gossip about scandalous conduct of some Texas Navy officers in New Orleans reached Texas. Lamar withdrew his nominations. The officers of the Navy served for three years without commissions.

This may seem an unimportant detail, but officers in those days frequently had to produce the authority of their commissions to legitimize captures, blockades, etc. Without commissions, they were neither men-of-warsmen nor privateers, having no letters of marque. Legally, the capture of a ship at sea by the Texas Navy ships might be argued to be an act of piracy.

John T. K. Lothrop became commanding officer of the *Zavala*. The special fittings for passenger cabins had been taken out; the galleys and ornate stairways were removed; additional guns, holds, and berthing space were installed. She received new parts in the main engines, a new foremast, replacement of about one third of the berth deck, and some new copper sheathing on the bottom.

Meanwhile, Commodore Moore had his own mission to perform. His vessel, the *Wharton* (formerly the *Colorado*), was about 110 feet long with displacement of 405 tons, and with sixteen 18-pounder medium-range guns. Her war complement was 19 officers and 112 men. She was allowed muskets, pistols, and cutlasses for her complement, and she had five boats.[9] Moore took her over to New Orleans in mid-November 1839 and then headed for New York.

The Neutrality Act of 1818 prohibited foreign navies to recruit in United States ports. The *Wharton*'s recruiting might not have been noticed if the port had been crowded with sailors so that all United States Navy ships could fill their crews, but it happened that for some time fewer and fewer sailors were on the waterfront looking for berths. Many guesses were made as to the reasons: that sailors were leaving the sea, that illness reduced their numbers, or that long overdue ships had not come into port. Whatever the cause of the shortage, Moore arrived at a poor time for inconspicuous recruiting.

The *Wharton* was greeted warmly. Close kinship was felt with the Texans struggling to be independent of Mexico. The sight of the beautiful little *Wharton* in the harbor, the fine reputations of her officers, the snappy appearance of her sailors in their new uniforms with pay in U.S. dollars in their pockets aroused much interest ashore. So, too, did the news of her swift voyage. She had left the southwest pass below New Orleans on 20 November at 6 A.M., and arrived on the evening of 10 December. Had she not run into a gale 158 miles off New York she would have beaten the mail.

The *Wharton*, towed up the narrows, passed in full view of the sailors in the Brooklyn Navy Yard, and then anchored so that the battery was between the *Wharton* and the yard, and small boats full of recruits could not be observed from across the East River. This anchorage was exposed to ice coming down the Hudson. Moore left orders for safety measures, but during one of his absences they were

---

[9] Harriet Smither (ed.), *Journals of the Fourth Congress, Republic of Texas*, III, 119.

not carried out, and the brig received some slight ice damage.[10] Moore did not immediately plunge into recruiting. He first set about giving the cruise an appearance of conformity with the Neutrality Act. He sent his powder ashore to the U.S. Navy magazines at Ellis Island, and started work on the *Wharton's* magazines. He bought fifty new-style rifles and fifty pistols which later became famous as the favorite of the Texas Rangers. He bought books on steam engineering and other subjects for the officers and midshipmen to study. He bought navigation equipment and instruments and the best lifeboat in the world at the time, a Francis self-bailing boat. He bought boats for the other ships. He spent $7,000 over the $40,000 he had been given, but this being allowed for in his orders, he drew on Navy Agent J. G. Tod for the amount.

Moore took justifiable pride in his rapid rise from a junior lieutenant, second in command of a U.S. naval vessel, to the senior officer in a rising little navy of six sailing ships and a steamer. He was received by his former seniors with all the pomp and ceremony which would otherwise have been denied him for twenty more years.

After a consultation with J. Prescott Hall, a lawyer, Moore was ready for recruiting. The good word had got around. A rendezvous was set up ashore with the assistance of R. and J. W. Benson (or Benjamin Benson) a tailor, Rufus Rowe (or Hughes) a butcher, and Robert Tilford (or Tolford) and James Jackson, watermen. Enthusiasm for the Texas cause swept the waterfront. Many sailors enlisted, signing statements that they were "sailormen hailing from Texas and calling themselves Texians," which made the enlistments practically legal. Texas Navy pay was the same as the U.S. Navy pay. Moore's men were subjected to the same discipline, privations, and poor food as those in the U.S. Navy. But adventure and prize money were to be had in Texas, for renewed war with Mexico awaited only the fleet's return from New York and New Orleans. Besides, the Texas Navy had Commodore Moore. He took back to New York many of the men he had earlier enlisted there; his character and leadership were well-known on the waterfront. Even the untrue story that tea

[10] Edwin W. Moore to General A. S. Johnston, 9 December 1841, Mrs. Mason Barret Collection of Johnston Papers (Howard-Tilton Memorial Library, Tulane University, New Orleans).

had replaced grog in the Texas Navy did not ruin recruiting. About
seventeen midshipmen and a hundred twenty men signed up. Recruiting was going all too well.

More than one U.S. ship was noticing empty hammock hooks,
while the *Wharton* had to install a hundred twenty-five extra hooks
for men signed on board above complement. Lieutenant Charles S.
Hunter of the U.S.S. *North Carolina* made official complaint against
Moore, swearing Moore was violating the Neutrality Act of 1818.[11]

Moore was arrested on 30 December 1839. His one-thousand-
dollar bail was posted by the Texas government, but he borrowed
$400.00 of it back. Arrested with him and held to the same bail were
his recruiters. Recruiting continued nevertheless, with Moore unable
to take receipts (to avoid possible legal complications) for the
twenty-dollar bounty money for enlistments.

While Moore was busy recruiting and fending off the law, there
was trouble in Texas. On 15 January the New York *Morning Herald*
reported a proposition in the Texas Congress to lay up the Navy and
sell the *Zavala*. To Moore in New York, it must have appeared that
the Texas Congress, having invested a third of a million dollars in
ships, and depending on the Navy entirely for forcing recognition
from Mexico, would not fall for a measure such as this in order to
save a few thousand dollars.

Moore was getting good men. With some drill they would soon be
ready to fight Mexico. When President Lamar gave the order, the
fleet would carry the brunt of the operation. It could take command
of the Gulf. Command could probably be maintained, because
Moore's ships could prevent the delivery of any single or small groups
of warships to Mexico, and could prevent trade from going on between Mexico and the outside world.

United States Secretary of State John Forsyth, never a friend of
Texas, did not forget Moore's recruiting. He wrote General Dunlap
a note about Moore. Dunlap, who had made the original suggestion
for recruiting in New York,[12] expressed horror at the thought that
anyone would so grossly violate United States neutrality, and assured Forsyth that Moore had explicit orders not to do such a thing.

[11] George P. Garrison, *op. cit.*, II, Part 1, 436.
[12] *Ibid.*, p. 411.

Forsyth rather brusquely reiterated the charges, and stated that if the offence was repeated he would bar all Texas Navy ships from U.S. ports.[13] Moore saved everyone embarrassment by bringing his powder back aboard on 4 January, and departing New York on 21 January 1840. Correspondence about the affair continued, but nothing more was done. Presumably the remaining $600.00 of Moore's bail was forfeited.

[13] *Ibid.,* p. 437.

Shaking Down

The *Wharton* arrived off Galveston on 8 February 1840, only three days after the Fourth Congress adjourned. It was generally known in Galveston that the Houston faction in Congress would cut down the Navy as it had furloughed the whole Army. When the news finally reached Moore, it was black. An act approved on the last day of Congress kept just two schooners in commission—and these for the purpose of making coastal surveys.

The Commodore and his sailors got a quick indoctrination concerning Texas legislative logic, and it is a wonder the new fleet did not begin its history with a full-fledged mutiny. The Republic had spent $120,000 (U.S.) for ships, Moore had invested $50,000 (U.S.) in New York, and Hinton had made it another $10,000, all together totaling nearly $200,000. With the price of the *Zavala*, the sum of par funds spent on the Navy grew to a third of a million dollars. The cost per month for running the fleet was $5,000 or $6,000.

There was no question in Moore's mind but that he could cover the initial investment cost of the Navy and pay operating expenses, as well as wring recognition out of Mexico, if given a free hand. He was then appointed to do the job. The ships were bought for it. He had shipped sailors to fight, to capture ships, and to lay cities under contribution. Mexico was weak, but rich. France had shown the way the year before in her Pastry War. She had left Mexico without a warship and with its principal sea fort in ruins, its government in revolution, and a $600,000-indemnity to pay. An aggressive Texas could do the same with sea power; this tiny Republic was capable of humiliating a country with a population fifty times greater.[1]

Was it the urge to economy which made Congress wreck Texas defence? Texas had always been in miserable shape financially. The Bank of the United States was in the middle of its financial rebellion against the United States and vice versa, and money was tight in American circles. Europe was suspicious of everything in the Western Hemisphere, and loans were hard to get. There was plenty of justification for financial worry, and cutting expenditures to the bone was a popular policy. A clever leader could use these predilections to economy to serve his own ends.

The Navy made a hit with the Texas people when it assembled in Galveston. There were few things besides visions and dreams that the Texans could be proud of. Their capital was a collection of log cabins. The principal seaport was a treeless, sun-baked sandbank, except at rainy times, when it was knee-deep in mud. Wrecked ships littered its harbor and beaches. But on the blue water of the bay rode the new fleet at anchor, visible evidence of Texas' partially realized hope. Texas money was engraved with pictures of the new ships, along with longhorn cattle and lone stars.

Yet these same ships were to be laid up, their sails taken ashore, the Lone Star flag lowered, the ammunition stored, the spars stacked in a warehouse, the sailors dismissed, the not-yet-commissioned officers discharged. When the *Zavala* returned in full fighting condition her costly engine would be allowed to rust. Sam Houston had seized leadership of Congress.

One by one officials came on board to see these vessels they had argued over, discussed, worked for, or voted against. A warship is

[1] George P. Garrison (ed.), *Diplomatic Correspondence of the Republic of Texas,* II (1), Part II, 761.

impressive; these visits to the snappy ships of the exacting Commodore Moore did not fail to stir the patriotism of the officials.

When Sam Houston saw how popular the fleet was, he, too, came on board. He said all the things that would later look well in print, and he found a Navy supporter to say them to, a man who would see that Houston's remarks were recorded. He told Senator Francis Moore of Galveston (who had been elected that autumn to the seat held the year before by Senator Wilson) that he regretted his opposition to the Navy and hoped the ships would be sent to sea immediately.

The words would be quoted in the country's newspapers. They would be quoted again by Houston in later speeches if necessary to show where he apparently had stood in regard to the Navy in March, 1840, and yet he was committed to little actual support.

Francis Moore, not related to the Commodore, who carefully recorded Houston's words as Houston knew he would, was a Navy booster.[2] He, as editor of the *Telegraph and Texas Register,* as a senator, and as a private citizen, supported the Navy throughout the existence of the Republic. He was particularly impressed with the vigor and enthusiasm of the officers, and he urged President Lamar to order the ships to Mexico, where he knew they would be worth ten thousand men in forcing recognition.

Commodore Moore at this point could have left his ships and rushed off to the capital to get the latest information or to convince the President that an emergency existed. A year or so later he might have done this, but he was not yet used to Texas politics. He trusted his superior, Secretary of the Navy Cooke, to fight for the Navy. Moore expected, like the good sailor he was, to concentrate on the preparation of his ships for sea, on training his crews by hard work, and on preventing, by vigilance, the desertion of his sailors. Some men had joined the Texas Navy with the intention of deserting in Texas, but Moore kept very small the opportunity to disappear into the wilderness. The ships were anchored out. Even if a sailor got ashore in Galveston, he was still on an island.

Twenty-nine-year-old Secretary Cooke was utterly uninformed on

[2] Charles A. Gulick, Jr., and others (eds.), *The Papers of Mirabeau Buonaparte Lamar,* No. 1741.

naval matters, and even lacked the political acumen which might have made up for inexperience. A year in West Point, a couple in college, and a little law practice made up all the preparation he had for his important job. Knowing nothing of the Navy and little of politics, and lacking personal conviction as to the importance of sea power, he was inevitably a weak secretary and, consequently, was able to do little for the department which he headed. But he was Secretary of the Navy, and Moore, so lately a junior officer and completely inexperienced in partisan politics, directed his attention to his first concerns: ships, officers, and crews.

Moore had an adequate number of problems to cope with right in Galveston. The ships, new as they were, had shown some faults in design, in construction, and in rigging. His sailing ship captains were all former passed midshipmen; none had adequate background for rigging his own ship. The Commodore took a team of ten or fifteen sailors to each ship, overhauled the rigging, checked equipage, changed faulty parts, and tried out new ideas. This was grueling, frustrating work, and it is no wonder that an exasperated boatswain's mate like J. Nevin lost his head and told off the Commodore and was broken for it.

The flagship *Austin* (formerly the *Texas*) had been delivered and commissioned 5 January 1840, while Moore was gone. She has been variously described as a corvette and as a sloop-of-war. She was ship-rigged. The *Austin* was of about the size and strength of Moore's old ships the *Boston,* the *Fairfield,* and the *Hornet,* with which he was long familiar. A newer vessel, the *Austin* was faster and handier than the U.S. ships. The *Austin* was 125 feet long, 500 tons, with heavy oak frames and copper sheathing. She had eighteen 24-pound columbiad guns with 25 rounds of solid and 13 of canister and 12 of grape, and powder for 25 rounds per gun. Her complement was to be 24 officers and 147 men, though she never was fully manned. The *Austin* was allowed 30 muskets, 10 pistols, and 30 cutlasses. She was to carry 8,000 gallons of water, a 26-foot launch and 4 smaller boats.[3]

Next, Moore turned to training. The ships were sent out one or

[3] Harriet Smither (ed.), *Journals of the Fourth Congress, Republic of Texas,* III, 119.

two at a time to exercise offshore. The schooners had trouble with ground tackle. Cables and anchors were too light for the sudden squalls which sweep down from the north on the Gulf. That fault in the schooners was never remedied, since the Navy did not get any money. During the next three years two, or perhaps all three, were lost because of poor anchor gear.

Sailing drills were not without hazard. One calm day off Velasco the *San Jacinto* lay at anchor conducting drill in handling sails, reefing, shaking out reefs, going through all the maneuvers and orders necessary to navigate the ships at sea or in battle. After a hard morning of it, the exercise was knocked off for dinner. Since all hands had been working sail the Captain foolishly allowed the deck to be left without a watch. A sudden squall came whistling in and in an instant laid the ship over on her side. Even if the skipper was not forehanded, he at least had presence of mind and good reactions; he ran up on deck, cut loose the boom which some lubber had lashed down, brought the ship's head up into the wind and righted her, while his dumbfounded crew looked on in amazement and terror. The Captain was probably James E. Gibbons, who had served in the U.S. Navy as a passed midshipman and found it hard to adjust as a senior officer in the new service. He was a strict disciplinarian who was free with the cat-o'-nine-tails. Gibbons did not last long at sea; he was sent to the fleet in ordinary (mothballs), where he worked under supervision of the Commander of the Galveston Navy Yard, and soon resigned.

About the same time, the ships began to convoy merchantmen carrying volunteers and supplies from the Louisiana line to the ports at the mouths of the Colorado and Brazos rivers. None of the vessels was molested, but the cruises afforded excellent training. The lubberly *San Jacinto* particularly needed it; she managed to foul her two anchors on each other, and it took the *Zavala* two days to clear them.

After the *Zavala* arrived 6 March she was of great assistance to the others, towing them into or out of port and saving $75 tug fee. The channel over Galveston Bar was long, narrow, unmarked, and quite shallow. Sailing vessels routinely anchored well to sea and awaited tug assistance to bring them up the channel to the east of the island, then to the area to the north, where the best sheltered anchorage was. To make the passage they needed tug assistance or stood good chance of grounding and being lost, as had two of the ships of the first Texas Navy in the face of the Mexican enemy.[4]

In late March 1840 Moore made the five-day horseback trip to Austin (the trip from Galveston to Houston was made by steamer at a cost of $20) to discuss naval matters with his superiors. It had never been Lamar's intention to lay up the Navy; he had invoked his emergency power when Congress adjourned. On 20 April President Lamar walked into the Navy office while Cooke was out and had Commodore Moore change the names of the ship and brigs from *Texas, Brazos,* and *Colorado* to *Austin, Archer,* and *Wharton.*[5]

While Moore was in Austin two Mexican Federalists appeared. General Antonio Canales of northern Mexico was rebelling against the Centralist government, and asked support for his Republic of the Rio Grande. Lamar refused formal assistance and made much public show of wanting to keep out of Mexican revolutions.

An agent from rebelling Yucatán also visited Texas. President Lamar became interested in keeping that rebellion going. Canales, after consulting frequently with Lamar in Austin, wrote a letter to General Juan Pablo Anaya, leader of rebel troops in Yucatán.[6] Lamar ordered Commodore Moore to deliver the letter to Anaya.

When Moore got back to his ships 7 May he found things in something of a mess. Idle men were becoming restless for action. On 9 May a marine was shot and killed while trying to desert. The next day three men deserted from the *San Jacinto* in the captain's gig. Moore had to disrate and imprison the English boatswain's mate, Hugh Schofield, for insolence to the Officer of the Deck. The Commodore transferred his cousin Alex from command of the *San Jacinto* to command of the *San Antonio.* Whether this was an endeavor to

[4] Jim Dan Hill, *The Texas Navy in Forgotten Battles and Shirtsleeve Diplomacy,* p. 91.

[5] Louis Cooke to A. S. Johnston, 4 April 1840, Mrs. Mason Barret Collection of Johnston Papers (Howard-Tilton Memorial Library, Tulane University, New Orleans).

[6] *Journals of the House of Representatives of Texas, Fifth Congress, First Session* (Archives, Texas State Library, Austin), pp. 232–239.

straighten out the *San Jacinto's* disciplinary problem or to make it possible for Lieutenant William Ross Postell, Alex Moore's relief, to leave port is not clear.

Lieutenant Postell was in serious trouble. The Commodore heard ugly rumors as soon as he got back to Galveston. He sought more information; he could get no worthwhile evidence. Nowhere does the correspondence indicate what the trouble was. There is one report of a plot by some officer to capture the *Austin* and turn pirate, but this was discredited as being invented by Edwin Nesbit, said to be a dismissed Texas Navy acting lieutenant.[7]

Moore ordered Postell to Aransas Pass in command of the *San Jacinto* with orders to survey that port. Meanwhile Secretary Cooke had heard the same rumors and on 19 May ordered Postell's arrest. The Commodore sent the *San Bernard* out after Postell, who returned immediately and was arrested as ordered. This time a formal court of inquiry was held, still without sufficient evidence to warrant Moore's framing charges. The regulations of the Navy required that an accused officer be furnished a copy of the charges against him within twenty-four hours after arrest; otherwise he could not be tried. As Secretary Cooke could not be found, the Commodore asked and received the President's permission to release Postell on 11 June.[8]

In early June Lamar and Secretary of State Abner Smith Lipscomb had come to Galveston, making separate visits to the *Austin* on the third and the fifth of June respectively. In the absence of Cooke, Lamar had Lipscomb write Moore's orders for his signature.

These orders, dated 20 June 1840, certainly were not the sort from which the young Commodore and his eager, untried captains and crews could expect to gain fame and fortune.[9] Moore was ordered to take as many ships as he could ready, and proceed to a safe anchorage near Veracruz. There he was to arrange for delivery of some messages to Texas secret agent James Treat via the British Consul to Veracruz and the British Minister to Mexico. After that he was to keep a ship off Veracruz for the next thirteen days, ready to carry

    [7] Galveston *Daily News*, 8 October 1899.
    [8] Charles A. Gulick, Jr., and others, *op. cit.*, No. 1815.
    [9] Harriet Smither (ed.), *Journals of the Sixth Congress, Republic of Texas,* III, 367.

Treat's dispatches back to Texas. Treat had authority to tell Moore that he could commence offensive operations, but Moore was otherwise ordered to remain out of sight and to fight only if attacked. Moore was also ordered to look in on Yucatán to deliver the letter from Canales to Anaya, and to reciprocate any friendly act by the Yucatecos. Moore's additional orders dated 23 June cannot be found, but apparently they ordered him to New Orleans for provisions before going to Yucatán.

For the cruise Moore moved over to the *Austin,* which he commanded, and took the *Zavala,* the *San Jacinto,* and the *San Bernard* to New Orleans, where he arrived in late June. The *Wharton's* sailors had been transferred to other ships; so she was left behind in Galveston with a skeleton crew under Commander Wheelwright, who was ordered by Moore to ship 140 men for one year's service and to join the other ships off Veracruz. The *Wharton's* sister, the *Archer* (formerly the *Galveston* and then the *Brazos*), had been delivered on 25 April 1840, but still had no crew; she also remained in Galveston. The *San Antonio,* partly manned, was left in Galveston to carry messages from the government to Moore.

The *Austin,* the *Zavala,* the *San Bernard,* and the *San Jacinto* were ready for sea off the Mississippi on 20 July. On the twenty-second Moore dispatched the steamer for Arcas Islands to await him there. The *Zavala* was to leave off the message from General Canales to General Anaya in Sisal, Yucatán. When the winds came up five days later, Moore sent the *San Jacinto* to Veracruz while he in the *Austin* with the *San Bernard* went first to Yucatán, intending a rendezvous with the *San Jacinto* and the *San Antonio* and the *Wharton* (if they got out) before the thirteen days were up. When the *Austin,* arriving at Sisal on 31 July, discovered that the *Zavala* had passed six days before, she went on to Campeche. At Campeche Moore met General Anaya, who was friendly, though he had not received Canales' letter. Since Moore knew that President Lamar had assisted in writing Canales' letter, he thought he had better see that it got delivered; he sent the *San Bernard* back to Sisal for it while he stayed in Campeche with General Anaya and conferred with the Governor-elect of Yucatán, Santiago Mendez.

Mendez offered the use of Yucatán ports to the Texas Navy. This was most important, as it was only three hundred miles from Campeche or three hundred sixty from Sisal to Veracruz, against six hundred twenty-three from Galveston and seven hundred eighty-nine from New Orleans. Better still, the Arcas Islands, only two hundred fifty miles east of Veracruz, could be made a base for operations.

Moore sent orders to Lieutenant Commanding William S. Williamson to keep the *San Bernard* at Campeche until 13 August while he went on 6 August to Arcas Islands in the *Austin* to look the place over and to confer with Lothrop in the *Zavala*. Moore, like Raphael Semmes during the Civil War, found the Arcas group just what he wanted.[10] Three tiny coral islands set in a triangle, they offered a secluded rendezvous. They were completely uninhabited, slightly off the usual trade routes, and well suited to provide a good place for rest and recuperation from the rugged life at sea without offering opportunity to desert. The water was crystal clear to the forty feet in which the *Austin* anchored. The beaches were littered with eggs of the gannets, sea gulls, and man-of-war birds that rose screaming and wheeling in the air.

During the afternoon the Commodore dove off the *Zavala*'s bridge and went swimming. Those who could not swim or had the duty could watch the Commodore put on an exhibition, which included swimming on his back faster than most people could on their stomachs.

To the wary the midday sun disclosed reefs offshore. This would be no place to enter at night or in rough weather. Reefs which can easily be seen in a calm, by noonday sun, are quite invisible on a murky day or in the evening. Arcas Islands certainly were not the ideal anchorage, but the location was strategically good, and though the highest point was only twenty-one feet above sea level the climate was dry and healthful, unlike the mosquito-ridden coasts of Yucatán and Veracruz.

Moore sailed early next day for Campeche, leaving the *Zavala* at Arcas to preserve her precious coal. She had received only 1700 barrels in New Orleans. If the coal had been good, this would have

[10] Raphael Semmes, *Memoirs of Service Afloat during the War between the States*, p. 538.

been enough for perhaps twenty-three days' steaming; but what she had was mostly slate and she had already used about a third of it. Moore wrote to Cooke requesting 2,000 barrels of coal for the *Zavala*, to be at the Arcas Islands by 1 October.

Moore met the *San Bernard* the fourteenth and departed Campeche the fifteenth for Veracruz. En route Lieutenant Armstrong Irvine Lewis of the *San Bernard* broke his leg falling down a hatchway while giving an order and looking aloft. The *San Bernard* put in to the Arcas Islands to leave Lewis, while the *Austin* proceeded alone.

On 18 August Moore in the *Austin* arrived off Point Mariandrea, thirty-five miles north of Veracruz. There he encountered, as expected, the *San Bernard* and the *San Jacinto*, but had no information as to the *San Antonio* and the *Wharton*, which he thought would have left Galveston by now, not knowing that President Lamar had countermanded the *Wharton*'s sailing orders. The first thing Moore had to do was to find out how Treat's negotiations were going so that he could plan his operations. Although the *San Jacinto* had stood off and on Point Mariandrea, as directed, since delivery of Treat's instructions on 1 August, no word had been received. Accordingly on 23 August the *Austin* went down to Veracruz, showing United States colors. Offshore, Moore intercepted the British brig-of-war *Penguin*, which had letters from Treat and some sailors' gossip.

The British Navy was, as usual, on top of the situation. For the small trouble of delivering messages between Treat and Moore, they were able to know all about what was going on, what was planned in the diplomatic way, and, by judicious delays, were able to influence events. For instance, Lamar's instructions to Treat had been delayed in delivery for long enough to make the thirteen-day time limit meaningless.[11] The delays were in keeping with the British policy of preventing the establishment of blockade and its consequent interruption of trade. Richard Pakenham, British minister to Mexico, well understood the situation and amazedly wrote his government about the preposterous Mexican attitude, that, though the Texas squadron held uncontested control of the Gulf, the Mexican

[11] George P. Garrison, *op. cit.*, II (1), Part II, 690.

government refused to consider a "cease fire" until after the Texas Congress had approved it.[12] Moore also saw and reported this as the time to deliver a decisive blow and achieve Mexican recognition, but neither the Texas government nor the British would allow it.

The captain of H.M.S. *Penguin* told Moore that the Mexicans were building up their naval forces, though at present they had none. A steamer, *Argyle,* had been chartered to tow vessels offshore from Veracruz. The Mexicans were expecting delivery of the sloop-of-war *Iguala* from France and were also considering the purchase of a French ship now in Veracruz. These additions, left uncontested, might hazard command of the Gulf. Individually the new ships could be handled, but as a group they would be a problem.

The Commodore wrote his reports to the Secretary of the Navy, the Secretary of State, and President Lamar, and enclosed Treat's letters. Moore wrote to one official:

[The Mexicans] are now assured by Mr Treat that our Vessels will not molest theirs, so long as his negotiations are "open" and "pending" they will of course keep them *so* as long as they can possibly find a pretext, and it will not be long before their Vessels will be running by ours, and they on board laughing at us.[13]

To another he reported:

With all due deference, I cannot refrain from the expression of the opinion that we have temporized too long already; and if we let them see that we really are in earnest, by capturing their Vessels and annoying their Sea Coast; which we can do with our Naval force, to at least some extent, I cannot but believe that they will very soon come to terms. I have no faith in their promises, unless they *feel* that they can be forced to keep them;— The whole history of their negotiations is strong proof of this position.[14]

To another:

. . . the Authorities of the State of Yucatan are, or profess to be our Friends; at all events their Ports are open to any Texan Vessel and they are anxious for the co-operation of our Naval force."[15]

[12] Ephraim D. Adams, *British Interests and Activities in Texas,* p. 47.
[13] George P. Garrison, *op. cit.,* II (1), Part II, 696.
[14] *Ibid.,* p. 697.   [15] *Ibid.,* p. 695.

To another:

The Centralists are allmost prostrate, and single handed with the means already at your Command [the Navy] you might, without the least prospect of being molested by them on the Frontier, dictate to, and no longer *ask* at their hands, that which they can be very soon made to *feel* is ours already, viz our perfect Independence of them; and in my humble opinion they will never acknowledge it until they are made to *feel* it.[16]

And to another:

With the Navy manned as indifferently as it is, every Mexican Vessel can be captured that dare put to sea, and their whole Sea Coast be kept in a perfect state of fear and trembling; why then should we temporize any longer with them, when, if they had the power they would annihilate every male Inhabitant of Texas and spread devastation and ruin throughout our devoted Country.

You may keep *Treating* with them until the expiration of your administration and will, in all probability leave for your successor, whoever he may be, to reap all the advantages of your efforts; now is the time to push them for they never were so prostrate![17]

[16] *Ibid.*   [17] *Ibid.*, p. 696.

Support of Treat's Mission to Mexico

Sending the *San Jacinto* to Galveston 25 August with the reports and letters, Moore went to the mouth of the Rio Grande as ordered by Lipscomb. These missing orders of 23 June evidently were directed at provoking hostilities off the Rio Grande so that Texas could openly support General Canales.[1] Moore reported that even though his ship showed the Texas flag within a thousand yards of Centralist troops the *Austin* was not fired upon. He stayed several days, watching the Centralists maneuvering ashore, but never was able to incite them into action against him. He was obviously disappointed both in this and in his inability to show the entire fleet there in accordance with his orders. The *San Bernard* was watching Veracruz; the *Zavala* was tied to the Arcas Islands by her shortage of fuel. A lack of sailors kept the *San Antonio* from joining the force. Commander Wheelwright of the *Wharton* had shipped a partial crew, but no one wanted to move over to the *San Antonio*. The Secretary of the Navy himself went aboard and talked twenty-six

[1] Harriet Smither (ed.), *Journals of the Sixth Congress, Republic of Texas*, III, 368.

men into accepting changes to their shipping articles to allow their transfer. The *Austin's* appearance made Arista retreat once more from his threatening position on the Texas border.[2]

Returning to his station off Point Mariandrea on 12 September, Moore learned from the *San Bernard* that communications with Treat were becoming difficult. Moore had tried to send in to the French minister some letters from the French consul at Campeche by a Colombian ship, and the captain had been imprisoned for carrying them.[3] Moore wanted to board all non-Mexican ships leaving Veracruz so that the Mexicans would not know who was carrying messages, and so Treat could leave by whatever ship he could and still be able to get to a Texas warship. Treat, however, continued to use the British men-of-war for his infrequent messages.

By mid-September the long cruise began to tell on ships and men. It had been two months since they had departed Galveston. The only provisions received were occasional turtles or fish bartered from Mexican fishermen who refused the Texas money Moore's ships offered them. Scurvy broke out; the *Austin* had twelve serious cases by the time the *San Antonio* joined her off Tampico on 18 September with provisions from Galveston.

In order to reprovision the ships Moore had to redistribute his forces. The *San Antonio,* fresh from port, would take up the position off Tampico. The *Austin* Moore wanted readily at hand to receive information momentarily expected from Treat. He did not want to go as far as the Arcas Islands; so the *Austin* would go to an anchorage at Lobos Island, sixty miles south of Tampico, and try to cure scurvy and rest the crew while awaiting information. The *San Bernard* was ordered to resupply the *Zavala* at Arcas, where she was remaining in readiness for the expected coal from New Orleans. Then the *San Bernard* was to proceed immediately to Veracruz. The *San Jacinto* was in Galveston delivering Treat's latest message. While there, she had a change of command: experienced, reliable Lieutenant Postell was relieved by his inexperienced First Lieutenant, James O'Shaunessy.

[2] George P. Garrison (ed.), *Diplomatic Correspondence of the Republic of Texas,* II (1), Part II, 712.

[3] Harriet Smither, *op. cit.,* p. 368.

Apparently Cooke had got new evidence in his charge against Postell, because on 7 August he disapproved Moore's court of inquiry and removed Postell from command. Postell resigned on 17 September without facing court-martial. Cooke then ordered Lieutenant J. O'Shaunessy to assume command until Lieutenant Thurston M. Taylor, Moore's First Lieutenant in the *Austin,* could take over. O'Shaunessy applied to Commander Tod of the Galveston naval station for an anchor to replace one lost when the *San Jacinto* was run down by the SS *Columbia* in June, but Tod said he had already sent him a replacement in the *San Antonio* a short time before.

Moore's arrangement of the ships would permit the Texas Navy to keep one ship off Veracruz, one off Tampico, one off Yucatán, the flagship in communication with Treat, and one ship available to supply the others, carry messages, and get a little rest in port.

The season of the northers had arrived, and the ships had to be ready for foul weather. Unlike hurricanes and summer tropical storms, northers frequently come completely without warning and from unexpected quarters. They are characterized by great suddenness, gusty winds, and drops in temperature of even sixty degrees in an hour. Frequently, heavy seas build up on shallow shelves open to the north.

On 1 October, while the *Austin* was off Lobos Island, a norther struck. For four days the *Austin* pitched and tossed, snugged down behind the reefs, her anchors holding firmly in the clay bottom. During the third stormy night the lookouts sighted a vessel in distress aground on treacherous Blanquilla Reef, four miles north. Moore sent three of his boats through the surf to the rescue. Two had to turn back, but Lieutenant Downing H. Crisp in the Francis lifeboat (the one with the gold medal and certificate as the best in the world) managed to get through. Crisp arrived at the wreck just in time to dissuade the panic-stricken crew from abandoning ship in a flimsy raft. Crisp could not get them off in his boat that night, but stayed until the next morning, when the crew and cargo were saved by the *Austin's* boat and brought to the *Austin.* The wrecked brig was the Centralist Mexican *Segunda Fama* with twenty-six men and a cargo largely of flour aboard.

Moore had moved his sick ashore under charge of Lieutenant

T. M. Taylor. Moore's treatment of scurvy seems a little strange: those ill were placed in holes dug in the sand. Moore thought that this together with vermacelli from the *Segunda Fama* and turtles bartered from the natives cured his stricken sailors. Limes, which grow on the island, were not mentioned, but they surely must have done the trick.

On 10 October, after the storm had abated, the sick men received a dramatic visitor. A gray-haired Mexican limped up to Lieutenant Taylor's Texas flag, seized its pole and begged sanctuary. He was General Pedro Lemus of the Federalist Army, who had been imprisoned in Matamoros fourteen months by the Centralists. While in Tampico awaiting transportation to Veracruz for trial he had contrived to get aboard the Yucatán schooner *Conchita,* which was in Tampico under false papers.[4] The *Conchita* had aboard Lemus' wife, six children, his brother Colonel Papa Lemus, and a letter from the U.S. consul at Campeche, John L. McGregor, for Commodore Moore. Moore took the Lemus clan aboard the *Austin* and kept them for twenty-eight days, until he could disembark them at Campeche.

With the *Austin* crowded with the rescued crew and the Lemus family, Moore departed Lobos Island on 14 October, arriving off Tampico on the 16th. There he sent in the *Segunda Fama* group in their own boat, which Moore had had repaired. They replaced their previous names for Texans—"cutthroat, pirate, robber"—with effusive letters of thanks, which Moore sent back home to be printed in the newspapers. Moore was anxious that his Navy be considered a well-regulated force, free of the rough-and-ready reputation of the 1837–1838 organization. After the *Segunda Fama*'s captain got to Tampico he sent out fruit, brandy, and further thanks to Moore.

The *Austin* was short of water. For three days her launch was sent about a mile and a half off Tampico to gather water where the flow from the river made it somewhat less salty. This was by no means a hygienic practice, and it is little wonder that aboard ship disease was so commonplace. However, ships had to stay on patrol, and this water was the best to be had.

Suddenly on 20 October a shore battery fired three shots close to the boat, drenching the crew with spray.[5] Since a sandbar lay a long

[4] *Ibid.,* p. 372.   [5] *Ibid.*

way offshore and the wind was blowing toward the land, there was
no point in working his ship in to retaliate against the seaport itself.
Moore contented himself with firing one shot in the direction of the
fort, picked up his boat and ordered the *San Antonio,* on patrol off
Veracruz, to start capturing shipping while he, in the *Austin,* rounded
up his forces to start blockading operations. As Moore wrote, ". . .
from that moment, fresh life and vigor was apparent in the counte-
nances of all on board, for we all felt that we could now do something
for the country, the Navy and ourselves . . ." He sent a note in to
Treat, reporting the incident and telling Treat that he was about to
commence hostilities, in accordance with his orders.

Moore planned a complete blockade of Mexico, and the capture
of every ship which came or went from her major ports. With the
Zavala he could seize ships in the harbors regardless of wind. Now,
he must ready and station the ships. He undoubtedly would have
preferred sending the *San Antonio* to round up the rest, but the
other two schooners were not off Veracruz as ordered, and the *Zavala*
was unreported for a month. If there were troubles the Commodore
was needed. Besides, with Lemus aboard, perhaps he could get
Yucatán to take a stronger stand against Mexico.

The *San Jacinto* had returned to Point Mariandrea on 9 October,
delivered her dispatches to the *San Antonio,* and, without orders,
had departed 20 October for the Arcas Islands, as she was almost out
of water. This left only the *San Antonio* off Veracruz, with the *San
Bernard* long overdue from her sweep south to Yucatán to resupply
the *Zavala.*

Moore considered the Arcas Islands the most likely place in which
to find the *Zavala* and the *San Jacinto.* He headed there. En route
he ran into a wet norther, which with all its unpleasantness brought
2500 gallons of sweet pure water to the *Austin's* slimy casks. Still
blown heavily by the norther, the *Austin* arrived off the islands 2
November and found two ships: the *San Bernard* idly at anchor, the
San Jacinto hard aground on her starboard side and abandoned.

Moore sent a signal for Lieutenant Williamson, the senior captain,
to board the flagship. Four hours later Williamson reported aboard
from the only remaining boat of the two ships. He reported the *San
Jacinto* a total loss—with a hole in her starboard bow half as big as

the Commodore's cabin. It was hopeless, he said, to try to save the *San Jacinto;* he had spent two days trying to pump her out. Commodore Moore prepared to take a look for himself as he brought the *Austin* carefully in to the south of the islands into the anchorage present-day sailing directions recommend.

Moore later got written reports from the two captains. He sent them on to the Secretary of the Navy with the comment that he had relieved Williamson of command for disobedience of orders. Lieutenant Thurston M. Taylor, previously ordered to the *San Jacinto,* but not now needed in her, he placed in command of the *San Bernard.* Moore took no immediate action with respect to O'Shaunessy, whose command was incapable of operations anyway. Moore ordered Taylor to find the *Zavala,* give her provisions, and bring her back to help salvage the *San Jacinto.* Williamson submitted his resignation and remained aboard the *Austin.*

Williamson's report was unacceptable. He had last seen Moore off Veracruz on 28 September, and had received orders to take provisions to the *Zavala.* Due to calm weather, then to the norther which had destroyed the *Segunda Fama,* he had not arrived at the Arcas Islands until 9 October. With only three men well enough for duty the *San Bernard* had grounded on the way in and had lost several sheets of copper off her bottom. Williamson got her off the reef in four hours and brought her into the center of the triangle formed by the three Arcas Islands.

There the *San Bernard* remained for nearly a month, her sick captain ashore with the rest. Two men died: John Harrington, seaman, and John De Hare, marine. Williamson found, but did not open, a box left on the island by Commander Lothrop of the *Zavala.* Only after the *San Jacinto* grounded did Williamson open the *Zavala*'s box to find out where she was. The *Zavala* had left the Arcas only a couple of days before the *San Bernard* arrived; she had been on half rations a week and had left enough food and water for only three days. The expected coal had not come.

The case of the *San Jacinto* was far more serious. O'Shaunessy said that he had returned from Galveston to Point Mariandrea as ordered by Secretary Cooke, but not finding the *Austin* there or off Veracruz, and finding himself short of water, and fearing for his foremast, he had made for the Arcas Islands, leaving word with Lieutenant Moore of the *San Antonio* of his destination. When he arrived off the Arcas, he saw the *San Bernard* and signalled for an officer to help him enter the anchorage. Lieutenant Williamson sent out young Midshipman Charles B. Underhill in the *San Bernard's* boat. Williamson misjudged a tack and collided with the *San Bernard* launch. It was sunk and two of its men were injured. Underhill was picked up by the *San Jacinto*, misjudged her anchorage, and brought her to anchor too near the reefs.

The norther which brought Moore the welcome drinking water brought heavy seas and high winds to the Arcas Islands, but Lieutenant O'Shaunessy decided it was a good time to go ashore; so he left his ship just when he was needed most. The *San Jacinto's* First Lieutenant Alfred G. Gray was aboard and fought long and resourcefully to save his ship. First, he tried to pull the schooner's stern out by heaving in on the line to the kedge anchor out astern. The anchor was too light and the bottom too hard; the anchor merely slid along the coral sand and "came home" under the schooner's stern without doing any good. Then Gray tried dropping one of the heavy guns over as a stern anchor. This did not stop the steady dragging either, and when the kedge anchor finally did dig into the ground it parted.

Gray decided to get underway and take her out to sea. He set his jib sail, intending to cut his line to the gun and shoot the *San Jacinto* forward fast enough that she would not drift down on the reef before she gathered enough speed to clear. It was a good gamble, but Gray lost. The schooner struck, first aft, then forward, and beat a great hole in her starboard bow. For ten hours Lieutenant Gray had kept the schooner off the rocks, but he finally lost her at 1:50 A.M.

As soon as the *San Jacinto* was beached, Gray got help. Sailors came from the *San Bernard* to take off navigational instruments, charts, firearms, ammunition, everything. By the time Commodore Moore arrived two days later, there was practically nothing left aboard, but little work had been done to try to save the schooner. The anchor which had dragged was recovered. It was broken at the shank, a sign of poor workmanship, since the cable is always made weaker than the anchor itself.

Moore went right to the wreck and surveyed the damage. He sent all available hands to try to free the *San Jacinto*. Using small pumps and bailing with buckets, they gained on the water. The hole couldn't be too big, after all. He had two big square pumps made to continue pumping while he tried something more radical.

He had salvaged two anchors and their cables from the wreck of the *Segunda Fama*. He took the anchors out over the high side and planted them firmly in the ground; then he had the sailors heave around on them inch by inch for two days until they turned the *San Jacinto* over on her good side. This left the hole on top, easily accessible for patching with wads and oakum on the outside and calking inside. The exhausted sailors pumped her down to four inches of water.

The only thing left to do was to buy material to patch the *San Jacinto* and to pray that no new storm would come before this was done. Moore left for Lieutenant O'Shaunessy, his officers, and some sailors with the wreck of the *San Jacinto*, a boat, some food, and five hundred gallons of the *Austin's* precious water, while he took the *Austin* to find the *Zavala* and the *San Bernard* (which he had sent on ahead to provision the *Zavala*) and to land his important political refugee, General Lemus. They arrived in Campeche 8 November and in Sisal 10 November. At Sisal they heard that the *Zavala* had been severely damaged in a norther. General Lemus landed at Campeche, became revolutionary Yucatán's Secretary of War and Marine, and began cooking up a plan of Texas Navy co-operation with Yucatán forces. Moore took the *Austin* to Frontera, where he finally caught up with the *Zavala* and the *San Bernard* on 14 November.

Lothrop had brought the *Zavala* from the Arcas Islands to Laguna. Fever had broken out. David Morgan and William Smith died. Low on fuel and food, but without money, Lothrop had to do considerable negotiating with the Yucatecos. They finally agreed to get him supplies on credit.

On 3 October, while anchored in the mouth of the Tabasco River to get the wood, the *Zavala* was struck by seas from the norther which had wrecked the *Segunda Fama* off Tampico. Lothrop decided to get underway, but just as he got ready to weigh anchor a sea struck his rudder, carrying it away. The steamer lay for three days wallowing in the great seas, pitching loose her masts and occasionally striking bottom as the anchor cable brought her up short. Lothrop had three guns tied together and dropped overboard to serve as an anchor. He avoided parting his anchor cable or dragging anchor by using the engines, but even that device began to look hopeless as the last of the coal and wood were used. Furniture, masts, decking were ripped up to furnish fuel for the engines. The space over one of the wheels filled with water, forcing the ship to take a heavy list. At last only one wheel was effective. With great skill and resourcefulness, Lothrop saved the vessel, though he was forced to throw all his shot and even guns over the side. He did save her, and limped into Frontera, where, lacking money and correct materials, he made a new rudder, pumped out the vessel, recovered his guns and shot, and made his steamer ready for sea. Lothrop's energetic action, good seamanship, and clear thinking in adverse circumstances marked him in Moore's mind as an outstanding officer and seaman who could be counted on in an emergency. It was a comfort to know that he had one competent captain.

The Navy was in dire need of supplies and money in order to salvage the *San Jacinto*, fuel the *Zavala*, and carry out Moore's plan of operations. Capturing prizes would gain the needed money, but the law was notoriously slow in judging prizes. What Moore needed was cash—immediately.

Lying some eighty miles up the wide Tabasco River was San Juan Bautista, a city of about 10,000 held by the Centralists but under attack by Anaya's Federal forces. Moore discussed matters with Anaya in the presence of French consul Eugene Elys and agreed to have his ships join Anaya's attacking forces. The Centralists had about six hundred soldiers to Anaya's 125. It would take a strong force on the river to cut off the troops. Accordingly, Moore agreed to have the *Zavala* tow three vessels up the river: the *Austin*, the *San Bernard*, and a Yucatán brig. If the town was captured, Anaya was to give the Texas Navy $25,000. On 19 November they started up the river, with General Anaya and the French consul in the *Austin*. The trip was broken by groundings, fouling of masts on trees, and such matters, but the vessels came to off the city on 20 November and captured it and its 600 soldiers without firing a shot. Moore controlled the river, the only communication to the city, and had heavy guns within easy range of the city. Sea power gripped San Juan Bautista.[6]

On the night of arrival Edward Thornton, Captain of the foretop of the *Austin*, got drunk and disclosed a plan for mutiny. Moore had him arrested and tried by court-martial. Thornton sobered up enough that he did not implicate anyone else. He and his friends may have had their eyes on the money Moore was to collect from the Mexicans. Thornton was convicted and sentenced to be hanged, with a recommendation that the Commodore commute the sentence to two hundred lashes. The Commodore so ordered, but Thornton died of the yellow fever. Before the body was sent ashore for burial, the sentence of the court-martial was read over it.[7]

Fever was raging, but Moore was not able to move his vessels from their unhealthful location. He and General Anaya had agreed that the Texas Navy was to get $10,000 before the city was captured, reduce the $15,000 still owed by the amount of the squadron's debt to Yucatán, and to wait twenty days for the remainder. Anaya tried to get Moore to leave with only part, but Moore knew that if he left he would never recover the remainder due him. After two or three broken promises, Moore seized the two Yucatán vessels on the river and threatened to close traffic entirely unless he got his money. Anaya found the money. And Moore had a large dance for the city. He then departed with only thirty able men aboard the three ships, and with the French consul astern in a canoe. Moore came down with the fever. And so did Lieutenant Downing Crisp and Purser Norman Hurd. The Commodore's steward, Edgerton, died, as did some twenty-four others between August 1840 and January 1841 aboard the *Austin* alone.

Moore ordered the *San Bernard* to proceed to Galveston by way of the Arcas Islands. On the way, the *San Bernard*'s chronometer became so erratic that Lieutenant Commanding Taylor was unable to navigate properly. He called a meeting of his officers, who recommended sailing direct to Galveston, especially with so few able-bodied sailors available to work ship in an emergency.

Moore met Lieutenants Gray and O'Shaunessy at Laguna and received the bad news that the *San Jacinto* had broken up during a

[6] *Ibid.*, p. 376.

[7] James L. Mabry, "Journal," Galveston *Daily News*, 13 February 1893.

norther and was a total loss. Midshipman Alfred Walke had been left on the island with a small group of men and enough whiskey and seagulls' eggs to "splice the main brace" for Christmas: "Spent this day very pleasantly indeed, quite a Paradise in the Dear Arcas. I shall never forget it. At 3 Oc'k set down o'er a kid of very good Egg Nogg. Drank all my absent friends healths and retired at 10.30 in a perfect state of happiness. Hurrah for the Arcas."[8]

[8] A. Walke, Log Book of Alfred Walke, 25 December 1840 (Archives, Texas State Library, Austin).

Spring 1841: Reorganization

The Texas Navy had established a reputation which would quickly add recruits to depleted crews; the ships were shaken down; officers had gained experience; Commodore Moore had lived up to expectations as a dynamic, resourceful leader with the strength of character and drive necessary to give stability to the little navy. He needed only men and supplies to put the blockade into operation.

Moore's plans were carried ahead to the Secretary of the Navy by the *San Bernard.* Moore intended to touch at Galveston and then to proceed immediately to New Orleans. Though enlistments of most of the sailors were about to expire, recruiting would be no problem. Texas sailors had prize money from the capture of Tabasco and there was promise of future prize money now that the fleet was free to act. The *San Antonio* had captured a ship which brought in $7,000.[1] Moore's pursers had money; buying stores and ammunition would be easy. The two schooners should be ready almost immediately; the *Austin* and the *Zavala* could follow within the month. All the way

[1] Harriet Smither (ed.), *Journals of the Sixth Congress, Republic of Texas,* III, 365.

back to Galveston Moore was going over in his mind every possible contingency and calculating means to bring his ships into contact with the Mexicans as soon as possible.

Touching the Arcas Islands on 13 January 1841 to pick up Midshipman Walke's group, Moore proceeded to Galveston, where he arrived 1 February. Here he found his plans cancelled.

In London General James Hamilton was making efficient use of the Texas Navy. Hamilton wrote Lord Palmerston, British foreign secretary, in October that within sixty days Texas would have its entire naval forces at sea blockading Mexico, and that Mexico had no fleet at all. He warned that if Great Britain did not recognize Texan independence it would be necessary for Texas to align herself with other European allies, as well as with Mexican Federalist rebels. Texas might seize some of Mexico's northern states, and would levy heavy duty on goods from countries which did not recognize Texas.[2]

Britain agreed to recognize Texas and to mediate between Texas and Mexico during a six-months' truce. The recognition in itself was sensationally good news, but the reaction of the Texas government was the worst possible. Instead of taking new heart in its fight for recognition by Mexico, the Texas government thought that the British government would settle things. Moore knew that Mexico would yield only to military or economic force, and that Great Britain would bring neither to bear. Texas political leaders were too faint-hearted or shallow-thoughted to realize the power they held in a naval force controlling the Gulf. Those who wanted to fight Mexico thought too much of pulling triggers and seeing Mexicans die, and too little of paralyzing enemy movement. In Moore's absence the *San Bernard* was sent out, practically breathless, to notify the first British man-of-war she could find that Texas had been recognized by Great Britain. Moore arrived in Galveston a week after the *San Bernard* left on her gay little errand; but instead of orders to proceed to New Orleans to replenish and to push the action against Mexico, Moore received orders to enter harbor, lay up his flagship in ordinary, and prepare for the dismemberment of the squadron, now in its most promising status. From the *Austin* alone he discharged twenty-two

[2] Enclosure in letter, Hamilton to Palmerston, 14 October 1840 (microfilm, Manuscript Division, Library of Congress), P.R.O., F.O. 75, 1–4.

men. Seven more were sent ashore seriously ill, and seven others died.

While Moore had been at sea for eight months his second in command, Commander John G. Tod, had been busily engaged in reorganizing the Navy at home. Every reorganization resulted in Tod's having more authority and the Navy's being smaller. When Moore took the fleet to sea in June 1840 he left Tod as naval agent and commander of the Navy Yard. By August Tod also had command of the *Archer* and the *Wharton* in ordinary. By November Tod was in Austin, Acting Secretary of the Navy, and was writing the bill which placed in ordinary most of the ships.[3]

Tod's background and ability should have made him the perfect rear-echelon officer for Moore. As Dunlap said when he recommended Tod for the position, Moore was not the man for laborious detail, and competence in handling detail was Tod's strong point. Tod had served in the Mexican Navy as one of David Porter's midshipmen; he then entered the U.S. Navy through Henry Clay's influence. After eight or nine years of service, most of it on the Gulf in small ships, Tod resigned as a passed midshipman in 1836 and came to Texas the next year. He applied for a commission in the Texas Navy before receiving appointment as Houston's naval advisor. Tod was a little fellow, methodical, orderly, and ingratiating, though lacking in confidence to make decisions under stress. He very much wanted the top job in the Navy and was resentful when it was offered to Moore. One of the tragedies of the Texas Navy is that Tod neither liked his superior nor shared Moore's enthusiasm for the Navy.

Tod and Moore must have met in 1839, though neither mentions it. Tod was sent to Charleston to supervise outfitting of the *Zavala* and later to Baltimore for the same duty with the sailing vessels. He traveled extensively up and down the Atlantic seaboard buying swords, boarding pikes, uniforms, and other items not included in the shipbuilding contract. He received assistance from Commodores Samuel Barron and Lewis Warrington and Naval Constructor Francis Grice of the U.S. Navy. At the same time that Moore was proving the new ships, Tod was exchanging glowing letters of congratulation with Dawson. This was courteous enough but not good business, be-

[3] J. G. Tod, Memorandum of Service, Navy Records (National Archives, Washington).

cause pretty soon reports of weak anchor chains, improperly made anchors, rotten masts, out-of-size fittings, and awkward rigging came in. Dawson had a testimonial to refute any later charges of poor material or workmanship.

Tod's reorganization bill would just about do away with the Navy. In it the number of commanders was reduced to one. Tod felt entitled by seniority to this station, but resigned in favor of another commander, probably Wheelwright. However, he, too, was disappointed; the place went to J. T. K. Lothrop instead. Actually, it appears that Tod left under a cloud. When his accounts were audited, he unsuccessfully tried to use some of Commodore Moore's vouchers from the New York recruiting expedition for his own.[4] Moore himself had to become naval agent as well as commodore in order to save manpower. The *Austin* was to be laid up, as were the brigs and the *Zavala*. Indications were that the *Zavala* would be sold. The *San Antonio* and the *San Bernard* were to be used for surveying the coastline.

One single ray of hope remained. As in the previous year, President Lamar was authorized to void the act, or any part of it, if invasion threatened.

While the *San Bernard* was flitting about the Gulf like a robin bringing the first news of spring, Moore was faced with a serious morale problem. He had to pay off the men he had enlisted the previous winter in New York, as their year's service was up. They were demanding their back pay as well as the clothing due them. Moore issued shoes and trousers to the amount in store. The $25,000 Moore got from Yucatán did not last long; the pay roll of the Navy amounted to about $100 per day, and no money had been received from the Texas treasury in a year. Ships began stagnating; food and repairs were costly; sailors became restive and sullen; cases of insolence and desertion began to show up again.

Even some of the officers began to give trouble. The worst case was that of Lieutenant James S. O'Shaunessy, whom Secretary of the Navy Cooke seemed determined to favor, even if it cost Texas every warship. On 15 January 1841 O'Shaunessy relieved fever-weakened

---

[4] Harriet Smither, *op. cit.*, I, 280.

Lieutenant Thurston M. Taylor, in command of the *San Bernard*, by order of the Secretary of the Navy while Moore was on his way to Texas from Yucatán. When the *San Bernard* got to Mexico on 10 February, O'Shaunessy had two merchant captains, John Breadford and George Williams, look at the *San Bernard*'s foremast. They reported that it was weak. On 5 March at Frontera O'Shaunessy deserted.[5] A year later O'Shaunessy and Lieutenant George Bunner of the Texas Navy met (probably in New Orleans), and O'Shaunessy confessed to having sold, with Captain's Clerk H. A. Goldsborough, thirty Colt revolvers and some carbines belonging to the *San Bernard* while she was in Laguna de Terminos.[6] Bunner reported this to Lieutenant J. P. Lansing, then Acting Commander of the *Wharton*. Lansing took matters no further, and after Lansing's death, 3 July 1843, Lieutenant William Tennison reported that he had seen correspondence between Lansing and O'Shaunessy indicating that the two had conspired in the theft and kept the money. Commodore Moore had already checked from pay due Lansing's estate several hundred dollars for illegal vouchers[7] and seventeen dollars for his coffin; it remained only for the Secretary of War and Marine to charge his estate $1,125 for the guns misappropriated.

Lieutenant Armstrong I. Lewis, the First Lieutenant, assumed command of the *San Bernard*, came to Veracruz flying a flag of truce, and anchored near H.M.S. *Comus*. Lewis boarded the *Comus*, and gave Captain Napier the dispatches from Lord Palmerston to the British ambassador to Mexico and the British consul in Veracruz. Napier says that at the same time he asked for protection of the British flag, and also for provisions. The British consul could not supply the provisions, but the Texas vessel was causing so much excitement in Veracruz that Napier sold Lewis £3–15/9 worth, just to get him out of port.

The Mexicans brought up three coast defence guns with about

[5] Log of the *San Bernard*, Navy Records (National Archives).

[6] "Special Report of the Secretary of War and Marine," 4 January 1845, Appendix to the *Journals of the Ninth Congress of the Republic of Texas*, pp. 75–90.

[7] Naval Returns, 15 June 1842, Texas Navy Records (Archives, Texas State Library, Austin).

eight hundred troops to serve them, Lieutenant Charles F. Fuller wrote in the log.[8] The second morning the *San Bernard* was in, a Mexican Army officer boarded the *Comus* and told the Captain that they were going to open fire on the *San Bernard* if she did not leave by 9:00 A.M. Napier suggested that Lewis get underway, but the *San Bernard* had only twelve sailors to work ship. The *Comus* lent her men enough to get underway. A norther blew up. The *San Bernard* could not beat to windward; so she anchored alongside the *Comus*. After four days the wind died down and the *San Bernard* finally left. Four months later Napier reported to his own government that the fortifications were actually only frauds upon the Mexican people to allow the Army officers to embezzle money.[9] He wanted Lewis out so that British trade to Mexico could proceed unmolested, and he achieved this end.

Another dismal failure as an officer was the Commodore's cousin, Alexander Moore. His career had been brief and embarrassing. In 1839 Alexander Moore had been the one who gave the U.S. Secretary of the Navy first concrete information on Texas Navy recruiting. Later he had been placed in command of the *San Antonio* as relief for William R. Postell when the latter went to the *San Jacinto*. The *San Antonio* was left off Tampico when the Commodore went down to the Arcas Islands and on up to Tabasco. She captured three ships, including the *Anna Maria*, and returned them to Galveston, together with the body of James Treat, who died aboard on 30 November, after he decided that his mission was a failure. The *San Antonio* also brought Juan Vitalba, a secret agent and Santa Anna's counterpart of Treat.[10] When the *Anna Maria* turned out to be the property of Commodore Moore's friend McGregor, the co-operative U.S. consul to Campeche, Alex Moore deserted. Captain John Clark of the *Wharton* went over to San Luis and persuaded him to come back. Commodore Moore returned about that time and forced his cousin to resign, 22 March 1841.

[8] Log of the *San Bernard*, 10 March 1841, Navy Records (National Archives).

[9] Napier to Douglas, 24 July 1841 (microfilm, Manuscript Division, Library of Congress), P.R.O., F.O. 75, 1–4.

[10] George P. Garrison (ed.), *Diplomatic Correspondence of the Republic of Texas*, II (1), Part II, 720.

On 24 March the *San Bernard* came slinking in from her useless cruise to Mexico. Moore sent Lieutenant Downing Crisp, his First Lieutenant aboard the *Austin,* over as relief for Lieutenant Lewis, who went on leave. Crisp, son of a retired British commander, had been in the Texas Navy since 1836. He was an excellent seaman, and was said to have been a former British midshipman.

The next week Moore went up to Austin to talk over naval problems with the new Secretary, Branch T. Archer, and President Lamar, who had resumed the office of President two weeks before. Moore stayed at Bullock's for twenty-five days, paying three dollars a day for board for himself and horse, and about a dollar a week for his twelve pieces of laundry.

For the immediate present the best Moore could achieve was to lay up the *Zavala,* to leave the *Archer* and the *Wharton* as they were, and to keep the *Austin* in reduced commission for harbor service. The *San Antonio* was to begin a coastal survey as required by the act of 18 January. The *San Bernard* had still another of Lamar's special missions to Mexico.

This time the agent was Judge James Webb, a former federal district judge in Florida. Webb was to be an official agent, a minister if accepted. He was to be Mexico's last chance. If he were not accepted, the *San Bernard* was ordered to take him on to Yucatán to negotiate with the Federalists there for joint action against Centralist Mexico. Secretary Archer diverted $15,000 of the appropriation for the survey to pay for the expedition, and Moore, who did not want to waste his time going along on one more futile diplomatic cruise, turned over the last $2,000 of the Tabasco money to Webb. The *San Bernard* arrived off Sacrificios Islands, near Veracruz, on 29 April, and fell in with the U.S.S. *Warren,* H.M.S. *Comus,* and the Spanish sloop *Las Alas* at anchor there. Naturally, Crisp wanted to exchange calls and to hear the latest news, but he felt so embarrassed by his tattered uniforms that he exchanged civilities by signal and letter. He sent Webb's credentials in by the *Comus* and anchored at Lobos Island to wait for a reply.[11]

The *San Bernard* waited a month for a reply. The Mexicans refused to go so far as to admit that Texas was an entity which could have a

[11] Harriet Smither, *op. cit.,* III, 396.

diplomatic agent. Finally, the French frigate *Sabine* brought out a
rejection on 16 June 1841. Webb wrote British Ambassador Pakenham that it was foolish to talk any longer. Crisp set sail for Yucatán
to allow Webb to carry out his negotiations there. About sunset on
the nineteenth, while very close to shore and making good speed, the
San Bernard's foretopmast snapped and left her crew to clear the
mare's nest of canvas, rigging, and spars from her upper works in the
dark, off a lee shore. A brave seaman went aloft, cut the stays, and
the whole mess came down on deck. When Crisp examined the break
he found the mast rotten in the center. He saved the rotten piece to
show his Commodore that faulty material, not faulty seamanship,
had caused the trouble. This was the same foremast Williamson had
complained about in October and O'Shaunessy in March. By nine
that evening the stump was re-rigged so that the ship could sail
safely enough in good winds and fair weather. Crisp and Webb
talked things over and decided to return home while they could.

Webb wrote his report to Lamar. He was dead tired of living in a
hot, close, cramped, six-foot square cabin in a tiny ship, but said
that he would do so again to serve Texas. He had left Texas believing Texas could not afford to fight a war, but now felt she could not
afford not to. He still thought a land expedition too expensive, but
felt that the Navy was ideally suitable. He recommended naval and
privateer action right away. As for Pakenham and the British, Webb
wrote that there was little use worrying over them. He said Pakenham was married to a Mexican lady and was practically a Mexican
by now. The British were out for themselves only.[12]

Webb's advice was the same which Commodore Moore had given
six months before.

While the *San Bernard* was away, Moore was carrying out his
orders for reorganization of the Navy. As soon as he returned to Galveston he formally relieved Tod as naval agent, commander of the
Navy Yard, and commander of the fleet in ordinary.[13] This meant that
Moore had to be in three places at once: as commander of the Navy
he should be at sea on a ship. As naval agent, he had to make pur-

---

[12] George P. Garrison, *op. cit.*, II (1), Part II, 760.
[13] E. W. Moore to J. G. Tod, 2 May 1841, Texas Papers (Navy Records, National Archives).

chases and ship crews in New Orleans. As commander of the fleet in ordinary and of the Navy Yard, he should remain in Galveston. There was still no naval officer in Austin. Moore particularly objected to the job of naval agent, but had to take it.

In Austin Moore had received $100,000 in promissory notes and a few thousand dollars in 8 per cent government bonds to pay off his sailors. Actually the notes were nothing but a promise to pay if Texas ever got any money, but gave the sailors a sort of IOU to show for their work. Even so, Moore was no sooner back in Galveston than he was told to return the notes. He replied that he had already promised the sailors this pay and so could not send back the notes.

The *Zavala* came in about then. Moore placed her out of commission, and gave Lothrop the Navy Yard and the ships in ordinary (*Zavala, Wharton,* and *Archer*). Lieutenant Alfred G. Gray took command of the *Austin* in reduced commission for harbor service. Moore as naval agent headed to New Orleans, where he shipped thirty-one new sailors and bought a few supplies.

Moore lost no time in taking advantage of the small appropriation to continue the charting of the Texas coast. The charts in use at the time he was doing his work were as much as seventy-five miles in error as to the positions of such important points as Galveston or Sabine Pass. Insurance rates were very high because of the hazardous conditions of navigation. Four of the sixteen British vessels which visited Galveston during 1841–1842 were lost on the coast because of poor charts.[14] The U.S.S. *Warren* was almost lost on 20 July 1842 as the result of a grounding caused by the poor charts, which showed the Texas coast sixty miles west of its true position. Also, depths of harbors were as much as four feet shallower than shown in earlier charts.

Commodore Moore had what he called congestive fever from his latest cruise to Mexico, but nevertheless he transferred from the *Austin* to the *San Antonio* for the tedious charting work.[15] Hundreds of difficult mathematical calculations, thousands of soundings with lead lines, and long hours of meticulous drafting were required.

[14] Kennedy to Bidwell, 8 January 1844, Ephraim D. Adams, *British Diplomatic Correspondence Concerning the Republic of Texas,* pp. 293–295.

[15] *Texas Treasury Papers,* No. 143, IV, 241.

From May to July 1841 the *San Antonio* was working to the east of Galveston, entering Sabine Pass to assist in establishing the Texas-United States border, and working back toward Galveston. Moore reported eight feet of water in Sabine Pass with mud so soft that ships of nine-foot draft could be towed across the bar.

From July to October Moore surveyed west to the Rio Grande, giving especial attention to Matagorda Bay, which he considered capable of taking a thousand ships in its anchorage. He also designed a breakwater at Brazoria to give a twenty-foot harbor to this port.

Results were excellent. Moore's charts were published by G. and W. Blount of New York City and by the British Admiralty. They were eagerly sought by all who approached the Texas coast. They easily paid for themselves through lowered shipping losses, with a consequent drop in insurance rates. Far more, they attracted visits by ships which otherwise would have avoided the hazardous coast. Approaching the Texas coast and harbors was changed from a chancey adventure to a proper seaman's routine. Risks still had to be taken, because of weather and sea conditions, but at least the navigator could trust his charts.

Lamar's Alliance with Yucatán

When Webb, Texas' third peace commissioner to Mexico in two years, was rejected, Lamar at last decided that the time was ripe for military pressure against Mexico. In northern Mexico there were still dissatisfied elements with Federalist leanings which might join up with the Texas forces, while the Yucatán-Tabasco group had already shown Moore friendship in the south. Lamar decided to employ a sort of pincer movement.

He publicly called for traders and adventurers to join an expedition to Santa Fe. Pay was to be in adventure and preferential position for trade. This expedition, 321 strong, departed Austin on 19 June 1841 with much optimism and very little topographical information.

While the Santa Fe scheme was progressing with such fanfare and folly, Lamar was working on a plan considerably more dangerous to Centralist Mexico. He started things off for this project in a letter 20 July to the governor of Yucatán in which he told of the fine reports Commodore Moore had given him of Yucatán hospitality and friendship. Now Lamar wanted to extend the friendship to a military alliance. He invited the governors of Yucatán and Tabasco to send agents to discuss mutual support.

Study of a map shows why a Texas-Yucatán alliance was a natural one. Texas is separated from Mexico by rugged mountains and semi-desert country; the only way of sustaining an expedition is over the Gulf. Similarly, the only way forces from Central Mexico could be brought to Yucatán and maintained there was by sea; the swamps were, and are, impenetrable.

Yucatán lies on the flank of Mexican sea lanes to Texas, closer to Mexico than Texas. Yucatán produced and manned most of the Mexican merchant marine of fifty- or sixty-ton coasters (called *canoa* or canoe) which took the place of trucks and railroads in the 1840's, as they do today. A necessary step for the reconquest of Texas was peace in Yucatán. As long as Yucatán could be kept in rebellion, Mexican ships, guns, and men had to be kept busy trying to subjugate it, and these resources could not be used against Texas.

Mexico was gathering its forces for an all-out effort to reconquer Yucatán by sea. A former Spanish brig was already in Veracruz installing an eighteen-gun battery and rigged for war. Now Santa Anna sent Commander Tomás Marín to the United States with instructions to buy two five-gun schooners for delivery in September.[1] Three thousand troops were training for an invasion of Yucatán in October. Yucatán intelligence had it that Texas would be next on the list after Yucatán had been reconquered and strengthened and her merchant marine had been restored to service.

Worse still, the Mexican government, said to be aided either by British abolitionists[2] or by a Catholic fund,[3] was contracting for the purchase of two great steam warships, the *Montezuma* and the *Guadaloupe*, in England. Their rumored date of delivery, January 1842, would make them of no value for a Yucatán conquest in October. It was apparent they were to be used for the reconquest of Texas.

The worried Yucatán government accepted Lamar's invitation.

---

[1] Captain Juan de Dios Bonilla, *Apuntes para la historia de la Marina Nacional,* p. 121.

[2] George P. Garrison (ed.), *Diplomatic Correspondence of the Republic of Texas,* II, Part 1, 529.

[3] *Ibid.,* p. 530.

Colonel Martín Peraza was immediately sent to Galveston in the Yucatán schooner *Campecheano*. He arrived on 5 September 1841 with six bags and one box of money, which he put in the Galveston customhouse for safekeeping, and proceeded to Austin accompanied by his secretary, handsome Donanciano Rejon, nephew of the Yucatán Secretary of State, and by Purser William Maury, Texas Navy, as official escort.

When Peraza's party arrived in Austin on 11 September Peraza called on Texas Secretary of State Samuel A. Roberts and asked for an appointment with President Lamar. This was set for 11:00 A.M. next morning in the President's office. Both sides were so anxious to come to agreement that the only question was the division of the loot. Peraza assured President Lamar that Yucatán would declare its independence in an October convention. This eased Lamar's conscience considerably. He was going to sign an agreement, not a treaty, since Yucatán was not a nation. At the same time, Lamar was a great believer in form, and it troubled him to humble his sovereign nation by signing an agreement with a country which did not yet legally exist.

The agreement was simple. Texas was to send three or more ships to Yucatán to co-operate with Yucatán ships in preventing the invasion of Yucatán by Centralist forces, and to capture Centralist ships and cities. The cities were to be turned over to Yucatán if strategically located; otherwise, Moore was to try to get the city to pay contribution, to be divided 50–50 after his expenses had been subtracted. If the city would not pay contribution, Moore was to take all public money and moveable property and destroy the remainder, leaving private property unmolested. The two countries were to share equally any proceeds from ships. Last, Yucatán would contribute $8,000 a month to help the Texas fleet keep the sea.

Lamar and Peraza exchanged letters of agreement on 17 September, and a great ball was held in the Capitol. Secretary of War and Marine Archer introduced the new ally to the people of Texas from the speaker's platform of the cedar-festooned Senate chamber. Transparencies of mottoes hung from the ceiling, and the Yucatán flag with its "Unidos" was crossed with the Texas Lone Star.

Peraza left Austin on 19 September, moved his six bags and one box of money to the *Austin,* and waited in Galveston while Lieutenant A. I. Lewis went out to locate Moore, who had been preparing charts for four months. It took Lewis until 13 October to locate his Commodore in Matagorda Bay. Both ships returned to Galveston. At this time Moore received two sets of orders; one set for preparation for the coming cruise; the other, sealed and secret, to be opened after he had gotten to sea in compliance with his general orders.[4]

Moore had to work fast. His powerful aid would hearten the discouraged Yucatecos and prevent defection. He had to arrive soon enough to defeat the Mexican ships one at a time as they arrived, for once assembled the Mexican fleet would be stronger than the Texan. At home the situation was even more urgent. Sam Houston had been elected President on 6 September, and had shown himself to be cool to the Navy. If the expedition were to take place the Texas fleet must get to sea before 13 December, Inauguration Day.

Moore's decision as to which ships to man was easy. He wanted the *Zavala,* but Lothrop's conservative estimate was $4,000 for repairs, which would have to include time-consuming towage to New Orleans, dry-docking, and the mysteries of shipyard cost-accounting. The *Zavala* could not be made ready for this cruise.

The Mexicans were buying a Spanish sloop of about the *Austin's* characteristics; so Moore must pull the *Austin* out of reduced commission, man her, patch her, and provision her. As for the other two ships, he must be content with the little *San Antonio* and the *San Bernard.* These were partially manned and in active service. Readying them for war would be cheaper and quicker than trying to recommission the larger *Wharton* or the *Archer.* The *Wharton* was in fair shape for a ship in reserve, but the *Archer* already had a foot of water in the bilges, her rigging was cannibalized or rotten, and some of her guns were dismounted. The *Archer's* only voyage had been that for her delivery, but already, within a year and a half, she was a wreck at her moorings.

Moore reported that the officers were still lacking commissions.

The *Austin* had no stores. The *San Antonio* and the *San Bernard* had been cruising since July without general replenishment, and so were low. Most of the stores could have been bought in Galveston,

---

[4] Edwin W. Moore, *To the People of Texas,* p. 12.

but Galveston prices were very high. Ammunition and sailors could be obtained only in the United States. Moore decided to take the first ship ready and go to New Orleans himself. The *San Antonio* bought a new foremast for forty-five dollars. She worked fast and well at fitting, stepping and rigging the 70-foot mast, and by 20 October was underway with Commodore Moore, Colonel Peraza, and the six bags and one box of money.

Moore had Peraza's advance of $8,000, and $3,800 which remained of the coast survey appropriation.[5] He wrote to the auditor, Charles Mason, for the $2,000 Moore had advanced Webb from the Tabasco expedition proceeds. Exclusive of pay, which no one ever got, the expedition was expected to cost about $22,000 par funds for three months. The cost of enlistments would be another $2,500. Moore had only half his immediate needs.

The *San Antonio* arrived at New Orleans 25 October during a fever epidemic. Moore contracted fever again, but had so much to do he remained in bed only two days. He needed 2,000 rounds of 24-pound shot, and had to do some tricky undercover work to get it, since a nearly six-inch cannon ball might be considered a munition of war and the purchase of 2,000 of them by a Texas vessel-of-war a violation of the Neutrality Act of 1818. Worse still, Moore could not locate any ready-made ones around New Orleans and had to arrange for their manufacture. He had ordered the shot one-tenth inch smaller than the diameter of the gun to allow for accumulation of rust at sea. However, since the order had to be disguised and also had to be made through a third person, the balls were made to army specifications: that is, with very small clearances, and so when rusty they would not fit into the bores of the guns. As soon as Moore inspected his first samples he sent the whole lot back to be recast. This caused delay before the projectiles were finally shipped commercially to Texas.[6]

Because of the fever, sailors were scarce. Those available wanted to

---

[5] August Seegar to E. W. Moore, 21 September 1841, Texas Navy Records (Archives, Texas State Library, Austin).

[6] Edwin W. Moore to General Albert S. Johnston, 9 December 1841, Mrs. Mason Barret Collection of Johnston Papers (Howard-Tilton Memorial Library, Tulane University, New Orleans).

see some cash before shipping aboard a Texas naval vessel. The Mexicans had been recruiting in New Orleans, too, and with cash. Moore reported that the Mexicans had enlisted more than 130 men in five months in New Orleans, including some former Texas Navy sailors who had been discharged without pay. Since a month had passed by now, Moore sent the *San Antonio*, with Lieutenant Commanding William Seegar, to Yucatán with Colonel Peraza for the second installment of $8,000. Peraza got six more bags of money (about $6,000) and the *San Antonio* returned with them to New Orleans on 27 November. Moore paid the bills and hurried back to Galveston aboard the *Neptune* with most of the stores, while the *San Antonio* followed with the remainder, plus the new crews.

He arrived in Galveston on 4 December. He had the *Austin* towed out to sea empty to receive her stores and ammunition. Fifteen or twenty times on the way out she bumped and touched, and then finally cleared the bottom. Moore felt sure she would never weather another such passage.

On 5 December the *San Antonio* arrived and anchored outside the bar. Night and day sailors worked in the chilly surf and drizzle bringing provisions from shore, loading stores from the *Neptune*, transferring men from the *San Antonio* and powder from the *Archer*, setting up rigging—in general, securing the vessels for sea. Inexperienced sailors make poor cargo handlers, and constant supervision by the officers was required to insure orderly stowage and to prevent pilferage or desertion. Midshipmen Creasy and Walke could no longer be excused from work because of having no shoes to wear in the wintry weather.

On 10 December, the *San Antonio*, almost completely provisioned in New Orleans, left first, headed directly for Sisal. Next day Lieutenant Commanding Crisp left with the *San Bernard*, to sweep by Tampico and Veracruz. Finally, on 13 December, Houston's inauguration day, Moore left Galveston in the *Austin* in the track of the *San Bernard*. All vessels were to meet off Sisal in early January.

As soon as the *Austin* cleared Galveston, Moore called First Lieutenant Alfred G. Gray, Dr. William Richardson, and Purser Norman Hurd to his cabin and opened his sealed orders dated 18 September. Moore was told to proceed to Sisal, Yucatán, and report to the governor, who was expected to have information as to the strength and whereabouts of a military or naval force which Moore was to keep from invading Yucatán. He was directed to capture any Centralist naval or merchant ships, but to consider that a neutral flag made any goods free of capture. Division of prizes and contribution was to be according to Peraza's agreement, a copy of which was furnished Moore.

Moore's orders of 18 September 1841 were to remain in effect until the Yucatán government said it no longer needed the Texas Navy, or until the Texas government recalled it.

While Moore was making his last-minute preparations to leave Galveston the fate of the expedition was being debated. On 23 November President Lamar notified the Congress that he had ordered Moore out to Yucatán and that the Congress could call the expedition back if it desired. This should scarcely have been a surprise, considering the ball in the Senate chamber, and all the newspaper comment. However, it brought on a lengthy debate. These were the last weeks of Lamar's presidency, when his control was weakest and his popularity lowest. Although the pro-Houston faction did not yet know of the disaster to the Santa Fe expedition, they found the expedition itself a good target for criticism. Now, in an effort to pull Lamar's prestige down further, they linked this land expedition with the naval mission to Yucatán.

For once Houston's boys overreached themselves. The preamble to the proposed resolution condemning Lamar for sending out the Yucatán expedition was so abusive and vilifying that the Houston moderates felt they could not support it. Three weeks and 118 pages of Congressional *Journal* later, they discovered that the Houston radicals and the Lamar forces had combined to refuse to allow the offensive preamble to be removed. Then, 14 December, the Houston moderates and Lamar faction combined to defeat the abusive bill, and thus, by a 20–18 vote on Lamar's character, the Navy was allowed to stay at sea.

The arguments were long, tedious, and generally pointless. It is easy to see why one congressman reported that it cost $4,000 for

Congress to pass a given resolution. Considering salaries were about $2 per day for the thirty-four men, the total cost in congressional salaries alone for arguing this measure was about $600 cash. The foolish thing about it all was that everyone thought that Moore had already sailed, though the ships were still readying in Galveston, and Congress knew very well that Houston would call Moore back as soon as he took office.

Houston sent out the recall on the fifteenth.

It got to Gail Borden in Galveston on December 28. He sent it on to the Texas consul at New Orleans for delivery, informing Houston of the nondelivery in Galveston, and offering to hire a boat to take it down to Moore if a receipt was desired.[7] Moore finally got the message in Yucatán on 10 March 1842 from the *San Antonio*. Meantime, Congressman Nicholas Darnell kept things interesting in Austin by saying that he thought Peraza was an agent of Santa Anna.

Moore himself thought he might be recalled. He wrote his friend General Albert Sidney Johnston at Johnston's request, outlining the possible political attacks which would be made on the ships and himself while they were gone. Moore stated bitterly that if this expedition were called off he would be humbugged no longer. He would resign from the Texas Navy and all his officers would follow him off the ships. Texas would be forever without a navy, as no self-respecting officer could put up with the treatment they had been receiving.[8]

While Moore was at sea, Yucatán offered to have the *Zavala* repaired and drydocked at the expense of Yucatán. With the other three ships on the Gulf and the *Zavala* operational, Texas could be kept supreme on the Gulf.

In the face of threatened invasion, and knowing that England was building and manning the two most modern war steamers in the world for Mexico to use against Texas, Houston refused the offer. He could not use economy this time as the reason for failure to repair the *Zavala;* so he cast about for some other excuse. The best he could say

[7] Gail Borden to George Hockley, 28 December 1841, Texas Navy Records (Archives, Texas State Library).

[8] Edwin W. Moore to General Albert S. Johnston, 9 December 1841, Mrs. Mason Barret Collection of Johnston Papers (Howard-Tilton Memorial Library, Tulane University).

was that he did not wish to enter Mexico's internal affairs, and, besides, did not trust the Yucatecos.[9] So the *Zavala* settled deeper in the Galveston sand, and Moore had to operate without his useful steamship.

[9] Harriet Smither (ed.), *Journals of the Sixth Congress, Republic of Texas,* II, 237.

The Texas Navy Helps Yucatán

Proceeding on ahead directly to Yucatán, the *San Antonio* arrived in Sisal on 19 December 1841. She operated in and out of that port for two weeks without incident, except for losing her port anchor and fifteen fathoms of chain on Christmas day. The *San Bernard* came in on 29 December, fired a twenty-one–gun salute and anchored long enough for F. and Luke Howard and H. Clausen to steal the first cutter and try to desert. The commandant of the fort seized them and turned them over to Crisp, who then stood out to sea to await his Commodore.

Meanwhile, Moore, in the *Austin*, had looked in on Tampico on the seventeenth, and had stopped two ships. One, the *Fortune*, turned out to be a Yucateco; the second was a Belgian galliot. Moore sent his surgeon, Dr. T. P. Anderson, to look at the sick Belgian captain, and to give him a Gulf chart. The *Austin* hove to for punishment on 29 December. William Stafford received the cat-of-nine-tails for stealing an unstated article, which may have been water, for by 1 January the *Austin* found herself down to a reported ten gallons. By draining the scum from several casks, she finally got 275 gallons. The *Austin's* capacity was 8,000 gallons; so that she had averaged about 450 gallons a day on the way down, some three gallons of water per man per day. Twentieth-century ships try to keep consumption below twenty gallons.

Three days later, forty miles west of Sisal, the *San Bernard* fell in. The next day the *San Antonio* reported. Both captains came aboard on the fifth to give the Commodore their reports of the cruise thus far. Next day all three vessels made their ceremonious entry into Sisal, and the *Austin* fired a twenty-one–gun salute, which was returned by the castle.

As soon as he anchored Moore took his senior captain, Seegar, and Dr. Richardson and headed for Mérida, the capital of Yucatán. The *Austin* he left under his First Lieutenant, A. G. Gray, and he ordered the *San Antonio* and the *San Bernard* to Mugueres Island for water, which was always scarce in Yucatán in the dry season.

Reaching Mérida on Saturday, 10 January 1842, the Commodore discovered that the political situation had changed. The Yucatecos had held their Independence Convention in October, but it ended the way many Latin conferences do: everyone took charge, introduced resolutions, made speeches. When it was all over, not only had independence not been declared, but the delegates had decided to ask for re-entry into Mexico, and, pending negotiations, had decided to forbid the Yucatecan Navy from attacking Mexican shipping or even helping Moore's ships. Rejon, the foreign minister, told Moore that the Yucatecos would not have agreed with Quintana Roo if they had known Moore was really coming.[1] This was absurd, since the *San Antonio* was in Sisal for the second month's rent on 19 November, and arrived at Sisal again on 19 December.

The leading Mexican mediator was Andrés Quintana Roo, a highly respected Yucateco. He had reached an accord with both sides on 28 December 1841, the week before Moore arrived. By the terms of this agreement, Yucatán would re-enter Mexico without prejudice to her rights to make treaties, and specifically was exempt from fighting Texas. Quintana Roo was preparing to return to Mexico with the agreement when Moore arrived in Mérida.

Quintana Roo's agreement strengthened Centralist Mexican hands, and the danger to Texas was real and great. Instead of fighting Mex-

[1] Edwin Ward Moore, *To the People of Texas*, p. 21.

ico minus Yucatán's power, Texas would probably eventually have to fight both. Moore saw the hazard at once, and used forceful persuasiveness to forestall the reunion.[2] In a meeting attended by the governor, the foreign minister, the secretary of war and navy, the vice governor, Colonel Peraza, and Lieutenant Commanding Seegar, Moore handed down what amounted to an ultimatum. Approval of the agreement would automatically make Yucatán a Texas enemy and hence her ships and harbors open to capture by Moore's vessels. The Yucatecos knew very well that Moore's ships could quickly close Yucatán ports as they had the ports of Veracruz and Tampico. Moreover, Yucatán understood the value of the threat of Texas Navy action upon Centralist diplomats, and was willing to continue the subsidy until she had won re-entry into Mexico upon her own terms. Accordingly, the Yucatán government agreed that the contract for the use of the Texas Navy should continue in effect until both Mexico and Yucatán ratified the agreement. Texas ships would be welcome, and the $8,000 a month would continue.

While Moore was up in Mérida negotiating with the Yucatán government, young Lieutenant Gray of the *Austin* was senior officer in Sisal. This was the same Lieutenant Gray who the year before had exercised such initiative and good sense in trying to prevent the grounding of the *San Jacinto* in the absence of O'Shaunessy. Gray had no notification of the negotiations between Mexico and Yucatán.

On the afternoon of 12 January the alert Lieutenant Gray noticed great activity aboard the American barque *Louisa* anchored nearby. Investigating, Gray was astonished to find that there were members of the Centralist government of Mexico as well as of Yucatán's provisional government aboard leaving for Mexico. This confirmed rumors of the last two days in Sisal of such a commission. Gray had received no word from Moore for four days, and felt sure that his chief had been captured as part of the accord between the two governments. He took action to assure Moore's safe return by sending Lieutenants Cyrus Cummings and Armstrong Lewis out in the cutters to seize hostages from the *Louisa*. The two boarded the *Louisa*, announced their purpose, and waited for their guests. While they were waiting, the captain of the *Louisa* came over to the *Austin*, blustering

[2] *Ibid.*

and threatening to report Gray to the United States government. Gray listened to the man rant a while, then ordered him off the ship. When the furious captain had left, Gray called Cummings' boat alongside and greeted Colonel José Lemus, Dr. Salvador Calcanio, José Benigo Gurman, and Colonel Anastacio Forrens, most of whom were passengers of the *Louisa*. Ten minutes later came the bigger fish: Andrés Quintana Roo, Dr. José Dolores Fernández (Yucatán Commissioner), General Juan Pablo Anaya, Diego Castillo, José Maldonado, and Antonio Peña y Barragán. He left the secretary of the commissioners, Miguel Arroyo, aboard the *Louisa*, since he was too sick to be moved. Gray told his hostages of their status, treated them courteously, and sent to Moore in Mérida by young Donanciano Rejon a report of his activity.[3]

The dusty rider woke Moore about 1:00 A.M. and gave him the message. Moore wrote a quick, reassuring note to Gray, ordering the release of the prisoners. He dressed in best uniform, and dashed across the dark, deserted plaza to the Governor's Mansion to reassure the governor, and to inform him of his order to release the hostages. Next afternoon, Moore got a formal note of protest from Foreign Minister Rejon, who had received belated word of the incident by another messenger. By 3:35 P.M. that same day Moore's messenger had arrived, the release order had been delivered via the commandant of the port. The hostages were released within five minutes of the receipt of the order. Moore sent a complete report of this event to Secretary of War and Marine George W. Hockley.[4]

The Commodore was back aboard the *Austin* by 22 January 1842, working on his report to the Texas government. To the hostile new President, Moore had to report a new set of circumstances which could only confirm Houston's distrust of Yucatán. Moore thoroughly and honestly reported all that had happened since he had left Texas, inclosing copies of laws, exchanges of letters, and other concrete data on the current situation in Yucatán. Then he made his plea for continuance of the Navy in Yucatán's service. Moore very much wanted to get along with the new administration, and did all he could to make a change of heart by Houston possible.

[3] Log of the *Austin*, collection of Mr. Harry Pennington, San Antonio.
[4] Edwin Ward Moore, *loc. cit.*

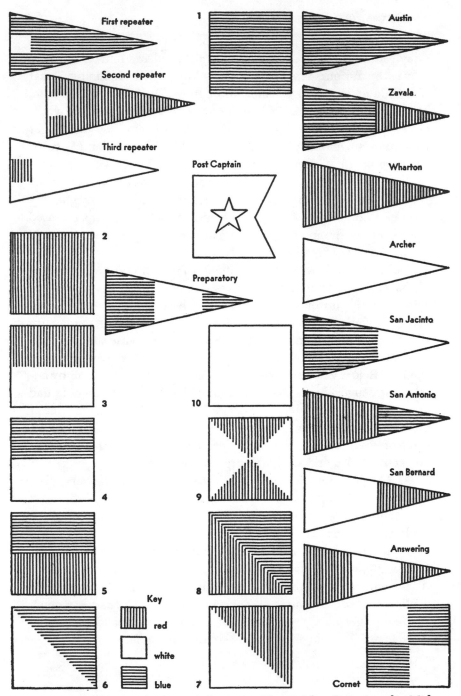

First repeater
Second repeater
Third repeater

1
Post Captain
Preparatory

2
3
4
5
6

10
9
8
7

Austin
Zavala
Wharton
Archer
San Jacinto
San Antonio
San Bernard
Answering
Cornet

Key
red
white
blue

Pennants and Signal Flags of the Texas Navy—After Drawings by Midshipman H. Garlick. Courtesy Rosenberg Library, Galveston.

Moore pointed out that, with the $8,000 subsidy money coming in each month, the Navy was kept in commission and ready. He said that he could get along until May without any money from Texas. The presence of the Texas Navy in the Gulf would prevent a Mexican offensive on Texas, and might even keep Yucatán and Mexico apart. If the *Zavala* were in commission Moore could blockade the whole coastline and pay for the entire cost of the Navy, though without her his work would be hard. Finally, Moore said that the material condition of the ships, particularly the *Austin,* was so bad that they would probably be wrecks if they had to bump their way across the Galveston bar before being repaired.

Continuing his letter, he recommended a complete blockade of Mexico, and asked for orders to establish it. One troublesome effect of his presence was already being noticed: foreign ships were beginning to take over Mexican coastal trade. His initial orders said that neutral flags covered whatever goods they hauled. He wanted his orders changed to allow him to capture coasters of foreign flag if they carried contraband. This was a decision his superiors had to make in accordance with the emphasis they wished to place on foreign help.

Moore had come to Yucatán as he had originally come to Texas, prepared to fight. Now he found the Yucatán government no more willing to attack Mexico at sea than Texas had earlier been. His orders from Lamar had freed him to capture Mexican war or merchant ships, but the Texas Navy could operate only as long as Yucatán subsidized it. Yucatán was afraid that the reopening of war at sea would jeopardize its negotiations with Mexico. Moore could only await his government's instructions.

Moore wished to send his report to Galveston in the *San Antonio,* but before she had arrived in Sisal an emergency at sea arose. On 24 January 1842 news was received from the Alacranes Islands that a ship was aground in a norther and in distress there. Moore, not having his two schooners yet, got the *Austin* underway, and beat one hundred miles north across the Yucatán Banks into the teeth of the norther. Arriving next day, he found some fishermen doing preliminary rescue work. Fighting through the unmarked, uncharted sandbanks and cross currents, Moore got close enough to send in his boats and take off the captain, passengers, crew, and most of the cargo of the *Sylph* before she broke up. He took them back to Sisal, the *Sylph*'s destination, and landed the cargo on the twenty-seventh.[5]

The captain, later sent back to New Orleans aboard the *San Antonio,* was profuse in his thanks, and wrote the newspapers and United States Secretary of State Daniel Webster asking for official praise for Moore.[6] Moore, in helping the *Sylph,* had acted in the opposite way from the Texas Navy of 1837, which had seized the cargo of the wrecked British schooner *Little Penn* on these same islands under similar circumstances.[7] The Texas government was still being sued and protested to over the affair. Moore was determined that piracy and looting should not be charged against his Texas Navy. The rescue expedition cost Moore two or three days' time, but more than paid for itself in the co-operation Moore always received from the United States and British men-of-war.

Upon his return to Sisal on 28 January, Moore found the *San Antonio* and the *San Bernard* lying at anchor there, having returned from Mugueres Island on the twenty-sixth after an absence of almost three weeks, 250 miles in the opposite direction from Centralist Mexico. This seems a long cruise for water, even on the arid coast of Yucatán during the dry season. It may be that water was that scarce, because the Yucatecos themselves lived off Mayan reservoir water from December to May, and hence suffered terribly from tropical diseases. The Navy of 1837—under Commodore Thomas M. (Mexico) Thompson—had put into Mugueres Island, even claimed it for Texas.[8] Crisp, one of the few officers left from the first Navy, went to Mugueres and returned with a chart, water, and report of plenty of wood and water in case the *Zavala* needed it later. Moore sent the report on to Texas.

The *San Antonio* left for Galveston and New Orleans on 1 February 1842 while the *Austin* and the *San Bernard* departed the same day for Veracruz via Campeche. There they took up stations as close

[5] *Ibid.,* p. 25.

[6] George P. Garrison (ed.), *Diplomatic Correspondence of the Republic of Texas,* II, Part 1, 555.

[7] *Ibid.,* II (2), Part III, 894.

[8] Wm. Kennedy to Lord Aberdeen, 6 August, 23 August, 29 August, 23 September 1843, Ephraim D. Adams, *British Diplomatic Correspondence Concerning the Republic of Texas,* pp. 245–249, 251, 252, 263–264.

inshore as the winds and visibility would let them. It was in this inshore work that Moore missed the steamer *Zavala* so much. In the winter months the trade winds blow strongly from the east or southeast most of the day. This meant that the sailing ships had to keep further east to avoid being caught against a lee shore without room to tack back off.

Hence, the two ships could approach Veracruz only when there were light winds or a not-too-strong norther. The first good day was 5 February. Moore came in to look over the harbor. He was dismayed to see, lying quietly at anchor, one of the two new schooners built in New York for Mexico, still flying the United States flag.

The new Mexican schooners had long been expected. On 22 September 1841 the Texas consul in New York had been instructed to investigate their construction. He was able to keep his government well informed as to their progress. They were built by Messrs. Hargous and Brother. They were similar to the *San Antonio*, but much cheaper, as Tomás Marín paid in gold ($25,000 for the two).

Texas had not protested the neutrality violation, because the Texas government wanted the ships to leave under the Mexican flag and therefore be subject to seizure. However, some helpful busybody reported the ships. They were delayed in New York by customs for possible violation of the Neutrality Act of 1818, and finally sailed under United States flag and $170,000 bond not to be used against Texas before delivery.

With sailing ships most successful interceptions were started in the very early morning or in poor visibility, because the difference in sailing qualities between two vessels was not very great, and visibility at sea is usually long. Under average conditions a sailing vessel was able to sight another's masts about ten miles away. A pursued ship tried to take a course which would delay action as long as possible, hoping to escape darkened in the night. A contact made by a single ship usually resulted in a chase of at least four or five hours, possibly more. Two ships acting in concert could herd an enemy ship into one or the other, and were much more effective than when operating singly.

In the early morning of 6 February the *Austin* and the *San Bernard* working together sighted the 180-ton brig *Progreso*, ran her down, and boarded her. The *Progreso* was on her way from Veracruz to Tuxpan with a cargo of sugar, coffee, and flour, which had a value estimated at $2,000 to $5,000. Also aboard was Lieutenant Luis Aragon, Mexican artillery, who tore off his epaulette and put it in his pocket when he saw the brig was about to be captured.[9] Moore put Lieutenant William Tennison, Midshipman Robert Clements, and a small prize crew aboard the *Progreso,* and ordered her to Galveston.[10] He took off the captain, crew, and Lieutenant Aragon, and kept them aboard the *Austin* for the time being. The *San Bernard* continued in pursuit of another vessel said to have specie on board, but failed to catch her. When the *Progreso* got to Galveston there was much optimism and speech-making. Lieutenant Tennison helped things along with a statement to the editor of the *Telegraph and Texas Register,* in which he said Moore was going to try to capture General Martín Perfecto de Cós, murderer of the Alamo, in Tuxpan, where the general was reported by the *Progreso* to be.

A peculiar thing happened to the *Progreso.* After she got to Texas she was sold, though no record of prize money or other profit to Texas or the Texas Navy is known to exist. Seven wagons belonging to a French citizen were removed by President Houston's express order.[11] Then Houston released her to go to New Orleans, where she loaded four hundred kegs of gunpowder. Although she sailed under the Mexican flag and was carrying gunpowder to Mexico, Houston in a letter to Moore dated 3 May 1842 gave her authorization for a free and unlimited passage to Mexico, explicitly ordering Moore to let her pass to any Mexican harbor she chose to enter.[12] She headed down the Mississippi River, and out the pass (where Moore could have easily intercepted her). From there she went to Tampico, carrying a letter from Arrangoiz to the general of the northeast forces of Mexico, warning him of preparations for a Texas invasion of Mexico.[13]

[9] William A. Tennison to Editor, *Telegraph and Texas Register,* 2 March 1842.
[10] Edwin Ward Moore, *op. cit.,* p. 36.
[11] Amelia W. Williams and Eugene C. Barker (eds.), *Writings of Sam Houston,* II, 535.
[12] Edwin Ward Moore, *op. cit.,* p. 61.
[13] Arrangoiz to Ministerio de Relaciones Exteriores, 16 May 1842. L-E-1066, Secretaria de Relaciones Exteriores, Mexico, D.F.

Sudden strong winds, heavy seas, and treacherous shoals were, and are, the worst threat off Yucatán and southern Mexico. In our Mexican War, twenty-three merchant ships were stranded in a single stormy night, many times as many as were lost by enemy action in the entire war. In the Texas Navy, the *San Jacinto* had been lost, the *Zavala* badly damaged in these northers. February 1842, was an unusually bad month. Moore hovered off Veracruz for about three weeks with the *Austin* and the *San Bernard,* plus the Yucatán schooner *Sisaleno,* present for a few days. Only three times in this period were the sailing vessels able to get in close enough to Veracruz to get a good look or to intercept anything.

Finally, on the evening of 17 February, another break in the weather came. The *Austin,* wearing United States colors, sailed right into Veracruz harbor. Moore picked up a pilot at the entrance, and from him got much useful information. He identified the new schooner *Eagle* (*Aguila*), still under United States colors. The pilot volunteered that the *Liberty* (*Libertad*), the other new Mexican schooner, had been wrecked on the Florida reefs while being delivered by the contractors. The most dangerous new enemy in Moore's eyes was a dirty little old commercial steamer, the *City of Dublin,* which used to chug about Havana harbor on her two sixty-horsepower engines. She did not have any guns yet; but her purchase by Mexico marked a new threat to the Texas Navy. She could tow Mexican sailing vessels through calms or into winds, and help them find the weak spots of his ships in light winds. If he grounded or failed to make a tack he could expect this miserable machine to tow a warship up and destroy him. This steamer, now to be called the *Regenerador,* was bought in Veracruz. There had been no opportunity for Moore to capture her. The pilot gave Moore the encouraging news that the two steamships building in England for Mexico would be delayed because Mexico had not been able to raise the money for them.

The addition of the *Regenerador* gave Mexico the more flexible force. Even with the *Austin's* greater fire power, she could not be considered the *Regenerador's* equal. The *San Antonio* and the *San Bernard* were almost identical with the *Eagle.* Mexico could take the initiative. The pilot told Moore that Tabasco's peace commissioner had left Veracruz, and that it was possible that Yucatán's re-entry agreement would fail. This meant that Centralist Mexico would start the business of reconquering Yucatán.

Moore then put Lieutenant Aragon, his captive, on parole and left him and all but four of the *Progreso*'s crew aboard the pilot's boat. Moore was none too sure of the wisdom of this act in view of the pessimistic rumor he had received of the fate of the Santa Fe prisoners. However, he was low on food and water, and could not afford the extra rations. Likewise, it had been the custom to parole Mexican officers throughout Texas history, even Santa Anna and Cós, bloody-handed as they were. Having put his prisoners off on the pilot boat, Moore departed Veracruz for Campeche, where he arrived 22 February with 10 per cent of his crew sick.

Moore wanted the rent for his ships. He got underway for Sisal the next day as soon as he got aboard a little water. From Sisal he sent up to Mérida for his February money, with a reminder that the March payment would be due before his present cruise was over. He got the first $8,000, fired a twenty-one–gun salute to Texas Independence, and headed up for the Arcas Islands for his rendez-vous with the *San Antonio*.

The *San Antonio* was not there yet. Moore could wait only a few days, since he was almost out of water—three days remaining at reduced rations; so he left orders for the *San Antonio* to rejoin him in Carmen, where he could get some water, paint ship, and overhaul his rigging. He departed Arcas 5 March, and stopped at Campeche for mail on the sixth. Upon anchoring, Moore started hoisting out his boats, intending to send in for water and provisions. The *Austin* was anchored near an American brig just in with late newspapers (only two weeks old) from New York, and the latest (30 January) quoted from Galveston. This item reported that the merchant sloop *Washington* had been sent out from Texas with orders for Moore to capture Yucatán warships. The Campecheanos had read the brig's news, too, mistook Moore's boat operations for an invasion of their walled city, and prepared to repel him. Moore sent in letters to the commandant of Campeche, to the governor, and to everyone else he knew, assuring all hands that he had no orders to seize Yucatán warships, did not expect them, and if he did receive such orders would notify Yucatán before complying with them.

The *Washington* had, indeed, been sent out with some sort of message for Moore on about 28 January, but failed to catch up, and arrived back in Galveston on 7 March 1842. The orders cannot be found. On 9 March the Mexican consul at New Orleans, Francisco Arrangoiz, reported that Houston had called Moore a pirate, and was going to recall him and lay up the Navy.

The more spectacular news that the American brig brought was the story of a mutiny aboard the *San Antonio* in New Orleans.

The *San Antonio* had gone directly to Galveston, where she anchored outside while her dispatches were delivered, and Lieutenant Commanding Seegar picked up the latest correspondence from Austin. Then, with the Yucatán contribution with which she was to buy provisions and stores for the squadron for three months' operations, she proceeded to New Orleans to land the *Sylph* survivors. Arriving about 9 February, Seegar anchored off Slaughterhouse Point instead of going alongside the pier or another ship.

New Orleans was a crowded port with few dock facilities. Ships were usually moored four or five deep all along the waterfront. A berth alongside probably would have been somewhat handier to ship chandlers and warehouses than an anchorage, but it took time and money to moor and unmoor. More important, a ship at anchor in a swift running river is hard to desert, while a sailor or a group of sailors could easily sneak off a ship nested among other ships. Prevention of desertion would be difficult, and recovery time-consuming. Seegar well knew that his men would desert at first opportunity, and likewise knew that even those not inclined to desert would do little to prevent others from sneaking off. He did have dependable officers, but they could not be everywhere. At anchor he could better control the situation.

On 11 February 1842 Lieutenant Commanding Seegar and the First Lieutenant, Alfred A. Waite, left the schooner in charge of Lieutenant Charles F. Fuller, one of the best officers in the Navy. Fuller's father was owner of Fuller's Hotel, favorite rendezvous of U.S. Navy officers in Washington, D.C. Fuller had Sailing Master

M. H. Dearborn assigned as Officer of the Deck, and had put him on
the alert for trouble as the result of a vague report by William
Barrington of unrest among the crew. Seegar left orders that no one
was to be allowed off the ship until he returned.

In the twentieth century this seems a harsh order after a three
months' cruise in the tropics; yet in the 1840's it was by no means
unusual. Neither in the navies of the world nor in the merchant
marine was it usual to grant liberty to sailors. Life at sea was hard
and crews difficult to obtain. Bounties were paid for enlistment, and
even the comparatively wealthy and well-manned United States and
British Navy vessels rarely allowed men off the ships before they
were finally paid off. Lord Nelson was once three years aboard his
flagship, never once going ashore. Dana, Melville, and Cooper talk
very matter-of-factly of how seldom the men were allowed off the
ships.

This does not mean that the men did not want to go ashore,
because of course they did. Many ways were devised to bring the
facilities of the shore to the ships at anchor. Harbors swarmed with
canoes, barges, and rafts laden with goods, knickknacks, fruits, and
food to sell. Laundresses came out, and so did ladies of other occupa-
tions. The Officer of the Deck had his hands full, day and night,
trying to separate legitimate tradesmen from sharpers, and eternally
inspecting stores, packages, and laundry for liquor. Many a dark
hand had passed a bottle of rum through a porthole on the larboard
side while the Officer of the Deck held his lantern up to a boat
alongside the starboard, and many a bottle of whisky has come
aboard with the laundry.

Sailing Master Dearborn unhappily noticed that some of the men
had managed to get drunk by 9:00 P.M. of his 8:00–12:00 watch on
the night of 11 February, and it was not long before the red-headed
sergeant of the marines was on deck, requesting permission to leave
the ship. Dearborn told him that he had orders to allow no one off
the ship, but added that the sergeant could make his request to the
captain when he returned. This did not satisfy Sergeant Seymour
Oswald, who loudly insisted upon going ashore. Several of his
companions joined him. The disturbance was enough that Lieutenant

Fuller heard it in his stateroom and came running out onto the darkened deck to take charge.

He took one glance at the unruly group and gave what should have been the correct order, "Call out the Marine Guard." This was the usual procedure on men-of-war. The traditional duty and reason for existence of marines aboard was to enforce the discipline of the ship, to protect the officers from insubordination. Naturally, the system broke down when the senior marine aboard as well as his corporal and at least one other marine were ringleaders in the mutiny.

Oswald readily responded to this order, and armed his men with cutlasses and muskets. Then he swung at Lieutenant Fuller with a tomahawk, missing, but bringing the officer down with a rifle bullet. Benjamin Pompilly, another marine, also shot Fuller, and then Antonio Landois, the corporal, viciously bayoneted the dying lieutenant's fallen body, kicking it and breaking off the point of his bayonet. When Midshipmen William H. Allen and Odell rushed out on deck to intervene, they were shot down and thrown down a hatch with Dearborn. Then the hatch cover was locked over them.[14]

The men now had control of the schooner, and with luck and a capable mariner at their head might have sailed out of the river. Fortunately for the official command, the Boatswain, Frederick Shepherd, as was later proved, refused to join them, and the other possible navigator, Midshipman Edward Johns, had been taken off the *San Antonio* in Yucatán by Moore's orders.[15]

The United States revenue cutter *Jackson*, a much stronger vessel, was anchored nearby and heard the shots and the disturbance. The *Jackson*'s boats, hurriedly manned, arrived in time to intercept most of the mutineers and the thirsty opportunists who accompanied them. The *Jackson* restored order, released the officers, and sent word to civil authorities ashore. Seegar received notice of trouble aboard his ship and hurried out. At his appointment the next morning with Leslie Combs he said he might have been able to stop the mu-

[14] Edwin Ward Moore, *op. cit.*, p. 100.
[15] Edward Johns, "Charges and Specifications Preferred against Midshipman Johns," Journal (Archives Collection, University of Texas Library, Austin).

tiny had he been aboard, by shooting two or three of the ringleaders. Seegar also reported that the midshipmen were not badly injured.[16]

The mutiny posed a difficult problem. Seeger knew that Moore needed him back in Yucatán, and that he could not delay in New Orleans. Thirteen men appeared deeply implicated in the mutiny. He could not take the whole lot with him for fear of a second outbreak. At the same time, Seegar felt that he needed to take at least some of the mutineers with him as examples to the rest of his crew. He selected Thomas F. Rowan and Frederick Shepherd, all he could safely take. Shepherd, apparently, was chosen because his authoritative position made him, if guilty, a most important example to set; and, if not guilty, most necessary to the ship.

The other eleven, some captured by the *Jackson* and the others ashore, including Landois, captured months later in New Orleans, were placed in a New Orleans jail until such time as the Texas Navy should call for them. They stayed there for over a year, during which time Pompilly died, and Sergeant Oswald contrived to escape.

In two weeks Seegar managed to overcome the bad publicity of a mutiny, reorganize the crew, prepare his schooner for sea, and sail with fourteen men to rejoin Moore at Laguna off Yucatán.

Subsequent testimony revealed that a mutiny plot had been formed in Mugueres Island by the crews of the *San Antonio* and the *San Bernard* to take over the schooners and sell them to Mexico. For some reason this never came about, but the seeds had been planted, and harvest had come in the Mississippi.

As soon as his cutter brought out the news of the mutiny, Moore locked in the wardroom all the firearms, posted a guard, called his crew to quarters, read the Articles of War, and notified them of the mutiny on the *San Antonio*. He solemnly told them of the consequences of the crime. He must have impressed young Midshipman Johns, recently in trouble himself, because Johns placed William Beatts, seaman, on the report for using mutinous and threatening language. Moore put Beatts in double irons, and next day broke the *Austin*'s boatswain, John Rice, for insolence and mutinous language.

Just before the *San Antonio* had left for Galveston two people were

[16] Leslie Combs to General Albert S. Johnston, 12 February 1842, Mrs. Mason

transferred from her: Midshipman Johns and William Beatts. Johns
was an immature young fellow of French extraction who was having
trouble finding his place as an officer. On this, his first cruise, he had
made a thorough mess of things. During the month of December
1841 Johns was reported for repeated failure to man his station for
bringing ship to anchor. Then he decided not to stand duty when it
was his watch. This cost him the friendship of his messmates, who
had to stand his duties until the First Lieutenant found out about
Johns and ordered him to stand extra watches. Driven outside the
little circle of officers, Johns began singing with the crew and otherwise associating with the men on the *San Antonio*'s cruise to Mugueres Island. The *San Antonio*'s First Lieutenant, A. A. Waite, preferred court-martial charges against Johns for "Frequent neglect of
duty, Disobedience of orders, and Ungentlemanly and Unofficerlike
conduct." Upon investigation, Moore dismissed the charges, but
moved Johns over to the *Austin* where he could personally see to
Johns' indoctrination.[17]

Commodore Moore permitted neither the informality of small ship
life nor the poverty of the Navy to excuse his midshipmen from indoctrination. Article 38 of the *Austin*'s regulations required all midshipmen to keep journals. The journals contained a record of important events concerning the ship, and a copy of the ship's Rules
and Regulations. Such problems as procedures for fighting fire, system for laying out a kedge anchor, or method of clawing off a lee
shore were written by the young officers, and Commodore Moore's
initials testify to their inspection by him. William Gordon, Professor
of Mathematics, saw to the academic end of things in the *Austin*.[18]

Moore had left a letter at Arcas Islands instructing the *San Antonio*
to meet him at Carmen, Laguna de Terminos. The *Austin* and the
San Bernard left Campeche 9 March and met the *San Antonio* off
Carmen next day. The three ships anchored, and Seegar came aboard
with his report of the mutiny, news of Texas, and, oddly enough, only

Barret Collection of Johnston Papers (Howard-Tilton Memorial Library, Tulane
University, New Orleans).

[17] Edward Johns, Journal, 29 January 1840 (Archives Collection, University
of Texas Library).

[18] A. Walke, Log Book of Alfred Walke, 18 April 1843 (Archives, Texas State
Library, Austin).

one letter from the Texas government. This was the one sent to Moore on 15 December 1841: "I am directed by his Excellency the President to order that the squadron under your command return forthwith to the port of Galveston, and there await further orders. Geo. W. Hockley."

Moore says that he was "compelled to disobey" this order, and Houston later agreed that Moore's action was correct.[19]

For the immediate future, Moore planned a week to get water for his ships, to receive stores from the *San Antonio,* to square away his weather-beaten ships alow and aloft. The ships anchored about two miles off the river's mouth. Moore felt it desirable to stay closer to Veracruz than he would be if getting water in the Cozumel-Mugueres area. His anchorage near the river was to make the boat trip as short as possible. The *Austin's* and the *San Bernard's* rigging was growing slack and could easily cost them a mast in a norther. Seams needed recaulking; rotten planking had to be repainted for preservation. If they were to be able to meet successfully a superior Mexican force the Texas ships had to be in the best possible condition.

It took almost three weeks to bring into town enough barrels of water for the *Austin* to get aboard 5,000 gallons. During this time Moore ordered courts-martial for the two accused mutineers whom the *San Antonio* had brought back from New Orleans. Frederick Shepherd requested delay to get more evidence. This was approved, and a year later he was found not guilty. Thomas Rowan was tried, and sentenced to one hundred lashes of the cat. This sentence was approved, and Rowan was probably punished aboard the *San Antonio* on 25 March, the day other punishments were carried out aboard the *Austin.* Moore wrote the Yucatán Secretary of War and Marine that he would get back the other mutineers and "mete out the uttermost penalties of the law."[20]

Beatts was tried and acquitted of the charges made by Midshipman Johns. Johns was reprimanded by the Commodore for making a charge he could not prove.

In addition to Rowan and Beatts, Midshipman John N. Postell was tried. Like those against Lieutenant William Ross Postell in

[19] Edwin Ward Moore, *op. cit.,* pp. 42, 51.
[20] *Ibid.,* p. 41.

1840, the charges against Midshipman John N. Postell are not known. Administrative discharge of a midshipman, who served under a warrant rather than a commission, was comparatively simple; so, since Midshipman Postell was court-martialed, he must have been accused of something very serious. He was convicted, sentenced to dismissal, and sent back to Texas in April 1842 for discharge.

In thinking over the causes of the recent mutiny in the *San Antonio,* Moore decided that his men should have some spot for recreation ashore. Carmen appeared to be the ideal place—there was no chance of running away; the city was small; it was on an island where few ships came. Accordingly, after a few days in Carmen, Moore allowed liberty ashore. Very promptly some of his sailors got themselves good and drunk, and started breaking things. The word soon got back to the *Austin.* Lieutenant Cummings, sent in in the second cutter to investigate, did not investigate very well; he returned to the ship and reported all quiet. A short time later, a boat passed close aboard the *Austin* and fired a pistol. Away went Cummings in hot pursuit. He soon lost sight of the boat in the dark. Hardly had he come back aboard when Lieutenants J. P. Lansing and Alfred A. Waite came aboard and excitedly reported murder and mayhem ashore, with the possibility that the Commodore might be in trouble. It would take more than this to faze Commodore Moore. He located the trouble, charged into its midst, threatened to burn down the town and imprison everyone involved, dragged out the ringleader, and dispersed the mob.[21]

The mayor released the other sailors to him for punishment, and Moore preferred no charges against Carmen's soldiers and civilians.[22] He court-martialed two sailors of the boat crew for leaving their boat and getting drunk. These men should have been a help in breaking up the riot, but participated instead. The sentence of the court was fifty lashes of the cat upon the bare back. One man, Burke, was pardoned.

Moore's use of the cat-of-nine-tails appears pretty liberal; it was also effective. Only one man, William Stafford, was twice punished

[21] Edward Johns, Journal, 26 March 1842 (Archives Collection, University of Texas Library).

[22] Report dated 6 April 1842, Archivo Militar (Mexico, D.F.) IX/481.3/1745.

with the cat. On the way down from Texas, Stafford was thus punished for stealing, and then on 22 January he got it again for drunkenness and insolence. Never again was it necessary to flog him.

On 28 March the watering was completed. Moore got $6,000 from Yucatán at Carmen, and stood out for Veracruz with the *Austin,* the *San Antonio* and the *San Bernard* in company. When they arrived off Veracruz on the thirty-first Moore took the *Austin* in for a look. Seeing the U.S.S. *Warren* there, he sent a boat in for the news while he passed close in under Sacrificios Island to reconnoiter the inner harbor.

To his delight he saw the steamer *Regenerador* start raising up steam, and the new schooner *Eagle,* now under the Mexican flag, warping herself alongside. They were going to get underway to fight him! Moore needed to lure them far enough out of the harbor to leave the guns of Castle San Juan de Ulúa. He picked up his boat and beat upwind to get a little farther off shore—and waited. They did not come. He tacked and wore all day in the harbor, trying to entice the Mexican ships out. Still they did not come. In desperation he passed inside the reefs, boldly challenging the steamer to take advantage of her better maneuverability in the light winds of the day. She never came.

Toward the end of the day the *Warren's* boat came out and gave Moore the latest information on happenings in Veracruz and Mexico. Santa Anna had 30,000 troops, and was massing to attack Yucatán. The Santa Fe expedition was a complete disaster; the prisoners were being badly mistreated. Thomas Lubbock, who had managed to escape, had gone to Laguna a few days before in an English ship.

More important, the Commodore heard of the capture of San Antonio by five hundred men under Rafael Vásquez. This was the first large-scale Mexican military effort against Texas in six years. Moore felt that this justified retaliation. He commenced an active campaign against Mexican shipping, taking the risk of antagonizing the Yucatecos. Though Moore did not know it for another month, President Houston had issued a blockade order on 26 March, which confirmed Moore's actions.

Moore sent the *San Antonio* to Laguna for Lubbock. The *San*

Bernard took the *Doric* as prize.[23] Crisp put six officers and men with rations for two weeks aboard her. That night the *Austin* stood northwest in company with the *San Bernard*. Next morning the two ships chased the small Mexican schooner *Doloritas*, and finally caught her very near land.[24] As the *Austin* came up, the Supercargo took the ship's papers, including the logs, and, with the crew, jumped into the ship's boat and succeeded in getting ashore. The boarding officer, Lieutenant Lewis, found Captain, Mate, and boy still aboard. Lieutenant William Oliver and Midshipman H. Garlick were put aboard as prize masters of the *Doloritas*. They headed for Galveston.

Two days later, near Tuxpan, the Texas vessels cornered the Mexican schooner *Dos Amigos* off Tuxpan with a cargo of salt and a crew of five; Lieutenant Cummings was the boarding officer.[25]

On 4 April 1842 Moore brought his prize, the *Austin*, and the *San Bernard* in to anchor under the lee of Lobos Island to shift prize crew, transfer men and money, and write his reports. On the way in, the *Austin*, while creeping with sails clewed up, ran upon a pinnacle near where Moore had rescued the *Segunda Fama* crew a year and a half earlier. She lost an anchor before the Commodore kedged her off two hours later.

By the *San Bernard* Moore sent a lengthy report, which included the proceedings of the courts-martial and Moore's plans for the future, together with the cashiered Midshipman Postell. He told Secretary Hockley that he would collect the $10,000 due the Texas Navy in Sisal, and return to Galveston, he hoped, by 18 April. He reported that provisions were low, and that almost all the sailors were due for discharge. He said that because the sailors would demand bounty and pay in good money instead of promises he wanted to go in to New Orleans with the last Yucatán installment in hand. In order to save a week's time and to get the blockade started within a month, he recommended that the vessels be allowed to proceed directly from Gal-

[23] Downing Crisp to Purser, 1 April 1842, Navy Papers (Archives, Texas State Library).

[24] Edward Johns, Journal, 2 April 1842 (Archives Collection, University of Texas Library).

[25] Edwin Ward Moore, *op. cit.*, p. 49.

veston to New Orleans. He made provision for Lieutenant Crisp of the *San Bernard* to notify him en route if this recommendation was approved. The *Dos Amigos* under Lieutenant Lansing went to Galveston in company with the *San Bernard.*

Slowed down by contrary southeasterly winds, Moore did not arrive in Sisal until 18 April. The *San Antonio* and Thomas Lubbock were waiting.

Moore received the disappointing but not surprising news that Yucatán no longer required the Texas Navy's service. Moore had counted upon Yucatán's help during his New Orleans overhaul, and had told President Houston that he could ship new crews and provision his ships without any extra money from Texas.

General Lemus wrote Moore that while the government did not expect another attack by Centralist Mexico for eight months or a year, because of Mexico's precarious political and financial state, Yucatán depended upon the help of Texas after the eight-to-twelve-month period—that the agreement was merely interrupted, not terminated—and that Yucatán ports would remain open to Texas warships.[26]

That very day the *Wharton* arrived at Sisal bringing the 26 March blockade declaration. Moore had the orders he had been wanting.

The next day the *San Bernard* came up with orders for Moore to return to Galveston as previously directed, and to proceed to Houston to confer with President Houston while the *Austin,* the *San Antonio,* and the *San Bernard* went on to New Orleans to get new crews and to refit. Moore received approval for his previous actions, and for the findings and sentences of the courts-martial of Shepherd and Rowan.

Seegar went up to Mérida to settle accounts with Lemus while Moore took the vessels back down the coast to Campeche. Moore advised the Yucatán naval commander to remain around Campeche until the Texans returned, in order to avoid surprise and capture. He also warned that, although Houston had excluded Yucatán from the blockade, as long as Yucatán ships flew the Mexican flag while entering and leaving Mexican ports they would be considered enemy and subject to capture. Seegar returned with an order for

[26] *Ibid.,* pp. 53, 54.

$12,208 from which the bills for supplies were subtracted. Yucatán was still short of specie. Moore had to take a thirty-day note for $4,000.[27]

The Yucatán warships, two brigs and two schooners, came out and dipped their colors three times to their departing comrades when the Texans sailed from the harbor on 26 April 1842.

[27] *Ibid.*, p. 49.

Congress and the Navy

While Moore was in Yucatán a great deal of legislative and executive activity concerning the Navy was occurring in Austin and Houston. Though Congress did not pass its annual abolish-the-Navy resolution, lack of understanding accomplished almost the same result.

Once the debate about the Yucatán expedition was over, the Sixth Congress began hearing the reports of the Naval Affairs Committee. One report dealt with former Commander John G. Tod. Tod's accounts from two years earlier still had not been settled. Uncomplimentary rumors had begun to fly, particularly after two of the three schooners had broken their foremasts and all together had lost four or five anchors, and after the *Austin* had required a new foretopmast. Charles Mason, auditor for naval accounts, wrote Tod for better explanations of his returns. Tod apparently thought better of counting votes than of counting receipts; so he petitioned Congress in November 1841 for clearance of his accounts.

The day before Mason completed his audit the House Naval Affairs

Committee introduced and the Congress passed a resolution not only exonerating Tod of any wrong doing, but also honoring him for having done an outstanding job in the purchasing and outfitting of these Dawson contract ships.

Mason objected to this high-handed kind of audit, and pointed out that Tod had used some of Moore's vouchers as his own and had also been completely unco-operative, hampering the completion of audit of Moore's accounts as well as Tod's own. From a report made a few days later it appears that because of the lack of vouchers from the people who assisted Moore in his illegal recruiting in New York, Moore's account with the government was in favor of the latter by $946.00. From an audit several years later it was learned rather that the government owed Moore about $6,000 as of December 1841.

President Houston vetoed the vote of thanks for Tod. He first pointed out the defects in the ships as reported by Moore, and then went on to state what should have been obvious: Congress should not waste votes of thanks upon people who merely fulfill the mission upon which ordered. Tod had been commissioned to supervise construction and fitting out of six ships, and had been given specifications and equipage lists. Even assuming that the ships had come up to specifications (and Houston did not believe that they had), no special resolution should be enacted.[1]

Both houses overrode Houston's veto, and passed a bill exonerating Tod and thanking him—and, last of all, requesting Houston to have the resolution read to the crews and entered in the logbooks of all the ships and stations. Houston apparently did not comply with the requests, because the logs which report rotten foremasts do not include praise for the man who purchased them.

A source of Houston's opinions on the Texas Navy was the 1841 Report of the Secretary of War and Marine. Hockley reported the foremast troubles, the poor condition of the *Zavala* and the *Archer*, and the cruises of the *Austin*, the *San Antonio*, and the *San Bernard*.

The Navy Yard in Galveston was in deplorable condition. Naval Agent William Brannum had diverted some of the fence-building money to other uses, and now cattle and horses were wrecking the

[1] Harriet Smither (ed.), *Journals of the Sixth Congress, Republic of Texas*, I, 330.

place. The powder magazine was poorly ventilated; the powder was deteriorating dangerously. Sailors from the ships had been using the blacksmith shop and foundry, and had taken tools back to their ships with them. Boats could not enter the Navy Yard without running aground, and what boats remained were rotting away with so few men for upkeep. The Navy had not been paid in months. Officers were still serving without commissions. In the Secretary's report no emphasis was put on the valuable service of the three vessels in Yucatán.

President Houston vetoed a measure which would have entitled Texas Navy sailors to the same Texas land bounty benefits as those received by the Texas Army.[2] His veto message said that sailors had no interest ashore, that the harpies who prey upon sailors on liberty would get all the land scrip and further increase land speculation in Texas. Whatever harpies might have been waiting would have had a precious long wait for anything worthwhile from the Republic of Texas sailors. Three partial paydays in three years, some cancelled promissory notes on the government not acceptable for anything, short rations, and inadequate uniforms were the lot of Moore's men. It is little wonder that almost no Texas Navy sailors finally settled in Texas: they owned no part of Texas, and they remembered the country only as a faithless employer with no interest in its defenders. Their Commodore and some of the officers were for them; the rest of Texas was a stranger to them.

The Naval Affairs Committee completed investigation of Captain Hinton's petition for redress for his dismissal. Hinton submitted to the House long-winded correspondence which must have worn Congress down. After one long, dry session of reading Hinton's papers, when a vote was called on another question, a quorum was not present. The sergeant at arms who was sent out to round up the necessary number of congressmen found several of the members at a square dance. Most of the men saw him coming, but one congressman was so intent upon his steps that he didn't see the sergeant at arms. There he stood, arms high above his partner, right foot in the air, waiting for the do-si-do that never came, for a silence fell upon the hall, and he looked up into the face of the representative of duty. When action

[2] *Ibid.*, p. 335.

was finally taken Hinton was cleared of any wrong-doing, but he was not reinstated.

Commander Wheelwright was complaining of an old slight, and he also asked for action by Congress. He said that Purser Hurd had reported financial irregularities allegedly committed by Wheelwright in 1838 directly to Moore instead of passing the report through the chain of command—which had included Wheelwright, of course.[3] Wheelwright had not heard of the report until recently, when his friend John G. Tod just happened to find it in the files. Wheelwright wanted redress of an unstated nature.

Another leftover of the free-and-easy first Navy had a few words to say. This was Lieutenant Thurston Taylor, now in command of the Galveston Navy Yard. Shortly before he left for Yucatán Commodore Moore had been trying to trace the missing pistols of the *San Bernard* and had found Taylor to be the last officer to have signed for them. He had directed Taylor to explain their absence. Taylor proved to the satisfaction of the Secretary of the Navy that he had turned them over to his relief, Lieutenant O'Shaunessy, when the latter relieved command of the *San Bernard*. Now Taylor, in a letter to the Secretary, accused his Commodore of wilful falsehood.

Also, came the case of John Appleman, sailing master of the *Wharton* in New York in the winter of 1839–1840, who had written critical newspaper articles about Moore's handling of the *Wharton* on the recruiting cruise to New York.[4] Appleman asked for, and was voted, $800 pay he had not received prior to being dismissed by the Secretary of the Navy in the spring of 1840.

Another measure to come up was a bill providing that the Dawson contract ships should be turned back to the seller in liquidation of the Texas debt. Surely no one expected this to be taken seriously! Dawson had built the ships to make money, and had invested a good deal of his own in the project. He would not want the rotten warships returned to him with a lot of promises. The act passed, but no action was taken.

[3] *Ibid.*, p. 277.

[4] E. W. Moore to General Albert Sidney Johnston, 9 December 1841, Mrs. Mason Barret Collection of Johnston Papers (Howard-Tilton Memorial Library, Tulane University, New Orleans).

Against the background of the hearings on the Yucatán expedition, possible malfeasance, decay of the Navy Yard and ships in ordinary, ineptness, and above all the miserably bankrupt condition of the Texas treasury, the Texas Congress took up the annual question of abolishing the fleet. This time, instead of pro-Navy Lamar, Sam Houston was president.

Houston wrote to Congress asking for money, not to operate the fleet, which was struggling against Mexico, but to install coastal defence guns at Galveston and Matagorda. All his life Houston was a militia man. He objected to regular armies in the United States as well as in Texas. Now he proposed the nearest possible thing to a citizens' navy in Galveston and Matagorda. Everyone, lawyers and teamsters, preachers and shoemakers, would rush to the waiting cannon at first alarm and repel the invaders. In the meanwhile, they would not have to be paid, and could continue their eloquent or "sole"-saving trades. This has always been an unworkable idea. Though Admiral Nelson said that a ship's a fool to fight a fort, he himself participated in dozens of expeditions in which mobile naval forces flanked or surprised fixed shore batteries or forts and captured them. The Texas coast offered many suitable landing beaches and even a number of harbors. An enemy squadron unopposed at sea could pick its time and place, land, and march to Galveston or Matagorda. For Texas, shore batteries in these two locations would have been, at best, nuisances to the Mexicans, and, at worst, false protection to Texas, the cause of useless expenditure of funds, and death traps for their defenders.

The most efficient places in which to stop Mexican sea power were the enemy's few seaports, not the trackless Gulf or the long Texas coastline.

The Texas Congress rightly rejected Houston's idea. It then expressed its opinion of the possibility of invasion, which can be summed up as: Maybe Mexico can, but we hope she won't. Therefore we don't have to protect ourselves.

When Congress appropriated $20,000 for the Navy, Houston got a provision added that he could reduce the expenditure if he desired. He reduced it well enough—he did not release any of the money at all, though $88,000 was due in back pay alone. In the case of the officers, the pay they did not get was cut to two thirds that of the officers of the same rank in the United States Navy, payable in Texas Treasury notes.

Houston's Secretary of War and Marine, George W. Hockley, wrote Moore on 17 February telling him of the lack of money and repeating the 15 December 1841 recall order. Moore did not receive the letter until 25 June 1842, but there can be little doubt that he knew of the act and its crippling provision. Moore was able to read Texas or New Orleans newspapers within a few days of publication, since it was customary for every ship to pass along such things, though official or personal mail frequently went astray, since ship movements were erratic and the Texas Navy, being at war, necessarily kept ship movements secret.

As events turned out, an earlier return to Texas would have been most fortunate. On 5 March General Rafael Vásquez and 500 to 700 men struck San Antonio, and the Republic was in an uproar. Although this raid had long been expected, the only preparations made were to evacuate some prominent families from San Antonio. President Houston wrote Moore a frantic letter. Just what he wanted Moore to do he did not say, but he certainly wanted him to do something right away. Since this letter, too, was delayed, not reaching Moore until 25 June, it did not matter too much that no concrete orders were given. However, it does show that Houston's attitude toward the Navy was the same as that toward the Army; hundreds of volunteers would pour aboard the ships, set sail, and miraculously become skilled sailors the way frontiersmen could turn into soldiers. To give the devil his due, Houston did point out the obvious in this letter; he said that his acquaintanceship with the Navy was less than that with any other department.[5] This he proved on every possible occasion.

Houston appointed John Wade to the command of Galveston coast guards on special service. Wade was to take command of the steamer *Lafitte* and the sloop *Washington,* and to search around the Corpus Christi area for possible supply or troop ships of the Mexicans. He was given considerably more latitude than was Moore, as he could capture not only Mexican ships but also neutral vessels carrying con-

[5] Edwin Ward Moore, *To the People of Texas,* p. 68.

traband goods to Mexican forces. Wade was to bring out his prizes to Galveston. Apparently the sailors on this expedition exercised militia rights and insisted on picking their own commander, because next day Houston appointed a Captain John Clark in Wade's place in accordance with the requests of the officers making up the expedition. Clark was a man of very considerable experience. Nathan Amory said that Clark had commanded a sixty-gun frigate in the Colombian War of Independence. He must have been in his fifties at least by 1842.

A newspaper says that the *Wharton* was also fitted out as a privateer at this time.[6] If this was so she did not operate very long under letters of marque, as she reported to Moore in Yucatán as a brig-of-war on 19 April 1842 under Commander J. T. K. Lothrop's command.

Commodore Moore's aggressive action off Veracruz following close upon Houston's March blockade order jarred shipping circles in London and Paris.[7] Foreign merchants were used to the threats and unsupported, unsustained efforts of the Texas Navy, which had caused temporary local delays and disruptions of trade.[8] Now, a sustained legal blockade of Mexico by a strong Texas naval force appeared likely, and Mexican stocks went down.[9] European diplomats began asking the Texans about Texas strength and potentialities. Ashbel Smith was delighted, and wrote Secretary of State Jones enthusiastically to maintain the blockade, that the great nations would force Santa Anna to accept reality and recognize Texas.[10]

[6] *Telegraph and Texas Register,* 18 March 1842.

[7] Lord Aberdeen to Admiralty, 15 June 1842 (Public Record Office, London, F.O. 50/158).

[8] J. Campbell to Lord Aberdeen, 21 and 24 May, 2 June 1842 (Public Record Office, London, F.O. 50/158).

[9] Arrangoiz to Ministerio de Relaciones Exteriores, 15 April 1842 (Secretaria de Relaciones Exteriores, Mexico, D.F., L-E-1066).

[10] Ashbel Smith to Anson Jones, 8 June 1842, Jones, *Memoranda and Official Correspondence Relating to the Republic of Texas, Its History and Annexation— Including a Brief Autobiography of the Author,* pp. 182–184.

Spring 1842: The Great Offensive

The ability to meet changing conditions of service has always been a requirement of a good naval officer. Moore's return to Texas gave him a chance to exercise this ability to the utmost. He knew that the latest communication received in Texas from him expressed a confidence in being able to refit his ships without receiving one cent from the Texas government. He had given this assurance when he had prospects of receiving $8,000 a month from Yucatán. Now, though he would no longer have the Yucatán subsidy, conditions in Texas demanded naval action which would increase his expenses. Moore must be prepared to fight for that $20,000 appropriated in February for the maintenance of the Navy.

Upon his arrival at Galveston, Moore reported to President Houston, who, with Secretary Hockley, happened to be in town, the capital being highly mobile just then. On 1 May 1842 Moore presented his reports of the cruise, and handed to President Houston copies of the letters from Lemus, together with copies of Moore's own exchanges with the Yucatán authorities.[1]

[1] Edwin Ward Moore, *To the People of Texas*, p. 36.

In these letters Lemus wrote that he considered the ship loan agreement only temporarily suspended, and Moore, signing as the Texas representative, concurred in this. Thus, Houston was informed that both Moore and the Yucatán government anticipated possible renewal.

Moore also handed Houston a letter to the President from the governor of Yucatán.

It did not take Commodore Moore long to see that Sam Houston was not really interested in the Yucatán expedition, the Navy, or even offensive war against Mexico. As far as Yucatán was concerned, Houston did not reply to the governor's letter. As far as the Navy was concerned, Houston held back all the $20,000 appropriated for it in February, except that he diverted $1,188 of it for another purpose. As for preparing for war, rumors were everywhere that Houston was letting the country cool off after the Santa Fe horrors and the sacking of San Antonio. Though he made speeches to volunteers and sent the men on to Corpus Christi, though he advertised and sent recruiters to the United States for supplies and more volunteers, offering adventure, fame, and loot, he did not call Congress to supply the money, and he did not begin the logistic build-up which he claimed would require 120 days.[2]

Houston, in spite of having made speeches since his inauguration concerning possible invasion by Mexico had, in fact, done nothing to prepare the country for the attack. He knew that the Army was leaderless. General Felix Huston had left Texas and submitted his resignation as head of the Army; yet Houston refused either to accept it or to order Huston to return. Lamar's Santa Fe expedition had depleted the Texas arsenal of firearms, but Houston failed to replenish it. In a message to Congress Houston reported the construction of the Mexican steamers *Montezuma* and *Guadaloupe;* yet he had refused Yucatán's offer to pay for the refit of the *Zavala.* The only concrete reaction of Houston to the expectation of invasion was to use it as a good excuse to try to get the capital moved from Austin to the city named after himself.

Houston was not even in the capital when the blow finally came

[2] Handbill enclosed in letter, British consul, New Orleans, to Lord Aberdeen, 30 March 1842 (Public Record Office, London, F.O. 5/383).

on 5 March 1842. Neither was Secretary of State Anson Jones. Secretary of the Treasury William H. Daingerfield was in New Orleans. Only Vice President Edward Burleson, no friend of Houston's, and Secretary of War and Marine Hockley remained at the seat of government. When the Vásquez raid on San Antonio came, Burleson immediately went to San Antonio, and was elected to command the volunteers. He headed for the Mexican border, bent upon a punitive expedition. Hockley took charge in Austin, where Houston would not go, and kept Houston as well informed as he could while Houston was issuing various forceful but ill-timed, illogical orders from the coast.

Five weeks after the attack Houston issued orders for Moore to bring the ships back to Texas, after issuing on 26 March, only nineteen days earlier, orders for the blockade of Mexico except Yucatán.

Houston gave the Army only confusing and negative orders. First, he ordered Burleson not to cross the Rio Grande in pursuit of the Mexicans. Then he ordered the senior brigadier, Alexander Somervell, to relieve Burleson in command. Somervell should long before have been ordered to the job, but the move just at this time was highly unpopular with the volunteers who saw in it the intention of Houston to hold them back. They refused to accept Somervell. Burleson, though he made a bitter protest against Houston's timidity, pleaded with the men to follow Somervell, and stepped down. For the moment the expedition into Mexico was stopped, but the people of Texas clamored for offensive war against Mexico and would not be quieted.

Houston's actions confused his contemporaries. In the following year after these erratic actions suspicion that he was insane was voiced in the newspapers.[3] Rumors started that he planned to give Texas to Great Britain.[4] A strong possibility is that he was deliberately making Texas vulnerable so that public opinion in the United States would bring about intervention, with resultant U.S. expansion to the west.

There was in Texas a strong and vocal war party, which was being reinforced by every company of volunteers which entered the coun-

[3] Galveston *Civilian,* 31 May 1843.
[4] Morgan to Swartwout, 8 November 1843, Morgan papers (Rosenberg Library, Galveston).

try. Houston decided to amuse the people with a plan for a land-sea invasion of Mexico.[5]

Houston invited volunteers to assemble in companies of fifty-six at Corpus Christi 20 to 28 July for an overland expedition. Men were to furnish their own guns, horses, and supplies for thirty days. The Navy under Moore was to capture Tampico.[6] The joker in the whole plan was that, although Houston said in March that it would take from 60 to 120 days to assemble the supplies and ammunition, and that there was no money in the treasury to buy them, he did not call Congress into special session until 27 June—far too late to do any good. An earlier session probably would have appointed a new general, levied heavy taxes to support a war, or declared offensive war. The session in June was late enough that no matter what it did Congress could be blamed for the failure of the expedition.

The President still vacillated between Houston and Galveston, pausing once in a while to tell Hockley to come on down from Austin with the archives, to write a blazing anti-Santa Anna letter or speech, or to try to get his Secretary of State to come back to work. In spite of the fact that the financial state of the government was as perilous as its military state, he made no effort to recall the Secretary of the Treasury. Instead, he finally got Anson Jones back to duty, and vainly sent him out to borrow a million dollars.

On 7 May almost all of Moore's officers turned in their resignations. They were broke, and saw no chance of getting their pay. The officers had an excellent case. They had been paid only three times since the time of Moore's entry two and a half years before: November 1839, May 1840, and May 1841.[7] Even these payments were partial and in Texas treasury notes discounted from 20 per cent to 50 per cent. Other government officials were paid almost every month, and had a chance to supplement their salaries. At this moment Secretary of State Jones was home practicing medicine for a while.

A naval officer at sea cannot have another job. The Texas Navy officers were tattered, some of them barefoot. It was a year since Down-

---

[5] Edwin Ward Moore, *op. cit.*, p. 87.

[6] Arrangoiz to Ministerio de Relaciones Exteriores, 27 May 1842 (Secretaria de Relaciones Exteriores, Mexico, D.F., L-E-1067).

[7] Edwin Ward Moore, *op. cit.*, p. 66.

ing Crisp had been too embarrassed by his threadbare uniform to exchange civilities with the United States and British navies; he had not been paid since. With debts over a year old, the officers had no more credit in New Orleans. Now these officers heard that the $20,000 appropriated for the Navy was not to be paid. If the government would not make a sacrifice to support the officers of the Navy, should they continue working for nothing?

It was true that Texas was in dire financial straits. This situation was largely due to misuse of the Navy, which, effectively used, would have stabilized the political situation, thus encouraging loans, attracting solvent settlers, lowering shipping costs, and thus bringing more imports and increased tax returns.

Misused, the Navy was a constant drain upon the treasury, and Navy personnel were called upon to make the greatest and most continuous sacrifices. The Army received land bounties, but the Navy got none. The farmers could establish headrights to land, but not men afloat. Indians received gifts, congressmen got per diem. Other people could electioneer, could make speeches; many had families to support them; others were protected by public demands for their well-being as Indian fighters, tax collectors, consuls, or diplomats. All these people received a considerable part of their pay. Money was available for coast defence, for printing a thousand copies of this or that speech or act of Congress. But for the Navy, even after Congress appropriated funds for it—nothing. Moore writes: "I have well attested assurances that the President of Texas (who pretended *officially* to approve of a grand naval movement against Mexico) was privately denouncing their extraordinary spirit of endurance, declaring that he had long tried to 'starve them out' and wondered how it was possible for them to 'hide their nakedness and procure sustenance for two years without pay.' "[8]

Moore's letter to Hockley reporting the resignations got two answers the same day, 7 May 1842. One was written in Houston's style, though signed by Hockley. This letter did not say anything, though it was emphatic about saying it. Moore was told to invoke a law of the United States Navy—if it was also Texas law (Hockley did not know)—dismissing the resigning officers.

[8] Columbia *Planter*, 17 August 1843, p. 2.

The other letter, apparently written by Hockley after Houston calmed down, was typical of a Houston afterthought. It neatly passed responsibility for the dissolution of the Navy onto Moore. It said that the Navy was going to get its money after all. The delay in printing the new exchequer bills in New Orleans was holding up the appropriation. The money would be ready in three weeks, when it would be turned over to the Navy. If the officers knew this and still wanted to resign, they could do so, and leave the Navy abandoned in Galveston, and Texas open to invasion and ruin.[9]

This hit Moore in a tender spot. Knowing how much depended upon the Navy and how the Navy depended upon him, he put all the great force of his personality and integrity into a plea for his officers not to leave the service. They stayed on to save Texas.[10] It was the spirit of John Paul Jones getting his own ship in France, of U.S. soldiers at Bataan fighting after their government had left them, of troops in Korea attacking despite a disinterested people at home.

Moore was ordered to proceed on to New Orleans with the *Austin,* while the *San Antonio* and the *San Bernard* would go to Mobile for supplies which the Texas consul would furnish.

Just before Moore shoved off on 7 May he reported to the Secretary of War and Marine that he had, in partnership with L. M. H. Washington, bought the efficient little steamer *Patrick Henry,* which they renamed *Merchant.*[11] They offered the *Merchant* to the government free of charge until Moore and Washington should need her. Thus the Texas Navy, through Washington's and Moore's funds and efforts, acquired a steamer to counter the *Regenerador.* Moore expected the steamer to be used to haul out volunteers in the great offensive which Houston was talking about starting. They left the *Merchant* in the hands of L. M. Hitchcock, Galveston pilot and ship chandler and former Texas naval officer. This was during the time that Houston's secretary, Washington Miller, was ranting at the privately owned *Neptune* and *New York* for not helping bring out the volunteers free.

Commodore Moore had had enough experience with Texas' weird

[9] Edwin Ward Moore, *op. cit.,* pp. 64 and 65.
[10] *Ibid.,* p. 66.   [11] *Ibid.,* p. 87.

financial arrangements not to expect much, but he could not have foreseen the mess things would be in at Mobile and New Orleans. At Mobile it was an uncomplicated case of false promises. When Lieutenants Crisp and Seegar in the *San Bernard* and the *San Antonio* reported to Consul Walter Smith and requested the supplies promised by the Secretary of War and Marine, General Smith could set them straight on that right away. There were no supplies and there was no money. The two schooners would be supplied and manned by whatever Moore could send from New Orleans, and by contributions from a city already sheltering those Alabama volunteers for the Texas Army who were awaiting transportation. The *San Antonio* and the *San Bernard* had orders to escort these men to Corpus Christi and on to the invasion of Mexico.

In order to get the ships out, Moore came over from New Orleans with Branch T. Archer and Washington to conduct a series of Texas rallies.[12] So successful were these meetings that the Texas-weary Alabamans once more contributed to the cause, this time enough to charter the steamer *Tom Salmon* for Texas transport service.[13] One lady even began to write a play about Commodore Moore.

At New Orleans the situation turned out to be no better. President Houston's written promise of the $20,000 in yet unprinted exchequer bills was completely worthless. Moore offered it, to no avail; then he turned it over to a Mr. St. John (possibly brother-in-law of Samuel Williams) to see whether St. John could find a taker in Mobile. None appeared, and neither did St. John for some time. Fortunately, Moore had not endorsed the worthless note; so it could not be negotiated, but it never reappeared. Though it was never paid, its loss embarrassed Moore, caused bad feelings between Williams and him, and became the basis of a subsequent charge against Moore made by Houston.

As usual in New Orleans, Moore ran into the always-present and quite familiar faces of Texas Navy creditors. This time they wanted money owed them by the Galveston Navy Yard from the winter be-

[12] Mobile *Register and Journal,* 23 May 1842.
[13] Arrangoiz to Ministerio de Relaciones Exteriores, 24 May 1842 (Secretaria de Relaciones Exteriores, Mexico, D.F., L-E-1067).

fore.[14] Moore did not pay them, and they did not help his credit rating, which was steadily becoming the Texas Navy's sole source of income. Arrangoiz happily reported Moore's troubles, but warned: "He is an active and resolute man. It is said that as soon as a steamer of war hoists the Mexican flag in Veracruz he will capture her. This bravado ought to be taken for what it is worth. It is very hard to know Moore's plans; he is very reserved."[15]

On 23 August 1842 the same writer described Moore admiringly: "Last night there was much excitement at Moore's going to Tobasco to fight our warships, and that he is doing all possible to get 5 or 6,000 pesos to recruit crews and get to sea and so far he has not succeeded, but as he is a man of extraordinary activity, has much talent, and strength of character, it would not be extraordinary if he fooled someone. I will write a letter to the Governor and Commanding General Tobasco by the 'Yazoo Planter' to try to catch him with the Mexican squadron."[16]

Even children were impressed by Moore's personality. At a ball once given by Richard Chinn, a friend of the Texas Navy, in honor of Moore, Chinn's nine-year-old daughter Eliza had eyes for only Moore, although Henry Clay and General Edmund Gaines were among the distinguished company. Seventy years later she still remembered, of all the dignitaries whom she had timidly watched, Commodore Moore and his fierce mustache, his imposing sword, and the huge gilt star on his uniform.[17]

Meantime, while Houston was taking no real action to defend Texas, Mexico was resuming the reconquest of Yucatán now that the Texas fleet had gone. Vice Admiral Sir Charles Adam, commander in chief of the West Indian Squadron, on 2 June 1842 ordered H. M. Sloop *Victor* to Galveston to protect British subjects during the invasion which would follow the reconquest of Yucatán.[18]

[14] Edwin Ward Moore, *op. cit.*, p. 69.

[15] Arrangoiz to Ministerio de Relaciones Exteriores, 21 June 1842 (Secretaria de Relaciones Exteriores, Mexico, D.F., L-E-1067).

[16] Arrangoiz to Ministerio de Relaciones Exteriores, 23 August 1842 (Secretaria de Relaciones Exteriores, Mexico, D.F., L-E-1068).

[17] Eliza M. Ripley, *Social Life in Old New Orleans*, p. 47.

[18] Vice Admiral Adam to Pakenham, 2 June 1842 (Public Record Office, London, F.O. 204/79, Part 2).

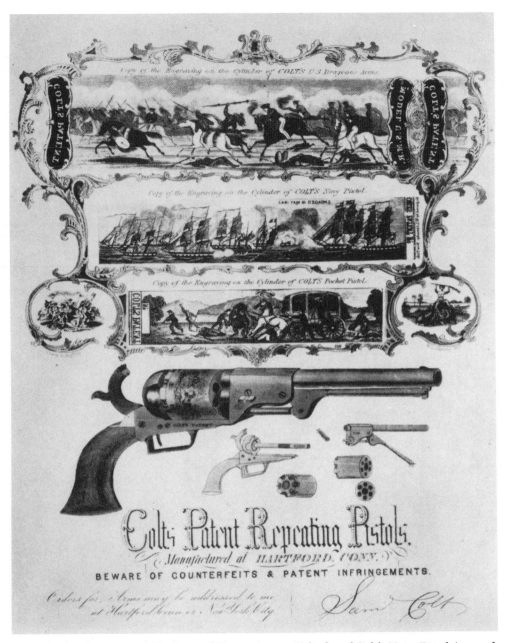

The Battle of 16 May 1843—Copy of Engraving on Cylinder of Colt's Navy Pistol (second from top)

From an 1855 Colt Advertisement

The *Guadaloupe*—A Contemporary Line Drawing

From the Texana Collection of Dr. Claude Elliott, San Marcos

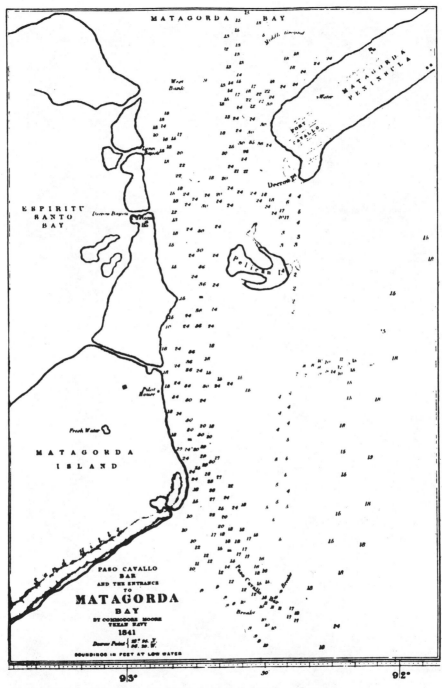

Chart of Matagorda Bay—From Soundings by Commodore Moore

Reproduced from British Admiralty Chart No. 1639 of 1844 with the Permission of H.M. Stationery Office and of the Hydrographer of the Navy and through the Courtesy of the Texas State Archives

The Texas Schooner *San Antonio*—A Contemporary Sketch

The Texas Sloop-of-War *Austin* –A Contemporary Sketch

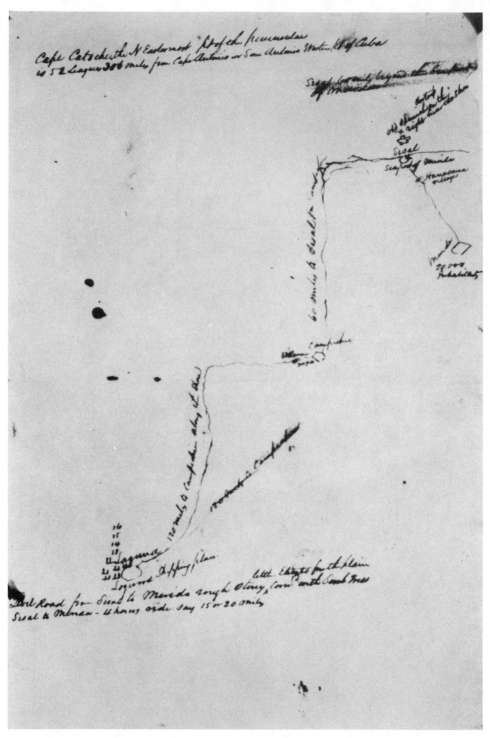

Campeche, Sisal, and Mérida—An Anonymous Sketch

TO THE PEOPLE OF TEXAS

AN APPEAL:
IN VINDICATION OF HIS CONDUCT
OF THE NAVY.

BY COMMODORE EDWIN W. MOORE, T.N.

AT GALVESTON. 1843.

Front Cover of Commodore Moore's *To the People of Texas*—Photograph of the Original
Courtesy Texas History Center, University of Texas Library

EN
CAMPECHE
EL DIA
16 DE MAYO DE
1843

LA ESCUADRA TEJANA
ORNUEBRO
ARATIO CON

Front and Back of a Mexican Medal

Courtesy National Museum of History, Chapultepec Castle, Mexico City

Moore could not cash the Yucatán draft for $4,000 given him in April; so on 26 May he ordered the *San Antonio* to Yucatán to collect the money, and to deliver to Lemus a letter from Moore, in which Moore said he could bring the ships to Yucatán's aid at once if Lemus would send money.[19]

Before the *San Antonio* completed her refit in Mobile, Seegar came over to New Orleans to present a demand on the civil authorities for the mutineers. Unfortunately, neither Seegar nor any of the other Texas Navy officers was able to produce his commission to give legal effect to his request. The prisoners remained in jail until President Houston should request their release. In the called session of Congress on 6 July the Senate approved Houston's nominations for commissions for Texas Navy officers. Moore's commission was back-dated to 21 April 1839, three months before he resigned from the United States Navy.

By the end of June so many hungry, suspicious volunteers were waiting in Galveston for the conquest of Mexico to begin that President Houston tried to charter the American brig *Retrieve* to take them to Live Oak Point. The *Retrieve*'s captain refused to trust Houston for the money (or take his watch, dramatically offered as security); so Houston sent Captain James Boylan and five armed soldiers to seize her.[20] They not only seized the ship, but impressed two officers as well.[21] Houston placed John Appleman in charge. In a foolhardy attempt to run over the bar without a pilot, Appleman grounded the vessel at Live Oak Point, unshipped the rudder, and almost lost the ship. On 5 July the troops were landed.[22]

Commodore Moore did not stand around the Verandah Hotel waiting for a sackful of gold to be sent from Texas. He had vessels to make ready for sea, crews to ship, provisions to buy, urgent blockade orders to carry out. Within three weeks he had enlisted his crews, had provisioned the two schooners for sixteen weeks, and had reported that he would complete the *Austin*'s refit in another ten days, just as

[19] Edwin Ward Moore, *op. cit.*, p. 76.

[20] Amelia W. Williams and Eugene C. Barker (eds.), *Writings of Sam Houston,* III, 70.

[21] George P. Garrison (ed.), *Diplomatic Correspondence of the Republic of Texas,* II, Part 1, 588.

[22] *Ibid.*, p. 587.

he had promised two months before in Yucatán. By 9 June at the latest Moore expected the three ships to be ready for extended operations. The *San Antonio* had sailed sometime before 1 June, and the *San Bernard* was cruising in the Gulf a few days later.

This was a remarkable job of organization and financing with no help whatever from the Texas government. Merchants trusted Moore on his personal signature while they refused to take President Sam Houston's power of attorney for the yet unprinted exchequer bills.

On 6 June, when less than three days' work remained for the *Austin,* the *Wharton* arrived in New Orleans with only nine sailors, no money, no provisions, and orders for Moore to add her to the expedition.[23] The *Wharton* had been left back in the Arcas Islands on 26 April when the other ships shoved off for Texas. She had stayed off Mexico until mid-May, performing a useful service in maintaining the blockade for an extra month, and returning to Galveston on 26 May. Now, she was a white elephant to Moore. She was a good ship, badly needed, but Moore had hardly enough money for the other three, and $6,000 was required to replenish, rearm, and recruit for the *Wharton.* Moore borrowed as much as he could, attached his own salary (at 50-per-cent discount) and began shipping seamen and contracting for provisions and ammunition.[24] Meanwhile, he desperately needed money from Texas or Yucatán. Since the *San Antonio* was not expected for another week or so, and since the exchequer bills should long since have been signed and released to him, Commodore Moore sent his brother James over to Texas to get the money. Moore wrote Secretary Hockley that with even half of the $20,000 due since January he might be able to get to sea. James Moore left for Galveston on 11 June. The Commodore contracted for the remainder of the stores, and shipped two thirds of the sailors for the *Wharton.*

By mid-June the *San Antonio* returned with the $4,000 cash owed Texas, but no advance, and James Moore was back from Texas without the exchequers. Houston sent word that he had publicly promised not to issue any more exchequer bills until after Congress met next

[23] Edwin Ward Moore, *op. cit.,* p. 70.
[24] Edwin Ward Moore to L. L. Ferrien, n.d., probably about 6 June 1842 (Archives, Texas State Library, Austin).

month.[25] Accordingly, he sent Moore another letter of credit for the same $10,000.[26] Moore was unable to negotiate it, either. It was rather like a parachute manufacturer offering a free replacement for the one that did not open. Houston added a new ruse: this one said that, since Congress would have to find some money to pay itself, there ought to be some way of paying the Navy.[27] He did not mention the previous session which came and went without the Navy's receiving a dime of the $20,000 appropriated for it.

Moore had recruited 230 men.[28] He had provisioned three ships. He had made temporary repairs to the *Austin*. He had contracted for supplies for the *Wharton*. If the $10,000 had been sent he would have been at sea within ten days. Now he was harbor-bound. Six of the sixteen weeks' provisions for the *Austin* had been eaten by mid-June. The sickly season was at hand.

Commodore Moore seriously considered resigning from the service and letting Texas shift for itself, but he was a stubborn and prideful man. He wrote: "I believe that the natural promptings in most bosoms would have been to abandon the service in disgust, at the failure of my Government to redeem its pledges, thereby involving me in its breach of faith. But I still hope[d] to redeem the enterprise from failure, which was so important to the very salvation of my country, and on the success of which I had been induced by my Government to stake my property, credit, character and life."[29]

As soon as he could he left for Texas to get the money. Consul Arrangoiz reported to the Mexican government that Moore was maintaining the Navy by his "extraordinary activity. Houston is a mortal enemy of Moore's. Moore never again will obey Houston's orders, but will act as appears best to him."[30]

Moore passed through Galveston on 1 July, eyeing the hulk of the *Zavala* lying where she had been beached to keep her from sinking—

---

[25] Edwin Ward Moore, *To the People of Texas*, p. 72.
[26] Amelia W. Williams and Eugene C. Barker, *op. cit.*, III, 71.
[27] Edwin Ward Moore, *To the People of Texas*, p. 73.
[28] *Ibid.*
[29] *Ibid.*, p. 74.
[30] Arrangoiz to Ministerio de Relaciones Exteriores, 29 June 1842 (Secretaria de Relaciones Exteriores, Mexico, D.F., L-E-1067).

a hundred-thousand-dollar ship settling into Galveston mud because the government would neither repair nor sell her.[31]

When Moore arrived in Houston Congress had just met. Moore made a written report to Secretary Hockley, and apparently button-holed a few congressmen as well as the President himself. Moore estimated $15,000 for repair of the *Zavala*, urgently needed to keep the worms from finishing her in six to eight weeks. Officers and men lacked pay. The *Austin* had to supply rations to the *Wharton;* both were running low. Bills in New Orleans were not paid. The entire $20,000 might barely see them through.

Moore was forced to wait three weeks for consideration of a Navy bill. Congress was largely concerned with the bill for offensive war.

The congressman who did most talking was brilliant, fiery, Houston-hating James S. Mayfield. Mayfield thought immediate, all-out war against Mexico was the only solution to Texas' troubles, and struggled to get a sensible war bill passed. He also had a few choice words to pass about Houston, with a tongue sharp enough to have brought out pistols in the winter session. He had beaten former House Speaker David S. Kaufman to the draw on that occasion, and had shot Kaufman down in the corridor between the House and Senate. This time he fired not pistols but words.

But he could not goad the Congress into straightforward action. A bill was passed giving Houston pretty much what he asked for. War was not declared, but Houston was given authority to call up troops' if he desired. Appropriations were made, but Congress shied away from strong revenue-collecting laws and left to President Houston the unpopular details of administration of customs. A strong, enthusiastic executive could have made the Congress' law work. Houston wanted to do nothing anyway, and could find a thousand excuses for not complying with the law, all the while insisting that he was bowing to the will of Congress. Mayfield saw the dangers of this war bill and railed against it. Then Houston, having maneuvered Congress into passing a bill giving him the almost unlimited authority that he had asked for, joined his bitterest critic and vetoed the bill he had called the Congress to enact.

Moore convinced Congress of the need for the Navy. Houston him-

[31] Edwin Ward Moore, *To the People of Texas,* p. 77.

self in his 27 June 1842 message to Congress supported the Navy, although he did take the opportunity once more to call the Yucatán expedition an unlawful one. He said that the Navy would soon be at sea, blockading Mexico, at no expense to the government, though only a few days before he had given James Moore another one of his powers of attorney for half the $20,000 appropriated in February. He asked for money for raising the sunken *Zavala*. In this he overruled Secretary Hockley, who wanted her sold.

"No *formidable* invasion, it is true, has been attempted since 1836 —nor do I believe they will be ever able to effect its accomplishment,"[32] Houston said, but he explained the presence of the recruits from the United States by saying of himself, "Under the conviction that immediate invasion was meditated, he felt himself fully authorized, under existing laws, to invite emigrants from the United States with a view of giving protection to our advanced settlements."[33] He went on to support the Navy: "I need not urge the high importance of this branch of the public service, and the necessity of maintaining it at all hazards in a state of efficiency. We are apprised that all the capacities and energies of our enemy are directed to the attainment of naval superiority over us upon the gulf; and unless we are in a situation to successfully compete with them our commerce will be ruined, and many calamities visited upon us. If our sea-coast is without this means of defence, we shall be in the most vulnerable condition for attack, and we may expect the infliction of wounds from which we could not readily recover."[34]

On 23 July Congress passed a naval appropriations bill for $97,659 to fulfill all the needs enumerated by Moore. An odd phrase was attached to part of it: the $15,000 for the *Zavala* and the $25,000 for outfit of the ships and provisioning them were to come out of the first money in the treasury or at the disposition of the President. Congress intended this to forestall any tricky business on the part of the President, whose dislike for the Navy was becoming more evident daily. Texas law required payment of normal appropriations on a first-come, first-served basis. This provision was intended to put payments

[32] Harriet Smither (ed.), *Journals of the Sixth Congress of the Republic of Texas,* III, 100.
[33] *Ibid.,* p. 101.   [34] *Ibid.,* p. 103.

to the Navy ahead of all other appropriations. The other $57,659 was appropriated for back pay owed the officers and men of the Navy.

Moore wrote:

I determined to bring matters to a close without further delay, and accordingly called on the President the day Congress adjourned, (the afternoon of the 23rd July) when he informed me that he had just signed the bill making a new appropriation of $97,659, for naval purposes. . . . and expressed his gratification in consequence thereof. He then enquired of me, as he had repeatedly done before, "when I would leave for New-Orleans?" To which I replied, "that it was useless for me to leave without the means of raising money to sustain the Navy," and again expressed a wish to get the appropriation of the *preceding* session of Congress, with which I hoped to get to sea. He refused to comply with my request, but offered to give a *bond* to be used in raising money on the faith of the appropriation. After the fate of the first two documents of a similar character, this was an evident *trifling* with the dilemma in which he had involved me. Viewing it in this light, and feeling assured that it was his intention to break up the Navy in a foreign port, I replied "that I had already fruitlessly tried to negociate similar bonds, as I had before stated to him, and that he need not try to *humbug* me with another bond or power of attorney, for I would not be *humbuged* by him.—That a power of attorney from the President of Texas for *one million of dollars* would not bring in New Orleans *one hundred dollars!*—That I had already exhausted nearly all my means and credit to sustain the Navy, and would not use another dollar, nor incur another dollar of debt until I saw a disposition on the part of the constituted authorities to aid me. That as to his inquiry of when I would leave for New-Orleans, I had to inform him that the steamer Merchant was waiting at Galveston for me, to which place I would repair the next day, and on my arrival in New-Orleans, would disband the Navy and leave the vessels to rot in a foreign port, as officers and men could not be kept on board without rations." This conversation occurred in the presence of a gentleman of known integrity, who is a citizen of the country. . .[35]

Houston thought things over a few days, trying to work out a way of disbanding the fleet without taking the blame, while Moore waited

[35] Edwin Ward Moore, *To the People of Texas*, p. 82.

for the boat to take him to Galveston. Then Houston lit upon a scheme which would rid him of the Navy and destroy Moore at the same time, without making himself obviously at fault. As the river boat was about to leave, Hockley sent for Moore. He said that Houston would sign the exchequer bills for $18,812 if Moore could get the boat to wait. Moore persuaded the boat's captain to wait one day; then picked up the money and some sealed orders to be opened in New Orleans.

Moore could enjoy his triumph all the way to New Orleans. When he opened his sealed orders—humbugged after all! No doubt the paint was singed off the cabin door! Houston had twisted Moore's statement that ". . . it is now barely possible that I can get to sea with the whole appropriation"[36] into ". . . the above sum is supposed to be fully sufficient for the purpose contemplated, the Department understanding clearly, from your estimate of the expense necessary for the accomplishment of the object, that the hypothecation of the above sum will enable you to . . . [accomplish the object].[37]

Moore was ordered to hypothecate, but not to spend, the accompanying $18,812.

Instead of the exchequer bills worth about $9,000 cash, Moore had another of those promises to pay in three months, only he had to be the promiser. This immediately cut their value in half once more—if anyone would take them. No one expected their value to rise in the three months of waiting to get the money. Texas money had always gone down before, and the exchequer stuff was not expected to be different. Moore could barely have got out with the exchequers; he could not go an inch on hypothecated notes. He was caught.

[36] *Ibid.*, p. 84.   [37] *Ibid.*, p. 85.

Autumn 1842: Baiting the Trap

Before the Commodore left for Galveston on 27 July 1842 he gave the Secretary of War and Marine a memorandum on the condition of the ships in New Orleans. He said that when he left New Orleans on 24 June he had expected to be in Texas only a few days instead of a month. At that time the ships had only two weeks' provisions, bought out of Moore's own credit, and he supposed Lothrop had used up his credit, too. If Lothrop could not feed his sailors, he would have to discharge them early and without pay, which would make recruiting more difficult and expensive.

The $20,000 appropriated in February was by Houston's own estimates only about half of the year's requirement. If Moore had received it all when he asked for it, he could have shipped crews, bought stores, repaired ships, and got to sea. There he would have been penniless, but he could have captured enough ships running the blockade to pay for food and ammunition. His directive from the Department of War and Marine said it was not doubted that he could sustain the fleet by captures—but since it was not an absolute certainty they would not give him the chance to try. Moore says that the objection to giving him the $20,000 was the insufficiency of this appropriation, "and the larger one is also withheld—because of its being too large, I suppose."[1] So, the whole bundle of near-worthless money went for food and housekeeping, with no possibility of getting the ships to sea or of getting more money.

His brief stop at Galveston did not make Moore feel better. Lieutenant Brashear, formerly of the *Zavala*, was in command of the Navy Yard now, and had just reported bad leaks in the *Archer*. Secretary Hockley, with Houston's sanction, instructed Gail Borden to help out, though as usual no specific orders were given and no money expenditure was authorized.

The *San Bernard* and the *San Antonio* looked a little better than the *Archer*, though both were short of men and provisions by now. In early June they had had crews and sixteen weeks' provisions aboard, but two months had gone by. Half the provisions were consumed, and sailors began deserting when they found they were not to be paid. However, the ships were at least active, convoying troops between Mobile and Live Oak Point, supposedly for the great invasion of Mexico.

Moore and Seegar went to New Orleans in the *Merchant*, arriving 31 July. Moore found the *Austin* leaking six feet of water a day; he opened his sealed orders to the sound of creaking pumps in the hold of his rotten flagship. In addition to the financial trickery, his orders contained a curious provision.

Enclosed was a blockade proclamation, quite similar to the one already in effect since 26 March, but undated, though signed by President Houston. Moore could not tell whether the omission of a date was negligence or was indicative of Houston's unusually great trust in Moore.

Moore was ordered to get out on the Gulf as soon as possible, prepared for an assault on Tampico or other Mexican seaport. His squadron this time was to fit out for four months, to take the *Merchant* along, and to reimburse itself out of contribution from the enemy cities.[2]

Moore had his orders; his problem was to carry them out!

[1] Edwin Ward Moore, *To the People of Texas,* p. 45.
[2] *Ibid.,* p. 86.

First, he had to put the *Austin* in dry dock to find the cause of the leak. In two days he had her up, and sure enough—the sloop had lost some copper sheathing. This damage had been incurred either in leaving Galveston the previous December or in touching the reef off Lobos in April. Now that she was inactive in the Mississippi the shrimps were picking the oakum from the seams, and the waterline strakes of the hull were rotting away. Checks aloft showed the main yard of the *Austin* and the foretopyards of both the *Austin* and the *Wharton* rotten to the core and demanding immediate replacement. Within a week the work was done, and the ships were seaworthy once more, though the *Austin's* hull needed a thorough overhaul.

Lieutenant Sebastian Holsinger, a German serving in the Mexican Navy, managed to get aboard the *Austin*. He reported her to Consul Arrangoiz clean and in such good shape topside that she appeared less than a year old, but that she had a crew of only thirty or forty men.[3]

Commodore Moore carried out his orders about not spending the exchequers—at least from the time he read his sealed orders. Mr. Lockwood of the firm V. Whitcomb Company spent the $2,360 Moore had put up as collateral for provisions before the 13 October date agreed upon.[4] It was obvious that $18,812, discounted to about one quarter of its face value, would not now get the ships out. There was no more money in New Orleans for the Texas Navy.

A possible source of money was from the sale of the stranded *Zavala's* machinery. The preceding July Secretary of War and Marine Hockley had recommended the sale of the *Zavala*, but Houston instead requested funds to put her in shape. He got his appropriation and then ignored it. Hockley, afraid of immediate sea-borne invasion led by the new Mexican steamers, searched for a way to help Moore. He once more proposed to sell the *Zavala's* engines.

This gave Houston an opening to be sanctimonious, and the Hero of San Jacinto rose in his most righteous manner as the defender of the Congress and of the Constitution. He would let that bunch of pirates, the Navy, rot and sink before he would lift a finger to make a

[3] Arrangoiz to Ministerio de Relaciones Exteriores, 23 August 1842 (Secretaria de Relaciones Exteriores, Mexico, D.F., L-E-1068 [1842]).

[4] Edwin Ward Moore, *op. cit.*, p. 106.

move unauthorized by Congress. Sam Houston would take no responsibility for selling a wrecked Texas Navy vessel, even if by doing so he could keep the other ships afloat.[5]

Hockley had been with Houston for fifteen years, from Houston's Washington days, when he was a clerk in the War Department through San Jacinto, when he was Houston's chief of staff. Hockley was no longer a young U.S. War Department clerk. He was a Cabinet minister, responsible for the defence of a country expecting attack. (A second raid on San Antonio actually came ten days later.) Hockley questioned Houston's judgment in keeping Texas' defences weak. Houston decided Hockley must go.

Knowing his man well, Houston bawled out and belittled Hockley in front of a stranger. Hockley had had enough, and submitted a bitter resignation, contending that Houston could have found a way for selling the *Zavala* if he had wanted to. On Hockley's recommendations Houston had appointed Army officers to posts which did not exist, had diverted appropriations, had given questionable orders to General Somervell. Now Hockley could only explain Houston's reluctance to act as prejudice against the Navy.

Houston, in his reply to Hockley, repeated that the Navy was useless, and changed the subject from the emergency procedure of a wartime government into a discussion of constitutional separation of powers. After reading the first couple of pages, Hockley threw it down, telling Attorney General Terrell that Houston was intentionally missing the point. Hockley's resignation from the Cabinet took effect on 2 September 1842, and his clerk, M. C. Hamilton, became Acting Secretary of War and Marine while Houston himself ran the Department and turned it into a bookkeeping concern.

Houston had silenced another advocate of preparedness.

Before Hockley had accused Houston of deliberately wrecking the Navy out of prejudice Moore had come to the same conclusion. Moore thought that Houston allowed malice toward a Navy which he identified with Lamar, and toward Moore personally, to cloud his judgment, or that he lacked the strength of character to risk war.[6]

---

[5] Hockley to Houston, 1 September 1842, Amelia W. Williams and Eugene C. Barker (eds.), *Writings of Sam Houston,* IV, 141–143.

[6] Edwin Ward Moore, *op. cit.,* pp. 92, 97.

In spite of Houston, Moore could and would defend Texas. He might have to use equivocation, stratagems, or disobedience. Admiral Nelson had achieved world fame and approval at Copenhagen for reading his superior's fainthearted signal through a telescope held to his blind eye. With complete legal justification, Moore might have waited in New Orleans for more money while the Mexicans came up and took Texas, but his sense of responsibility for Texas made him stretch his authority to the utmost. He felt that Yucatán would now underwrite another cruise by the Texas Navy. He ordered the *San Antonio* to Sisal with a letter to Lemus offering help. He waited two months to report this to the Secretary of War and Marine.

While the *San Antonio* was on her way to Yucatán, the *San Bernard* remained in the Galveston area, cruising between that port and Copano Bay (near Corpus Christi). On 31 August Lieutenant Commanding Crisp wrote from Galveston to Commodore Moore that the *San Bernard*'s hull was leaking badly. Moore instructed Crisp to bring the schooner at once to New Orleans, but the *San Bernard* was in such poor condition below decks that Crisp feared for her safety and asked the Department of War and Marine for $100 to effect temporary repairs to make her seaworthy for the voyage. He received nothing. When the great September 1842 hurricane hit Galveston, the *San Bernard* was short-handed, and further endangered by a leaky hull, by her location in shallow water, and by the very light anchors and cables Tod had bought.

Crisp was a good seaman. He had watched barometer, sea, and sky, and fully expected the storm long before it broke. He had struck all the topmasts, yards, and other gear which would offer sail area to the coming wind. Then he put down his extra anchors and veered chain to sixty-five fathoms to starboard and forty-five to port. He secured his hatches, set a sea watch, and rode out the storm. The seas carried the *San Bernard* farther and farther to leeward, dragging both anchors until they caught on the mud bank. The stern smashed against the *Merchant*; then she grounded and blew into two feet of water, heeled over on her starboard side where she lay stranded in the mud. It was 3:00 A.M., 18 September 1842. A brig and three merchant schooners were stranded in the same storm. The Episcopal and

Presbyterian churches were knocked down; there were four to six feet of water in the Tremont Hotel.

The *San Bernard* appeared only slightly damaged during these troubles. As soon as the seas subsided, Crisp moved the valuable gear off her and commenced preparations to put her back into the water. His plan was to take his twenty remaining sailors and bring the hulk of the *Archer* in as close as possible, lift out the *San Bernard's* lower masts, and then use jack screws and lines to the *Archer* to bring the *San Bernard* to an even keel, repair her, and launch her once more. Hamilton asked Gail Borden to help Crisp. Houston sanctioned the request. As usual, neither authorized Borden to spend any money. Borden lent Crisp some manila lines, but furnished neither jack screws nor provisions. Crisp did all he could with his few men until he ran out of food.

He appealed in vain to Borden, to Hamilton, and finally to Moore in faraway New Orleans. Moore sent Crisp three barrels of beef, three of pork, one each of beans and raisins from his own scant supply, but Crisp's crew were starved out. Only two men and two boys remained when Moore's supplies arrived. Lieutenant Crisp, his five officers, two men, and two boys moved over on the *Archer* to obtain shelter and to await better times. The government had long since stopped paying them. No issue of government food arrived after Moore's shipment in November. Threadbare, starving, except for the charity of friends ashore or a lucky windfall, they held on, determined not to be run out of their ship as long as there was a chance to restore her to service, because all wanted a hand in repelling the Mexican sea-borne invasion.

By now the *Archer* was nothing but a hulk with seams open wide enough to put a hand through. The sails, tackle, yards, and other rigging which had not been removed to put on the *Wharton* the spring before were on the spar deck. The *San Bernard's* gear was aboard, too, to add to the confusion. Her guns took the place of the *Archer's*, which had been moved ashore for Galveston's coast defence during the emergency.

Two boys and one man were discharged without pay, leaving only the cook, the six officers, and Crisp's pet pig. Even this happy animal finally disappeared, though he never left the ship. There were few dishes; the gale which stranded the *San Bernard* sent a hail of crockery to the railing. The little band drank yaupon tea and occasional coffee out of a handleless mug, a pitcher, a basin, a tin can, and a flowerpot.

Once in a while Crisp would brush off his coat, hide his cuffs, borrow bits of uniform from the others, and get into the gig to be rowed to a visiting ship by his five officers and Hussy, the cook, all dressed in old sailor clothes.[7] In January 1843, Lieutenant Crisp left the ship on leave to England. Most of the officers went ashore with friends. Lieutenant Charles B. Snow, left aboard, hocked his epaulette to get food for himself, Sailing Master Charles S. Arcambal, the only other officer on board, and the one sailor. Finally, starved out, with no prospect of ever receiving pay, Lieutenant Snow put the brig in charge of a Mr. St. John, took Arcambal, carbines, pistols, cutlasses, Roman swords, chronometer, sextants, and other navigational instruments, reported his actions to the Secretary of the Navy, and reported in to Moore on the *Austin*. Snow also got recommendations from Lothrop and Moore to help find another job. Lieutenant William C. Brashear began gathering recommendations for entry into the Russian Navy.

In New Orleans the ships were a little better off because they had a few more men and the firm hand of the Commodore. But they, too, had their troubles. Nineteen men deserted between 6 June and 15 September, some with less than a week's service. It was necessary to discharge in early November fifteen others who had not received pay from Texas. The men enlisted in May and June were finishing their six months' enlistments. Fever broke out; Marine Captain Robert Oliver died of it.[8] Arrangoiz reported that Moore was pursued by creditors everywhere he went, and that the officers worked in tattered dress coats.

Robert H. Chinn wrote: "Commodore Moore is still here without

[7] Anonymous, "The Dismasted Brig; or Naval Life in Texas," *Colburn's United Service Magazine,* October 1845, p. 264.

[8] Edwin Ward Moore to General Albert S. Johnston, 15 October 1842. Mrs. Mason Barret Collection of Johnston Papers (Howard-Tilton Memorial Library, Tulane University, New Orleans).

means of leaving. He cannot get off without money. His officers are dissatisfied, wavering as they say between a severe sea battle on the gulf and Mexican prisons and a dishonorable confinement in New Orleans. The most anxious and nervous persons I ever saw to meet the contest although the Mexicans have the Supremacy in point of Naval force besides being manned by Englishmen. . . ."[9]

Aboard the *Wharton* the officers showed the effects of despair and monotony. Midshipmen Fielding R. Culp and George W. White fought a duel, and the former died on 4 October. Midshipmen Callender Fayssoux and Peyton Middleton had a duel. Fayssoux shot the hammer off Middleton's pistol while having his own hat shot off. First Lieutenant A. I. Lewis came aboard one midwatch and ordered the steward to open the spirits room. Purser F. T. Wells complained to Captain Lothrop, and Lewis resigned 7 October 1842.

On 1 October Arrangoiz reported to his government that two Texas officers, one of whom had been captain of the *San Bernard* (as Lewis had been) came into his office, trying to enter the Mexican Navy. Arrangoiz was afraid they were spies. Besides, he resented their insolent American attitudes. He turned them down, and also refused to give them passports to Veracruz.[10]

Though he could not get his ships to sea, Moore did his utmost to harass the Mexicans, nor could they ever be confident that Moore would not at last be able to sail.

One October afternoon Arrangoiz was indulging in his usual occupation of spying on Moore when he saw the Commodore board the American merchant steamer *Alabama,* have an animated conversation with her skipper, and then leave for the *Austin* in his launch. The *Alabama* got underway at sunset, and made circles in the river while eighteen men in the *Austin's* launch tied up astern of the *Alabama.* They all headed down the river. The Mexican brig *Rosa Alvina* was about to shove off. Arrangoiz reported Moore's maneuver to the New Orleans merchants who had goods aboard her. They

---

.[9] Chinn to General Albert S. Johnston, 27 September 1842, Mrs. Mason Barret Collection of Johnston Papers (Howard-Tilton Memorial Library, Tulane University).

[10] Arrangoiz to Ministerio de Relaciones Exteriores, 1 October 1842 (Secretaria de Relaciones Exteriores, Mexico, D.F., L-E-1068 [1842]).

got the customs to assign an escort for the ship.[11] Moore found out about this precaution, and had the escort ordered dropped five miles at sea. However, the forewarned *Rosa Alvina* left by the northeast pass instead of the logical southwest pass, and thus escaped the waiting Texans.[12]

A successful expedition led by James Boylan did capture the *Mary Elizabeth*, but she was lost in Galveston in the storm which wrecked the *San Bernard*.[13] Moore then gave Boylan command of the *Merchant*.

One of the factors which made Moore impatient to leave New Orleans was the impending delivery of the *Montezuma* and the *Guadaloupe* to Mexico.[14] The two steamers were ultramodern in every sense. The *Guadaloupe*, 788 tons, 183 feet long, with 180-HP engines, was built by Lairds in Birkenhead.[15] She had two 32-pounder long guns and two 68-pounder swivel Paixhans pivots, the guns with the explosive shells "as large as a good-sized pumpkin,"[16] which would render all other armament obsolete. She was the first iron steam warship in the world to be launched, and when she was launched, the largest iron vessel ever built.[17] Another unusual feature was construction in watertight compartments.[18] The *Montezuma*, wooden-hulled, was even larger—1164 tons, 203 feet long, with 280-HP engines and two 68-pounder swivel and six 42-pounder long Paixhans guns. She was built in London. Both ships had been built from models furnished by the Admiralty, and with the intention of selling them to the Admiralty, but they had not been accepted.[19] The Admiralty kept a close eye on the *Guadaloupe*'s performance, and adopted many of her features for newer ships.

---

[11] *Ibid.*, 9 October 1842.
[12] *Ibid.*, 11 October 1842.   [13] *Ibid.*, 26 September 1842.
[14] Robert H. Chinn to General Albert Sidney Johnston, 27 September 1842, Mrs. Mason Barret Collection of Johnston Papers (Howard-Tilton Memorial Library, Tulane University).
[15] Sir Allen Moore, BT, *Sailing Ships of War*, p. 55.
[16] George P. Garrison (ed.), *Diplomatic Correspondence of the Republic of Texas*, II (1), Part III, 986.
[17] James Phinney Baxter, *Introduction of the Ironclad Warship*, p. 34.
[18] George P. Garrison, *op. cit.*, II (1), Part II, 983.
[19] Ashbel Smith to Sam Houston, 1 September 1842, Unpublished Letters of Sam Houston (Archives Collection, University of Texas, Austin).

From the first, Texas Chargé d'Affaires Ashbel Smith recognized the danger of these great ships. He started inquiries in January 1842, and made protest after protest to the British Foreign Office and the Admiralty.

On 28 April 1842 Mexican Minister to England Thomas Murphy had signed an agreement with Lizardi and Company to purchase the two steamers. Smith protested. On 8 June Smith wrote Texas Secretary of State Anson Jones to report that it looked as if the ships would be sent to Mexico with British approval, since British sympathies follow British trade. He was quite sure that the ships would be used against the Texas coast, probably with British officers. He urged Texas to put the *Zavala* into operation to capture these steamers one by one on the way out.

The Texas consul general to London was William Kennedy, a British subject who was soon to become British consul to Galveston. Before he left the Texas service Kennedy expressed to Foreign Secretary Aberdeen his belief that Texas would withdraw the blockade if England so requested.[20] This no doubt influenced Aberdeen to allow the sale and arming of the *Guadaloupe* and *Montezuma*. The *Guadaloupe* sailed with guns mounted, ready for action. Smith protested. The *Montezuma*, which sailed almost four months later, had her guns dismounted, and her commanding officer, Commander Richard F. Cleaveland, resigned his Royal Navy commission. However, all her officers, 150 seamen, and 12 marines were British.[21]

Moore apparently received reports from England directly from Smith. He expected the *Guadaloupe* to sail about 1 July, and she actually sailed on the fourth. By the end of August, after a passage of fifty days from Liverpool, she was in Veracruz.[22] Smith also wrote Reily, Texas chargé d'affaires in Washington, D.C., and warned him of the *Guadaloupe*'s sailing.[23] Reily went to President Tyler, who immediately ordered one of the two steamers of the United States,

[20] Kennedy to Aberdeen, 3 June 1842, Ephraim D. Adams (ed.), *British Diplomatic Correspondence Concerning the Republic of Texas*, p. 66.

[21] Murphy to Aberdeen, 20 August 1842 (Public Record Office, London, F.O. 75/18, 145).

[22] Pakenham to Aberdeen, 29 August 1842 (Public Record Office, London, F.O. 204/77).

[23] George P. Garrison, *op. cit.*, II (2), Part III, 986.

the *Mississippi,* to the Gulf. Smith also reported that the *Montezuma* sailed on 29 September 1842.[24]

The *Guadaloupe* was captained by Commander E. P. Charlewood, RN, an active-duty officer of the British Navy on leave. Likewise, the eighty sailors were British, though British diplomats denied that they were active-duty sailors. The officers apparently originally intended only to deliver the ships, though the Mexicans recruited most of them for six months' or a year's service. Charlewood demanded and received the then tremendous sum of $450 a month,[25] the pay and allowances of a post captain; the other Englishmen were paid in proportion.[26] Four fifths of the prizes were to go to the crew, who were told, after they got to sea, that they were going to fight a kind of half-breed Yankee called "Texians."

Yucatán's troubles with Mexico had returned soon after the departure of the Texas Navy. Young Commander Tomás Marín with 57 men in the merchant schooner *Margarita* boarded the brig *Yucateco,* and took her by surprise at Campeche on the night of 5 July.[27] On 30 August he captured the brig *Iman,* the schooner *Campecheano,* and a schooner or small boat at Carmen, when that city surrendered.[28] Eight thousand troops who landed near Campeche blockaded that city and Lerma.[29] British consuls in Mexico were predicting the defeat of Yucatán.[30] Moore was expecting every day money from Yucatán to enable his squadron to get to sea. Pakenham wrote to the Earl of Aberdeen that the forces to be used against Texas were collecting, and only lack of money was delaying the expedition.[31] General Albert Sidney Johnston had information that Mexico would invade Texas early in the spring with an efficient

[24] *Ibid.,* p. 1033.

[25] J. M. Tornel, "Report," 17 January 1843 (Departamento de Archivo, Correspondencia y Historia, Mexico, D.F., 117D/111.6/1923).

[26] Record (Public Record Office, London, F.O. 204/79, Part 1, p. 198).

[27] Barbachano and Carbó, *El Estado de Campeche,* p. 91.

[28] Report dated 30 August 1842 (Secretaria de la Defensa Nacional, Mexico, D.F., XI/481.3/1741).

[29] Edwin Ward Moore, *Doings of the Texas Navy,* p. 6.

[30] British consul, Veracruz, to Pakenham, 20 October 1842 (Public Record Office, London, F.O. 204/79, Part I, p. 232).

[31] Pakenham to Aberdeen, 10 September 1842 (Public Record Office, London, F.O. 50/155).

army.[32] On 11 September 1842 the Mexicans sacked San Antonio once more. General Woll announced in San Antonio that this was the start of the reconquest of Texas.[33]

Woll's raid on San Antonio came the day after Houston revoked his 26 March blockade of Mexican ports. This revocation had been the first major project of the new British consul general and chargé d'affaires, Captain Charles Elliot, RN.

Elliot, fresh from having brought on the Opium War in China, which gained Hong Kong for Queen Victoria, had been instructed to be merely a spectator and reporter in Texas.[34] Lord Aberdeen told Elliot and Pakenham that the British government did not care whether Texas was independent of Mexico or not, but under no circumstances must Texas join the United States. Elliot worked earnestly to keep Texas, "this flotsam or derelict of the Prairies,"[35] as he called it, apart from the United States.

Meanwhile, British trade interests, particularly the Mexico and South American Association, were clamoring for an end to the blockade. Elliot achieved the lifting of it. He got along well with Houston and Anson Jones, and reinforced Houston's desire to weaken the Navy.

Elliot was instructed by the Foreign Secretary to convince Houston that the construction, manning, and outfitting of the *Montezuma* and the *Guadaloupe* did not indicate British favoritism for Mexico, but were only commercial ventures with a precedent in the Dawson contract in the United States.[36] Captain Elliot wrote back to England that he would have no trouble with Sam Houston on this subject, and he had none. Houston was so eager to ingratiate himself with Great Britain in order to worry the United States that he apologized

[32] A. T. Burnley to General Albert Sidney Johnston, 21 October 1842, Mrs. Mason Barret Collection of Johnston Papers (Howard-Tilton Memorial Library, Tulane University).

[33] William R. Manning (ed.), *Diplomatic Correspondence of the United States, Inter-American Affairs, 1831–1860*, XII, 254.

[34] Foreign Office to Elliot, 1 July 1842 (Public Record Office, London, F.O. 53/18).

[35] Elliot to Aberdeen, 5 February 1843 (Public Record Office, London, F.O. 204/83).

[36] Elliot to Addington, 15 November 1842, Ephraim D. Adams (ed.), *British Diplomatic Correspondence Concerning the Republic of Texas*, pp. 125–130.

to Elliot for Ashbel Smith's zeal in trying to delay or stop the transfer
to Mexico of the steamers that were to lead the invasion of Texas![37]

In Houston's 12 September 1842 proclamation revoking the blockade he gave as his reason for this action that he wished to ease the
tension while Great Britain and the United States mediated between
Texas and Mexico. This deliberately missed the point of the failure
of Bee's, Treat's, and Webb's missions. Webb had pointed out that
Texas could deal with Mexico only from a position of strength.

Houston authorized Somervell to cross the Rio Grande,[38] and, before the raid actually came off, had George W. Terrell (now Acting
Secretary of State) formally ask the United States, Great Britain, and
France to get Mexico to agree to stop border raiding.[39] He continued
the inconsistency (which Webster called to the attention of Texas
Chargé d'Affaires Van Zandt)[40] by challenging Mexico to make a
major attack on Texas, withholding money from the Navy, disbanding U.S. volunteers, recruiting more, and repeating orders for Moore
to get to sea. Great Britain, France, and the United States accepted
the mediation job, which all knew to be useless, and Houston granted
permission to Warfield to invade Mexico as a commercial venture, at
no cost to the government—and no profit either, as later events
worked out.

A month after the *San Antonio* had sailed from Galveston on 27
August 1842 with an offer of help to Lemus, and had been unsighted,
Moore reported her possible loss. A schooner of her description
(black hull, raking masts) was later reported as a West Indian
pirate, but she is generally thought to have foundered in the September hurricane.

Moore wrote again to General Pedro Lemus. In early November
he received a noncommittal reply. Mexico sent three thousand more
troops and a brigade of artillery to Yucatán. Wind and weather were
favorable to them.[41] Captain Charlewood reported that there was no

[37] Ephraim D. Adams, *British Interests and Activities in Texas*, p. 114.

[38] Houston to Somervell, 3 October 1842, Unpublished Letters of Sam
Houston (Archives Collection, University of Texas).

[39] C. E. Lester, *The Life of Sam Houston*, p. 226.

[40] George P. Garrison, *op. cit.*, II (1), Part II, 152.

[41] British consul, Veracruz, to Pakenham, 20 October 1842 (Public Record
Office, London, F.O. 204/79, Part 1, p. 232).

doubt of the Mexican success; Campeche could hold out only a month or six weeks longer.[42] On 1 December 1842 Mexico proclaimed a blockade of Campeche.[43]

In early October, near Atchafalaya Bay, the *Merchant,* uninsured, sprang a leak and sank, a total loss. The loss meant the end of Moore's income and of his best source of credit.

On 14 and 26 October the Commodore reported his inability to get underway without money. This called for another order, written 29 October 1842:

". . . If you cannot with the means at your command, prepare the squadron for sea, you will immediately with all the vessels under your command sail for the port of Galveston, and on your arrival there . . ."[44]

This order was written by direction of the military genius who allowed two inferior forces to combine the day before San Jacinto.

Six days later Hamilton repeated his desires (but not orders) for the ships to return to Texas if Moore did not have money properly to fit them out. He hoped, however, that ". . . some kind fortune may have enabled you to accomplish your purpose."[45]

Moore sent back the muster lists of his two ships, showing that he did not have enough men even to get one ship underway, much less to sail her through the enemy squadron expected daily off Galveston.[46] The *Wharton* had a surgeon's steward, a boy, and two marines.[47] Arrangoiz reported nine men between the two ships.[48] Moore's letter was answered with another order to carry out the impossible order.[49]

Consul Bryan was ordered not to furnish the Navy with supplies.[50] Moore was informed that no money was to be forthcoming, that

[42] *Ibid.,* 17 November 1842, p. 255.

[43] U.S. Consul, Campeche, to Secretary of State, 1 December 1842. Letters from U.S. Consuls (National Archives).

[44] Edwin Ward Moore, *To the People of Texas,* p. 104.

[45] *Ibid.,* p. 107.   [46] *Ibid.,* p. 116.

[47] Muster List, 18 December 1842, Dienst Papers (Archives Collection, University of Texas).

[48] Arrangoiz to Ministerio de Relaciones Exteriores, 21 December 1842 (Secretaria de Relaciones Exteriores, Mexico, D.F., L-E-1068 [1842]).

[49] Edwin Ward Moore, *To the People of Texas,* p. 117.

[50] Anson Jones to Bryan, 18 November 1842. Consular papers, 1838–1845. (Archives, Texas State Library).

the $97,659 appropriation of 23 July was a dead letter and never had meant anything.[51] The appropriation bill had been passed by the Congress, signed by the President, with the provision in it that it was to be paid out of the first money at the disposition of the President or in the treasury, but it was still a dead letter!

Yet money was paid out for such items as: $300.00 for a porter, $114.00 for printing, $350.00 to Houston for secret service, $354.84 to W. D. Miller for extra services, $675.00 to L. M. Hitchcock for charter of schooner, and many more.[52]

By 2 December Moore had told Houston that he had sent the *San Antonio* to Sisal to see about renewal of the naval agreement, that he was expecting money from Yucatán, but was afraid that Yucatán would fall before it could send any.[53] Houston still did not tell Moore to stop asking Yucatán for money, and apparently still hoped "some kind fortune" would intervene.

Houston called the Seventh Congress (in the election of which regular Navy Texans had cast absentee ballots aboard the ships for the last time in over a hundred years) to meet three weeks early in Washington-on-the-Brazos. So many members dallied that a quorum was not reached until four days before the regular convening date of 5 December.

Houston delivered various public messages to Congress, but kept secret his message concerning the Navy. This message, and Hamilton's report, painted the Navy in the worst possible light.[54] Houston said that Moore had run through every dime Congress had appropriated, that Yucatán had defaulted her payments, that the Navy would cost $300,000 a year to keep up, and that Moore would not go to sea even if he could. Houston held Moore incompetent and disloyal for failing to get to sea and stay there for nine months on what amounted to less than $5,000, given months too late.

No Mayfield or Francis Moore arose to defend the Navy. The only argument in favor of a navy was Houston's own analysis of the mili-

[51] Edwin Ward Moore, *To the People of Texas*, p. 117.

[52] Treasury warrant 414, Unpublished Letters of Sam Houston (Archives Collection, University of Texas), IV.

[53] Edwin Ward Moore, *To the People of Texas*, p. 112.

[54] E. W. Winkler (ed.), *Secret Journals of the Senate, Republic of Texas*, p. 244.

tary situation of 10 January 1843, intended for an entirely different purpose: to set Houston up as the military dictator of Texas, with powers similar to those in the war bill he had vetoed seven months before.

Houston desired:

. . . to communicate the substance of certain intelligence, on that subject, which he has very lately received, with such suggestions as he deems it his duty to make.

This intelligence is from the city of Mexico, and dated the 8th of November. It indicates to the Executive in the most authentic and impressive terms, that Mexico, in the event of being successful against Yucatan, will immediately invade Texas with a formidable force both by land and sea. And the Gentleman who communicates the intelligence does it with a view that Texas may so provide, as to ensure the repulse of the troops of the enemy sent against her. He is not now in Mexico, but has transmitted the information with the greatest despatch, that it may be laid before Congress previous to its adjournment. It is additional to any that was in the possession of the Executive, at the time his last communication on this subject was made.

It seems to be a fact established by reason, that if Mexico meditates the invasion of Texas, it will be attempted during the ensuing spring. She cannot expect that the civilized powers will tolerate in her a protracted war with Texas, unless she make some demonstration to them that would create a reasonable belief that she is capable of subjugating and reannexing it to the Mexican territory. Hence it may be supposed, that all her available energies will be called into action and employed with the greatest efficiency.

The question then arises, is Texas in a situation to repel a formidable invasion? If she is, we have nothing to fear from it; if not, she ought to be so. Every means in our power should be called into action, and be in readiness for any event we should anticipate.

We should calculate the probable effect and influence, which the employment of our troops on the Rio Grande might produce upon Mexico, as well as the events which might result to Texas from the same cause. If disaster should befal our men on the Rio Grande, their return to Texas will be well calculated to create sensations not only of an unpleasant nature, but cast a gloom upon the spirits of our people that would be unfavorable to prompt action on our part. A state of great excitement is always unfavorable to military operations; and with the advance of the enemy in great strength, confusion might soon mature into panic, and cause the removal of families. With them, also, a large portion of those who should rally to the field, would recede from the scene of action, leaving but comparatively a small force to contend with the invaders. If an insufficient force should rally, and be compelled to give back before the enemy, it would only increase the panic, if any existed; and, if at the commencement, there should be no actual panic, it would have a tendency to create one, or, at least, to depress the ardor of our troops.

In regarding our enemy, we ought not to rely so much upon their inefficiency, as upon our own preparation and readiness to meet them. By underestimating them, we neglect to husband our own strength, and to use that forecast and precaution, which might alone ensure success to our arms.

We have yet time to organize our forces, by sending expresses to the several colonels commanding regiments throughout the Republic, with contingent orders, so as to meet, or rendezvous, at certain points, to enable us to counteract the probable movements of the enemy. This may be done at an expense not exceeding two thousand dollars; and an appropriation of that amount for the purpose, is respectfully recommended.

If Texas is invaded, the object will certainly be to overrun the country by a formidable force, entering it probably in two divisions; the most numerous by San Antonio, detaching to upper Colorado a sufficient force, composed principally of cavalry, to sustain itself; and after ravaging the upper part of that river, fall down to La Grange, and there unite with the main body, advanced from Bexar. The lower division will probably enter the country by Victoria, and advance along the seaboard in cooperation with the fleet destined for Galveston, inciting, if possible, an insurrection amoung the negroes of the lower Colorado and the Brazos; supplying them with arms and munitions of war, and forming, finally, a junction with their fleet at Galveston. The division at La Grange may be expected, in the greatest force, to advance to Washington, whilst the remainder of the division would diverge by San Felipe, and those at this point cross the Brazos, descend to the bay, and there concentrate with the entire force of the invading army. They would thus have the entire command of our waters, and the gulf, and could sustain themselves, receiving supplies by water, and by the aid of cavalry, harrass the country eastward as far as the Trinity, and forage upon the stock and numerous herds of cattle which abound in Texas.[55]

[55] *Ibid.*, pp. 270–271.

Houston's speech was the most logical possible reason for Texas to slash its internal spending to nothing in order to build up the Army and to allow the Navy to get to sea. Any drastic means were justified to destroy the Mexican ships before an invasion of Texas could be mounted.

Yet on 16 January 1843 Congress passed and Houston immediately signed a secret act to provide for the sale of the Navy of Texas:

An Act to provide for the Sale of the Navy of Texas.

Sect. 1. Be it enacted by the Senate and House of Representatives of the Republic of Texas in Congress assembled, That the President be and he is hereby authorized and required [as] soon as practicable, consistent with the public interest, to dispose of the vessels comprising the Navy of Texas, to wit, The Ship Austin the Brig Wharton at the highest price which can be obtained either by sale or in exchange for and redemption of the entire liabilities of the Government contracted in the purchase of said vessels, and the Brig Archer and the Schooner San Bernard together with the Steamship Zavalla her tackle furniture and apparel, also the property of the Navy Yard with all the Naval Stores be sold for cash or credit as the President may deem proper, and the proceeds of sale from the Archer, San Bernard and Zavalla with the public property at the Navy Yard, shall be disbursed in the following manner, to wit, fifteen thousand dollars for the payment of claims due the present or former officers, seamen and marines of the Navy in proportion to the time they have served and the amount which may be due, and the ballance to be paid into the Treasury of the Republic.

Sect. 2. Be it further enacted That the President be and he is hereby authorized to appoint some trustworthy and suitable person or persons, to act as agent or agents, in affecting [sic] at as early a period as practicable the object of this act.

Sect. 3. Be it further enacted That this act take effect from and after its passage.

N. H. Darnell
Speaker of the House of Representatives
J. A. Greer
Presdent Pro. Tem. of the Senate,

Approved 16th Jany 1843
Sam Houston[56]

[56] *Ibid.*, p. 316.

The Navy Commissioners

Toward the end of January 1843 while Moore was still in New Orleans awaiting a reply to his offer to help Yucatán, and a month after the giant *Montezuma* had entered the Mexican Navy, President Houston appointed commissioners to sell the Texas Navy. They were Samuel May Williams, James Morgan, and William Bryan, with Purser J. F. Stephens, secretary.[1] Williams, who had initially bought the Navy, declined the appointment. James Morgan, a wealthy landowner and speculator from near Galveston, though he thought the sale of the Navy would leave the coast at the mercy of the enemy, accepted, since he estimated that Santa Anna did not have enough men to attempt an invasion.[2]

President Houston followed what, even for him, was a devious route. He had secured the passage of his bill to abolish the Navy, at

[1] G. W. Hill to Stephens, 27 January 1843 (Archives, Texas State Library, Austin).

[2] Morgan to General Swartwout, 20 February 1843, Morgan Papers (Rosenberg Library, Galveston).

the same time warning that sea-borne invasion was imminent. Daniel Webster warned Texas in early December of 1842 that Mexico would land in Texas in two to four months.[3] Pakenham predicted Mexican operations against Texas in the spring of 1843.[4] The Texas consul in New York had information that the British would not prevent the *Guadaloupe* and the *Montezuma* from leading a Texas invasion. Mexican Foreign Minister to Washington Juan Almonte urged his government to defeat Texas immediately.[5]

Houston kept the news of the secret act from his own naval commander and from the general public, but he told Captain Charles Elliot, RN, and the collector of customs in Galveston. He offered the ships back to Frederick Dawson, and began feeling out customers to buy the Navy. Even the Mexicans got the word.

To prepare his country for defence against invasion Houston offered it another scheme for amusing the people while he threw the country open to the invaders. Even though the assumption of the clairvoyance to predict the details of enemy tactics is one of the most dangerous things possible in warfare, Houston's prognosis of Mexican tactics in the impending invasion of Texas apparently represented Houston's own best belief.

His plan was to make himself the military dictator of Texas, with authorization to command the Army in person and to order up the militia:

. . . The constitution declares that the President shall be the Commander-in-Chief of the Army and Navy. At the same time, it restricts him from personal command, unless he should assume the same by authority of Congress. Although he sincerely deprecates the necessity which might render it proper for him to be invested with personal command, yet he can anticipate an emergency which might render it very proper and necessary to the interests of the country for him to do so. He would therefore, respectfully suggest to the honorable Congress, if a formidable force

[3] George P. Garrison (ed.), *Diplomatic Correspondence of the Republic of Texas*, II, Part 1, 616.

[4] Pakenham to Aberdeen, 24 February 1843 (Public Record Office, London, F.O. 50/161).

[5] Almonte to Ministerio de Relaciones Exteriores, 7 February 1843 (Secretaria de Relaciones Exteriores, Mexico, D.F., L-E-1069).

should invade the country, and it should be necessary to rally our greatest strength, for the purpose of arresting their advances, that he be authorized to assume the command in person.[6]

Under this plan the magic of Houston's name would insure a magnificent army which would somehow equip itself and destroy the Mexicans when they came east of the Guadalupe. In short, it was no plan at all.

Houston sent $500 to the Indians as payment for using them against the Mexican soldiers and civilians, explaining that this was different from the objectionable way the Mexicans had used Indians against Texans.[7] He spent $9,000–$10,000 to fortify the 370-mile Texas coastline at three places, Galveston, Velasco, and Matagorda.[8] He let the men of Galveston march up and down the streets with their guns, practicing scaring off the Mexican ships. Some Galveston merchants sent their goods inland; others wanted to surrender at first sight of the Mexican fleet. The more rugged proposed to burn the city to keep it out of Mexican hands.[9] Matagorda was practically closed down. Finally, Houston sent a letter to Charles Elliot asking him to get the British minister to Mexico to persuade Santa Anna to recognize Texas independence.

Moore was not ignorant of what was going on in secret session. For one thing, Lieutenant Crisp left the Texas Navy on leave without pay about 1 February 1843, having sold a broken bell and several pieces of old copper for $27.08 with which to buy food.[10] Undoubtedly he passed through New Orleans to pay his respects to Moore before returning to Europe to look for a commission in another navy, and undoubtedly he reported to the Commodore what was going on in Texas. He was sick, hungry, depressed, and he saw no future for the Texas Navy.

[6] E. W. Winkler (ed.), *Secret Journals of the Senate, Republic of Texas,* p. 275.

[7] *Ibid.,* p. 250.

[8] Houston to Hockley, 18 January 1843, Amelia W. Williams and Eugene C. Barker (eds.), *Writings of Sam Houston,* IV, 154.

[9] William R. Manning (ed.), *Diplomatic Correspondence of the United States, Inter-American Affairs, 1831–1860,* XII, 254.

[10] Receipt, 21 January 1843, Texas Navy Papers (Archives, Texas State Library, Austin).

The midshipmen aboard the *Wharton* were restless, so ashamed of their appearance and hopeless situation that they had a meeting and submitted their resignations in a body. This time Moore did not even forward the resignations to the Navy Department, as he had done when the officers resigned the year before. He simply ignored them. He needed officers.[11]

Some former Texas Navy sailors who had been discharged without pay were so angered that they tried to burn the ships. A group of Moore's friends lent him money to pay out and quiet them.[12] Again, a storm parted one more anchor cable and caused the loss of twenty-eight fathoms of chain from the *Austin*.

But Mrs. Matilda Houstoun, an Englishwoman visiting New Orleans with her husband, was quite favorably impressed by the Commodore of the Texas Navy, despite his sad economic state:

There is a beautiful corvette lying near us, a long low hull, and raking masts; at the mainmast is flying a small flag, with one star on its brilliant white ground; it is the star of the young Republic of Texas. "Boat alongside!" "Side ropes!" It is the gig of the Texan Commodore. He had sent a lieutenant from the San Jacintho with many kind offers of assistance and civility. In about an hour Mr. Houstoun returned the visit, and brought the Commodore back with him. The latter gave us a good deal of information as to the state of the Texan country, and some news from the army. His countrymen and the Mexicans are continuing a desultory warfare, and with but little present prospect of coming to an amicable settlement. . . . The San Jacintho, though of eight hundred tons, drew but ten feet; she was fully armed and equipped; all the Commodore wanted was money, and that seemed very scarce with him just then; had he but possessed that necessary article, he "would go to sea, take the Montezuma and Guadaloupe, and whip the Mexicans all around!" And so he very likely would, for he enjoys the reputation of being a good officer, and a very fighting one. Mr. Houstoun went on shore with the Commodore, and was introduced to the British Consul. . . .

. . . The day after our arrival our new acquaintance Commodore Moore paid us a visit, accompanied by General Euston; The former certainly did spin us some wonderful yarns, concerning the new country we were about

[11] Midshipmen to Moore, 15 February 1843, Navy Papers (Archives, Texas State Library).

[12] Edwin Ward Moore, *Doings of the Texas Navy*, p. 8.

to visit; but it was all very amusing, and only made us the more determined to see and judge for ourselves. The poor Commodore since those days has done many wonderful things, besides saying them. I was quite sorry to read in a Texan paper, that he had been accused of piracy; he certainly appeared ready to do any thing, (as the schoolboys say "from pitch and toss to manslaughter") for his country.[13]

As soon as Moore felt sure that the Navy was to be offered up for sale he borrowed another $800, chartered the fast little schooner *Two Sons*, and, with Boylan as captain, sent a Mr. McDonald of New Orleans to the governor of Yucatán and the commandant at Campeche with Moore's offer to renew the old Navy contract.[14] By coincidence Moore signed the letter the same day that the secret act to provide for the sale of the Navy was passed in Texas.

At this same time, in late January, 1843, the idea of asking for Texas aid occurred to the authorities in Yucatán. Sisal was blockaded, Laguna captured, but Campeche, besieged by land and by sea, held out long after every prediction of its fall.[15] Colonel Martín Peraza had left Campeche for New Orleans a few days before the *Two Sons* arrived, and by 7 February 1843 was in New Orleans with his welcome sacks full of money for the Texas Navy.

The governor, lieutenant governor, and Campeche commandant sent urgent letters to Moore by the *Two Sons*. The governor wanted help in ten to fifteen days. He apologized that for so long his countrymen had failed to realize their need for the Texas Navy, and explained that Lemus, naturally without telling Yucatán authorities of Moore's repeated offers to help, had joined the Centralists. The first the Yucatecos knew of Lemus' treachery, he added, was when two of their land forces opened fire on each other.

Peraza and Moore signed an agreement on 11 February.[16] It was essentially the same as the previous agreement, but required only two ships. The $8,000 was to be paid to Moore or his successor, and Moore signed as duly authorized agent of his government.

[13] Mrs. Matilda Houstoun, *Texas and the Gulf of Mexico*, I, 155–166. "Pitch and toss" was a gambling game.

[14] Edwin Ward Moore, *To the People of Texas*, p. 119.

[15] Consul at Campeche No. 2, 1 February 1843, Letters from U.S. Consuls (National Archives, Washington).

[16] Edwin Ward Moore, *To the People of Texas*, p. 125.

As soon as Moore got money from Peraza he once more began shipping men. Peraza gave him $4,713, then $2,500 more. New Orleans business men found $5,000, and then $5,000 more available to lend to a man with a war to fight and with aggressive Yucatán support behind him.

The stores and food for a three-months' cruise were quickly got aboard. The ammunition magazines were filled, including 600 of a shell shot Moore had perfected in June, a sort of poor-man's Paixhans.[17] Furloughed officers were recalled. The problem lay in recruiting sailors. The men who had tried to burn the ships were bound to be the worst kind of reference for the Navy. The United States was recruiting in New Orleans at the same time, offering $75 advance pay in U.S. cash. Mexican agents were spreading anti-Texas Navy propaganda to a susceptible waterfront. Moore had to take what he could get—a rough, undisciplined lot—but by late February he had shipped almost half the crews for the *Austin* and *Wharton* in an urgent effort to get to sea. The British consul at New Orleans reported that Moore shipped forty men from New Orleans workhouses and jails.[18]

But, on Saturday, 25 February, before he could get underway, the commissioners arrived to sell the Navy.

Moore went to the Texas consulate. There, in the late afternoon, he greeted Morgan and Bryan with, "Well Gentlemen, I understand you have come for the vessels under my command."[19]

Before they recovered from the surprise of that remark, or their amazement at seeing Moore in New Orleans when they thought him out of the way in Washington-on-the-Brazos, Moore continued with some such remark as: "You don't get them. You shan't have them," and "I have the reins in my own hands and I intend to hold them."[20]

---

[17] *Ibid.*, p. 71.

[18] John Crawford to Sir Charles Adam, 10 April 1843 (Public Record Office, London, F.O. 75/8, p. 38).

[19] *Telegraph and Texas Register*, 28 August 1844, p. 1.

[20] Thomas Johnson, "Argument of Hon. Thos. Johnson," *Documents Relative to the Dismissal of Post-Captain Edwin Ward Moore from the Texian Navy consisting of E. W. Moore in 1843; the Argument of the Hon. Thos. Johnson, Judge-Advocate; Proclamation of President Sam Houston; Veto of President Anson Jones*, p. 15.

It appeared to the commissioners that their job was not going to be easy. Weary from travelling, they decided to let business go until the following Monday.

As Moore, Morgan, and two or three others stepped into the street at the consul's door, a messenger came up to Moore with a letter which had arrived that day on the same steamer with the commissioners. Moore opened the letter, and saw that it was an order from the new Secretary of War and Marine, G. W. Hill, for Moore to come to Washington before final action was taken on a secret act concerning the Navy. Since this important letter was over a month old, the Commodore handed it to Morgan, saying, "I am glad you are present; this is the first time I have seen this letter or heard of it." Moore asked Morgan to remember seeing him receive the letter and break the seal.

On Monday they met again. The commissioners gave Moore a letter from themselves enclosing a second letter from Hill written the same day as the first and addressed to Commander J. T. K. Lothrop or Officer in Command of the Navy. This letter directed that control of the ships be turned over to the commissioners together with muster rolls and reports of the ships' conditions.

The intent of these two sets of orders was clear: the first, which had made a slow journey by mail, was to get Moore out of town and let a less dynamic commander deal with the President's commissioners. Moore had for the past three years studied political strategy under that master of chicanery, Sam Houston. He rejected the first order because he received the second one of the same date two days later. Also, he now had $1,800 worth of travel claims against the Texas government and could not afford to make any more trips at his own expense. Furthermore, the second letter and the presence of the commissioners in New Orleans indicated that final action had already been taken—and actually had been taken a week before the letter was even written.[21]

Moore at once reported the condition and manning of his ships. However, he would not turn the ships over to the commissioners, as then he might not be able to carry out the sealed orders he had from his superiors. Besides, the authority of the commissioners was not

[21] Edwin Ward Moore, *To the People of Texas,* p. 130.

clearly defined. Moore wanted certified copies of the secret act; he was ready to co-operate with the commissioners as far as possible until he got it.

Morgan was overwhelmed by Moore's enthusiasm and persuasiveness. He had expected to see a duplication of the *Archer*'s hulk, complete with pig and moldering canvas. Instead, he found well disciplined men-of-war preparing for sea under a resolute commander who had a strongbox full of secret orders himself and more real money than Texas had seen in months. Morgan and Bryan took Moore's report and their instructions and hurried ashore to see a lawyer friend of theirs for advice.[22] This was apparently William Christy, for he was soon corresponding with Houston in Moore's behalf. Christy recommended that the commissioners send Bryan back to Texas for instructions. Commodore Moore had gained a few more weeks, and an opportunity to talk alone with Morgan.[23]

Bryan departed for Texas about 10 March and was ushered in to see Houston himself. Houston, greatly angered, flayed about in fine style. He ordered the commissioners to get those ships at all costs. He wrote them, "Post Captain E. W. Moore has no authority from this government, to ship men, appoint officers, enlist marines, or to do any other act, or thing, but to sail to the port of Galveston" or to turn over command to Lothrop. He could not make agreements with Yucatán. The commissioners were to get control of those ships, or get the United States or Louisiana authorities to help them do so.[24]

Mexican consul Arrangoiz continued his excellent reports on the Texas ships, and by March was sending off a daily dispatch to his Foreign Minister. He apparently had sources right aboard the flagship, his reports were so accurate, so frequent, and so immediate after developments. Occasionally he complained about Moore's secrecy, particularly in financial matters. By 20 March Arrangoiz was expecting the ships to leave daily. Recruiting was about completed; Moore was now insisting on the very best seamen.

[22] James Morgan, *To the Public*, p. 2 (Rosenberg Library).
[23] Arrangoiz to Ministerio de Relaciones Exteriores, 28 April 1843 (Archivo Militar, Mexico, D.F., XI/481.3/1973).
[24] Amelia W. Williams and Eugene C. Barker (eds.), *Writings of Sam Houston*, III, 336.

Arrangoiz was particularly interested in Boylan, whom he rightly suspected of being Moore's liaison with Yucatán.[25] Boylan, captain of the *Two Sons,* was carrying powder to Sisal through the Mexican blockade. Yucatán had built a number of *canoas,* each with one or two 6- or 9-pounders for use as gunboats. Boylan and Moore had worked out tactics for Yucatán and Texas forces combined under Moore's command to capture one of the steamers if they could catch her alone.[26]

April 3 Morgan handed to Moore a letter dated 21 March 1843 from the Department of War and Marine. There was a seal and stamp of the Republic on the envelope, but it was not closed by the seal.

Moore observed, "The letter is unsealed."

"Yes."

"It's strange the department should send a letter in that manner. Do you know the contents?"

Morgan replied yes, that he had a copy of it, and then left Moore. After Moore had read it and thought it over, he searched out Morgan.

"You see the situation I am now placed in: I've been at a vast expense to get these vessels fitted and ready for sea; you know in what a situation the vessels are now. I entered into a contract with the Yucatán government, which I felt myself legally authorized to do, and am now suspended from command of the vessels by this order. If I obey this order and leave the vessels in the port of New Orleans, every officer under me will resign; the vessels will be left at the mercy of the sailors, who will be sure to mutiny and destroy them, which they threatened to do once before when I could not pay them off."[27]

Morgan answered that the orders to the commissioners were painful to him. "I accepted this commission with a great deal of reluctance, but I mean to execute the orders regardless of consequences."

Moore was looking for a way to get along with the commissioners without losing control of the ships. He asked quickly, "Do you have

[25] Arrangoiz to Ministerio de Relaciones Exteriores, 4 March 1843 (Secretaria de la Defensa Nacional, Mexico, D.F., XI/481.3/1971).

[26] *Ibid.,* 20 March 1843.

[27] Edwin Ward Moore, *Doings of the Texas Navy,* p. 10.

a communication for any officer under my command?" Someone must have been appointed in his place.

"I had another communication for Captain Lothrop, to take charge of the vessels."

"Have you delivered it?"

"I put it under a sealed cover and handed it to Mr. Stephens [who was secretary to the commission] to deliver to him; supposing him to be on board the brig under his command . . ."

Moore explained again his situation, the probability that the vessels would be destroyed if he left, the loss to the government, and bargained: "If you will withdraw the communication to Captain Lothrop, I will proceed with the vessels immediately to Galveston and go with you direct to the President and endeavor to satisfy him that I never intended to do anything wrong with the vessels, nor anything that would compromit my own honor or that of my adopted country."[28]

"Now, that is precisely what I want done with the vessels. If Captain Lothrop has not received and read the communication I have sent him by Mr. Stephens this evening, the arrangement proposed shall be made, and you shall continue in command of the vessels until our arrival at Galveston."

Colonel Morgan could not find Stephens, but soon ran across Lothrop. He asked whether Lothrop had received a communication from him, but Lothrop said he had not. Morgan remarked, "Capt. Lothrop, if you do receive a communication from Mr. Stephens under a sealed cover, it is from me, and I would be glad if you would not break the seal, but return it to me with the seal unbroken."[29]

Lothrop took a letter from his pocket and held it out for Morgan to see.

"Is this it?"

Morgan, taking the letter, answered that it was, and that it was from the Department of War and Marine.

Lothrop replied shortly, "Any communication from the Department of War and Marine to me, should come through Commodore Moore." This was in keeping with naval custom, which requires de-

---

[28] Senator James Jones, *Speech to Senate . . .*, 3 August 1854.
[29] Edwin Ward Moore, *Doings of the Texas Navy*, p. 10.

livery of communications via the chain of command. Morgan did not linger in the chilling company of Commander Lothrop, but returned to Moore.

"I have got the communication from Captain Lothrop, and he had not broken the seal."

That was a relief to both, and they went over their plans, Morgan summing them up: "The understanding between us now is, that you continue in command of the vessels until we get them into Galveston, where we are to proceed immediately."[30]

Moore replied, "Yes, I pledge you my honor there shall be no delay, and we will go immediately to Galveston."[31]

Morgan prudently suggested, "As it will be saving the Government some expense, I will take passage with you if you have no objection."

Moore replied that he would be happy to have Morgan's company. Bryan, when Morgan told him of the arrangements, also thought it a good idea.[32] Morgan thought that the best way of getting Houston's approval for the retention of Moore in command would be to tell Houston personally when the ships got to Galveston. Bryan agreed to this, too, and so delayed writing to Houston of the arrangement until after the first mail steamer following the departure of the vessels.

It was a couple of days later, after Morgan and Moore had exchanged letters confirming their conversations, that Morgan remarked, "I feel particularly gratified that matters have taken the turn between us that they have; for if you had been obstinate or disposed to act incorrectly in any way with the vessels I had a paper that would have controlled you."

Moore smiled and asked what it was.

Morgan told him it was a proclamation from President Houston. He handed it to Moore to read.

Moore read it.

"Good God!" he exclaimed. "Did the President think I was going to run away with the vessels or turn pirate?"[33]

It was a proclamation signed by Houston suspending Moore from command, cancelling all his orders previous to 29 October 1842, and

[30] *Ibid.*, p. 20.   [31] *Ibid.*, p. 10.
[32] *Ibid.*, p. 11.   [33] *Ibid.*, p. 13.

ordering him to report in person to the Secretary of War and Marine. The document, dated 23 March, asked all nations in amity with Texas to seize Moore and his ships and return them to Galveston if Moore sailed without authority.

Since the document included the allegation that Moore had refused to deliver the ships to the commissioners, but Moore had not actually refused, Morgan considered the proclamation undelivered and without effect.[34] Thus, Morgan had a weapon to enforce any instructions he might want to issue to Moore. If Moore at any time took action which Morgan did not approve of, the proclamation could be published and Moore would be deprived of his authority. Meanwhile, Moore's previous orders remained in effect.

Moore got the *San Antonio* mutineers aboard, minus Sergeant Oswald (who had escaped) and Pompilly (deceased). Using his authority as commander in chief of the Texas squadron, and carrying out President Houston's orders, Moore ordered Commander Lothrop as president to conduct the general court-martial while final preparations were being made to get the ships to sea. The court, which included Lieutenants Alfred G. Gray, J. P. Lansing, Cyrus Cummings, and Daniel C. Wilbur, with Dr. Thomas P. Anderson as judge advocate, first met aboard the *Austin* very near the spot where the mutiny had taken place, and rendered final verdict on 13 April, after the ships reached the mouth of the Mississippi. The trials took place while the United States was debating the execution of three mutineers aboard the U.S.S. *Somers* on 1 December 1842.

The *Austin* had 146 officers and men while the *Wharton* had 86 out of complements of 171 and 121 respectively. Lieutenant G. C. Bunner reported in from leave. William G. Cooke, captured and imprisoned commissioner of the Santa Fe expedition, later a member of Somervell's expedition, joined as the *Austin*'s marine officer, ready for patriotic revenge. On 15 April Moore paid off the drydock company and the bakery, got Morgan aboard, and after dark cleared New Orleans with the *Austin* and the *Wharton*. As the ships passed close aboard the U.S.S. *Ontario* in the night, that ship manned her yards and gave three cheers for the brave Texas Navy vessels on their way—they thought—to tackle a stronger enemy.

[34] *Ibid.*, p. 9.

At the Belize on the seventeenth such a dense fog set in that the ships had to anchor for three days until it cleared. Captain Ducey of the American schooner *Rosario,* three and a half days from Campeche, the captain of another American ship, and a passenger boarded the *Austin* as she lay near the northeast pass of the Mississippi.[35] All had the same story: Mexican General Ampudia was concentrating his forces off Campeche for a sea-borne invasion of Texas. Campeche was defending itself against a fleet of three steamers, five sailing ships, and a large force which had blockaded, bombarded, and besieged that heroic fortress city for six months. The walls, parts still encircling the city today, three hundred years after their construction, stood, but the great Paixhans of the *Guadaloupe, Montezuma,* and *Eagle* had commenced to batter the city down.

The Yucatecos, aided by Indians, fevers, and poor Mexican logistics, had defeated a Mexican thrust through Telchac toward Mérida. General Peña y Barragán, who only five weeks before had relieved General Miñon (who was imprisoned for failure to deliver a victory), capitulated, and agreed to leave Yucatán by 13 May.

The Mexicans had brought to Lerma General Ampudia from the Texas border. Ampudia was fresh from his victory over Fisher's Mier expedition. With him came his best troops, largely by chartered American ships. He started a diplomatic offensive at the same time he redoubled the military pressure against Campeche. He proposed to re-embark the soldiers at Telchac and unite them with their former enemies, the Yucatecos, in a sea-borne crusade against Texas. He was taunting the Yucatecos with Moore's continued absence, trying to make them believe that Moore had been bribed to keep the Texas ships away from Campeche and pocket their money.[36]

Moore's chance meeting with the ships' captains at the Belize brought him the news that the *Montezuma* was alone at Telchac, 150 miles to the northeastward of Campeche, embarking the invasion troops. If the *Montezuma* could be captured in a surprise action, she would furnish the means of taking the rest of the Mexican squadron.

Moore and Morgan also heard a rumor (evidently current both in New Orleans and Yucatán) that Great Britain and Mexico had

[35] Edwin Ward Moore, *To the People of Texas,* p. 145.
[36] *Ibid.,* p. 155.

agreed that if Mexico did not recapture a major Texas seaport by 15 May, Mexico would recognize Texas Independence. Beyond all doubt, Texas would have the Mexican Navy to fight within a month, and had a choice of doing so in Yucatán waters with the help of the Yucatán gunboats, or alone at Galveston with the ships laid up in ordinary and the crews scattered.

Houston had told Morgan the winter before that "there was to be a formidable invasion of the Country; that it was gone; that it would cease to be a Republic in six months."[37]

Morgan wrote:

. . . I felt justified in taking the Coast of Yucatan on our way. The fact was, I found our vessels in such apple pie order—the officers so anxious to proceed on the Cruise—such bully crews: and knowing if the vessels did go into Galveston Harbor they would never come out again as *Texas* vessels— if at all—considering still farther that many of the Officers had never recd one cent of pay for the last two years—and if the navy was laid up or sold they probably never would,—That now an opportunity offered to do something for themselves & their adopted Country—a full stop was to be put to the expedition & close it at Galveston—For these & other *still more cogent reasons,* I concluded to stretch my authority as Commissioner, a little, and authorize Com. Moore to go ahead: believing we could visit the Coast of Yucatan & accomplish every object we had in view, in 20 or 30 days, at fartherist. . . .[38]

On the evening of 19 April, "a moonless night, as black as a crow's wing" Midshipman Fuller called it, the *Austin* and the *Wharton* set sail for Telchac. Morgan wrote to Houston. Moore wrote to the *Texas Times* saying that in the event the President proclaimed him a pirate Moore wanted it known that he sailed with the Commissioner's permission, that ". . . the officers and men are all eager for the contest. We go to make one desperate struggle to turn the tide of ill luck that has so long been running against Texas."[39]

Victory would not be easy. The *Montezuma's* Paixhans considerably

[37] Charles A. Gulick, Jr., and others (eds.), *The Papers of Mirabeau Buonaparte Lamar,* No. 2500.

[38] Morgan to J. Reed, 11 May 1843, Morgan papers (Rosenberg Library).

[39] Moore to F. Pinkard, 19 April 1843, Ephraim D. Adams (ed.), *British Diplomatic Correspondence Concerning the Republic of Texas,* p. 193–194.

outranged all the *Austin*'s 24-pounders and the *Wharton*'s 18-pounders. The light spring winds would allow the *Montezuma* to choose the range at which an action might be fought. If the sailing ships were to be able to close in to lethal range for their own guns they must be prepared to take a lot of punishment on the way in. This required the kind of discipline which would keep men aloft under heavy fire while their shipmates far below were unable to return it. Moore had seven convicted mutineers aboard. Almost every other sailor had been aboard less than a month. For the most part they were a hard lot, the leavings of the U.S. Navy and merchant ships, men either unfit for other service or with an eye for a fast dollar. Moore knew that he had aboard most of the ingredients for a mutiny. He had the strength of character to take the action to insure that none would come about.

On 21 April the Commodore had all hands of the *Austin* fall in while he had the accused mutineers brought forward. Moore himself read the findings and sentences of the court-martial. Frederick Shepherd was acquitted. John W. Williams was sentenced to receive fifty lashes, but the Commodore pardoned him.

On 22 April, William Barrington, sentenced to 150 lashes, was given 100. On the twenty-fifth Edward Keenan got the same.

After this punishment the Commodore read the sentences for Antonio Landois, Isaac Allen, James Hudgins, and William Simpson: death. Commodore Moore then read the laws for the government of the Navy which made him, as commander of the Navy, responsible outside Texas for the execution of the sentences. Moore made a talk to his men. He hated to execute these men. He had never before even seen such punishment. He hoped to God he never would again. They had had fair trials and competent counsels, New Orleans lawyers in some cases. But they had committed the crime of mutiny, had killed one officer and wounded two others. The men were then told to make themselves ready for execution next day.[40]

At noon, 26 April 1843, the *Austin* lay to. All hands assembled for the execution. None of the crew would admit to knowing how to tie the hangman's knots. Lieutenant A. G. Gray tied the knots himself. The four noose lines were married together, and all hands were

[40] Edwin Ward Moore, *Doings of the Texas Navy*, p. 14.

ordered to hoist the culprits with a rush. This was done. The men died instantly. They were left hanging at the foreyard for an hour, then turned over to their messmates for preparation; the funeral services were read by Dr. Anderson, and they were buried.[41] Moore then made a few solemn remarks to the crew which deeply affected them all.

The *Austin* filled away for Telchac at the best speed the light wind would give her.

[41] *Niles Register,* 3 June 1943.

One Last Desperate Struggle

Captain G. B. Elliot of H.M.S. *Spartan* (cousin of Charles Elliot) wrote his superiors on 25 April 1843: ". . . Campeche will very shortly have to surrender and leave the squadron free to engage in operations against Texas."[1]

Van Zandt on 21 April 1843 reported to the Texas Secretary of State that Daniel Webster frequently told him ". . . the favorable or unfavorable termination of that [Yucatán] campaign would determine the ability or inability of Mexico to reinvade Texas."[2]

By now it was no surprise to the Mexicans that Moore was coming. Arrangoiz had warned Commodore Lopez;[3] Lopez chartered the American schooner *Fanny* to order the *Montezuma* and the *Eagle* to rejoin the main forces.[4] The *Austin* and the *Wharton* arrived at Tel-

[1] Elliot to Adam, 25 April 1843 (Public Record Office, London, ADM 1/5529).

[2] George P. Garrison (ed.), *Diplomatic Correspondence of the Republic of Texas*, II (1), Part II, 168.

[3] Peña y Barragán to Minister of War, 16 May 1843 (Archivo Historico, Secretaria de la Defensa Nacional, Mexico, D.F., XI/481.3/1928).

[4] Lopez to Secretary of State, 29 April 1843 (Archivo Historico, Secretaria de la Defensa Nacional, Mexico, D.F., XI/481.3/1986).

chac on the afternoon of 27 April just twenty-four hours after the *Montezuma* left.[5]

Hoping to overtake the *Montezuma*, Moore skirted the Yucatán coast as closely as those shallow, unmarked, and unlighted waters permitted. Off Sisal Moore sent the word of his arrival up to Mérida. On the night of the twenty-ninth he estimated his position to be off Campeche. He had the *Austin* and the *Wharton* anchor with orders to be underway by first light of morning. He expected to meet some or all of the Mexican squadron, and wanted to meet it while the early morning breeze still allowed his ships to maneuver. He ordered his ships to make preparations for their own destruction by magazine explosion if capture appeared likely.[6]

Dawn broke on the thirtieth with the Texans underway fifteen miles northwest of Lerma,[7] and the breeze from ESE. The Mexican ships *Montezuma* (8 guns—Paixhans), *Yucateco* (17 guns), *Eagle* (7 guns—Paixhans), *Iman* (9 guns), and *Campecheano* (3 guns) were sighted about ten miles to the south. The *Guadaloupe* (flagship of Lopez) was coaling ship close inshore to Lerma.[8] Moore mistook her slowness in getting clear as indicating she was aground.

Pressing all sail, the Texans darted eastward, trying to get upwind of the Mexicans. The Mexicans first headed north; then, seeing how fast the Texans closed, turned south momentarily. Both Texas ships gave three hearty cheers as they approached the enemy. The little Yucatán squadron (*Sisaleno* and *Independencia* plus five little gunboats each mounting one 6-pounder) under Boylan sortied from Campeche, and, keeping to the north, joined Moore's forces to the leeward. It was 7:00 A.M. The *Montezuma*, which had many Spaniards aboard, broke the Spanish flag.[9] The *Guadaloupe*'s sailors, still mostly Englishmen, refused to fight except under their own colors, so flew the Union Jack. Moore broke the Texas flag at his mastheads and the United States and British colors at the foretop.

[5] Edwin Ward Moore, *To the People of Texas*, p. 172.

[6] *Telegraph and Texas Register*, 28 August 1844, p. 2, col. 1.

[7] Edwin Ward Moore, *op. cit.*, p. 147.

[8] Lopez to Secretary of State, 1 May 1843 (Archivo de Cancelados, Mexico, D.F., Caja 546).

[9] Doyle to Aberdeen, 29 August 1843 (Public Record Office, London, F.O. 204/80).

By 7:35 the Mexicans were able to open fire, first short, then over the *Austin*.[10] They tried the 68-pound explosive Paixhans shell, but only one damaged the *Austin*.[11] As far as is known, this was the first use of Paixhans shells in action between warships.

Moore observed to Lieutenant Gray: "They don't intend to let us get any nearer to them; they are paddling off stern foremost faster than we can come up to them; keep her away a little, so our broadside can bear, and damn them, give it to them."[12]

The *Austin* and the *Wharton* bored on into the space between the steamers and the sailing ships. Engaging the steamers to port, they exchanged five broadsides; then turned their attention to the weaker sailing ships to their starboard or downwind side. The sailing ships fled while the steamers came to their rescue, skirting outside Texan gun range. No one had yet been hurt.

It was now 8:40. The breeze died down. While the ships lay to, and the Mexicans remained cautiously out of range, Moore had his weary crews retire from battle stations for grog.

Hope for more wind died. The ships anchored with springs to their anchors. This was done by attaching a line from well aft on each side up to the anchor cable. By heaving around on one line and slackening the other, the ships could be turned without having to depend on the wind. Then Moore sent his crew to breakfast, keeping a sharp lookout for attacks by the steamers or signs of wind.

Not until 11:15 did the steamers reopen the battle, trying to pass under the sterns of the Yucatán and the Texas ships. The *Austin* and the *Wharton* sprung themselves about to bring their starboard batteries to bear. The breeze came up again, this time from the north. The ships slipped their anchors and filled away on an easterly course toward the Mexicans. The steamers and Texas vessels exchanged broadside after broadside. Moore and Gray saw one 68-pound shot from the *Guadaloupe* coming toward them. They dodged. The solid shot went right over where their heads had been, cut the starboard

---

[10] Edwin Ward Moore, *op. cit.*, p. 151.

[11] Morgan to Reed, 11 May 1843. Morgan Papers (Rosenberg Library, Galveston).

[12] Edwin Ward Moore, *Doings of the Texas Navy*, p. 15.

aftermizzenmast shroud, smashed through the Commodore's cabin, and out the stern. The ships continued firing at each other until the Mexicans pulled out of range upwind of the sailing ships and ran off. Moore was now between Campeche and the blockading fleet, with no chance at present of being able to close in on the steamers. Taking one of Boylan's pilots, he headed for the anchorage. On the way in, the pilot grounded the *Austin*.

Lothrop hailed from the *Wharton*, "Shall I heave to?"

Moore replied, "No, Sir, keep on to your anchorage."[13]

A number of little Yucatán gunboats under Boylan came skimming across the water like seagulls to offer their assistance. Until the tide came in an hour later to float the *Austin* clear, she lay there. Still, the Mexicans made no effort to close the *Austin*. When she reached the shallow water anchorage, where the Mexican steamers could not venture, and their sailing vessels would not, Moore gave his exhausted crew a chance to rest.

Morgan wrote:

. . . But the way we knocked H——ll into them & out of them was a caution. We thrashed them soundly & the whole fleet ran off. Here we gain the advantage of steam over wind and calms.—It enabled the enemy to choose his distance & keep it & after fairly whipd. to clear himself & save his fleet—and now keep in full view & laugh at us! We can do nothing with their steamers except by stratagem & the moon will prevent that at this time by night while calm & light winds will place it out of our power by day.

.   .   .   .

I could not imagine more coolness & determination than was displayed by the Officers & crew in the fight—all appeared delighted & the young middys & powder boys made a perfect Jubilee of the affair! For my own part I had much rather been at a feast—For d—— me if I saw any *fun* in it! I summoned up courage enough to keep on the deck during the action to be sure & like a frightened child who will make a noise to keep fear away— I huzzaed for Texas most of the time as loud as I could howl: but I could not help *bowing* instinctively to the enemy's 68 lb shot as they came over

[13] George Fuller, "Sketch of the Texas Navy," *The Quarterly of the Texas State Historical Association,* VII, 223.

my head—They did command that respect of me! Nor could I help laughing to see the glee it afforded the *powder boys*—(some 5 or 6) and thought of the fable of the Frogs & the boys![14]

No one was hurt aboard the *Austin.* The *Wharton* lost two killed, three wounded. Although Moore did not know it, Commander Richard F. Cleaveland, RN, captain of the *Montezuma,* had died of yellow fever the night before, and forty of Cleaveland's men were incapacitated. In this action the *Montezuma* lost thirteen killed; the *Guadaloupe* lost seven killed.[15] Her British captain, Charlewood, had resigned and returned to England; Commodore Lopez had assumed command of the ship in addition to command of the squadron. When word of the action reached Mexican authorities, Lopez was relieved, arrested, and tried by court-martial for allowing the Texans to break the blockade.[16] His superiors demanded revenge for the dishonor. Commander Buenaventure Arajuo of the *Eagle* took command of the *Montezuma.*

The President himself had to order reluctant Don Tomás Marín to take command of the Mexican squadron in its poor condition.[17] Marín had his share of braggadocio, but he was a capable and prudent naval officer. He reported the poor state of the ships, undermanned with tired and poor-spirited sailors. British technicians were sick and dying of yellow fever. Marín said that Moore's men were rested and well cared for. He complained that his own men had not been paid in three months.[18]

Moore's arrival heartened the Yucatecos:

. . . When we first appeared off the City they were about to make a treaty for an Armistice, but no sooner than our Flag was seen than one universal shout of joy was heard throughout the City and the stipulations for the Treaty rejected by the Governor of Campeche with scorn and during our

[14] Morgan to Reed, 11 May 1843, Morgan Papers (Rosenberg Library).

[15] A. Walke, Log Book of Alfred Walke, 30 April 1843 (Archives, Texas State Library, Austin).

[16] Commandant, Veracruz, to Minister of War, 8 June 1843. Archivo de Cancelados, Mexico, D.F., 546D/111.4/7219).

[17] President to Ampudia, 5 May 1843 (Archivo Militar, Mexico, D.F., XI/481.3/1973).

[18] Marín to Ampudia, 5 May 1843 (Archivo Militar, XI/481.3/1973).

engagement all the Tops of Houses, walls, and all other places that could command a view of us was crowded with spectators including Men Women and Children, shouting and Huzzaing for us and evincing every demonstration of joy.[19]

Governor Mendez said that when the Mexican ships opened fire on his friends, the Texans, the truce was broken automatically, and the struggle was resumed.

Moore borrowed two long-range 18-pounders from the Yucatecos to extend the range of his ship,[20] already armed with sixteen medium 24-pounders and two medium 18-pounders (apparently borrowed from the *Archer*). The *Wharton* borrowed a long 12-pounder to go with her fifteen medium 18-pounders.

Moore sent the Yucatán gunboat *Republicano*,[21] under Captain Charles Cox, to Galveston on 10 May with his action report to the Secretary of War and Marine, and Morgan's reports to Secretary Hill and President Houston.[22] The *Republicano* was ordered to wait ten days for communications from the Texas government.

To James Reed, Morgan wrote: "I expect 'Old Sam' will *'hang me'* —for I have travelled out of the course his instructions dictated. But as we have played h——ll with the enemys arrangements and calculations in this quarter He may be afraid to overlook the matter!"[23]

Moore knew that in this season there was the chance of a good strong offshore breeze, when, taking advantage of the speed and maneuverability of his little vessels with their greater number of short-ranged guns, he could quickly pass through the dangerous longer Mexican ranges and get into the area where he had the superiority. Each dawn Moore's ships were out on the early morning breeze, hoping that it would last, or that the breeze which usually came up from seaward would change to one from the east. On 5 May he wrote, "If I had a steamer here, I would give ten years of my life,

[19] A. Walke, Log Book of Alfred Walke, 1 May 1843 (Archives, Texas State Library).

[20] Marín to Minister of War and Marine, 11 May 1843 (Archivo Militar, Mexico, D.F., XI/481.3/1973).

[21] Morgan to Reed, 11 May 1843, Morgan Papers (Rosenberg Library).

[22] Edwin Ward Moore, *Doings of the Texas Navy*, p. 16.

[23] Morgan to Reed, 11 May 1843, Morgan Papers (Rosenberg Library).

as with it I could get to close action at once and decide the Fate of Texas."[24]

At the same time, Marín had no desire to meet Moore in a strong or (to Moore) favorable wind. He avoided Moore's efforts to approach him by keeping his sailing ships far to sea and by backing his steamers up into the winds where Moore could not follow.[25] He sent the *Mexicano* and *Zemperaltca* to Carmen and stripped them of sailors for use on the other ships.[26] He sent the *Regenerador* and some transports to continue the re-embarkation at Telchac while the *Montezuma,* the *Guadaloupe,* and the *Eagle,* the heavy-gun ships, watched Moore at Campeche.

Santa Anna announced the formation of his expedition to reconquer Texas.[27]

General Ampudia grew weary of Marín's cautious handling of Moore, and told him to press for action. This Marín did by steaming back and forth off Campeche, outside of range of Moore's ships, in the noonday calms. Moore did not come out. He could not.

Ampudia then had Marín challenge Moore to come out to three fathoms of water and fight. Even before the captain of the American schooner *Fanny* could deliver the message to Moore, Ampudia gave the press his *Official Bulletin No. 1,*[28] which was intended to make the Yucatecos despise Moore for refusing the challenge, and join the Centralist cause.

Moore did not hear of the challenge until the evening of 16 May,[29] but to Marín it looked as if he had. The breezes held a little longer than usual that morning. Moore's force sailed right out into twenty fathoms of water. Marín had to make good his challenge—for a while at least.

Morgan ran out onto the roof of his hotel and saw the beginning

[24] Alexandria *Gazette,* 24 May 1843.

[25] Edwin Ward Moore, *To the People of Texas,* p. 149.

[26] Marín to Commandant, Yucatán, 5 May 1843 (Archivo Militar, Mexico, D.F., XI/481.3/1973).

[27] Doyle to Captain Elliot, 24 April 1843 (Public Record Office, London, F.O. 50/161).

[28] Boletín Oficial Numero 1, 15 May 1843 (Archivo Militar, Mexico, D.F., XI/481.3/1974).

[29] Clipping from *Daily Tropic,* n.d., Morgan Papers (Rosenberg Library).

of the action. All of siege-weary Campeche was on the walls and church towers: men, women, and children, to cheer; thousands of brunettes waved snow-white handkerchiefs at the brave Texans.[30] General Ampudia was watching from his post in Lerma. As the *Austin* took the fire of the steamers and returned it double, he saw scenes far different from those during his rout of the Texans at Mier six months before.

The wind died down at 10:00 A.M. with the two squadrons only about three miles apart. The Mexicans opened fire with their big 68- and 42-pounders, while the Texas sailors could only curse the noonday calm. Still firing, the Mexicans came in close enough for the *Austin's* borrowed long 18's to speak. On the second salvo, down came the *Guadaloupe's* flagstaff, colors and all. The Texans let out three hearty cheers. Twenty minutes later the *Austin* took in rapid succession three hits, which wounded three men, but did no great amount of damage to the ship. Both the Mexican and Texan squadrons opened fire with their medium guns by now.[31] The Yucatecan gunboats, except one commanded by a Frenchman, held off, in spite of Moore's repeated signals for them to join in the action.[32]

The *Guadaloupe* and the *Montezuma* fell upon the *Austin*, one on her port quarter and the other on her port bow, pouring their heavy shot into the little sloop. Occasionally a great Paixhans shell burst overhead, raining its fragments through sail and rigging. Morgan said that time and again he lost sight of the *Austin* in the smoke and flash of engagement only to see her three graceful masts again when the smoke drifted away.[33]

All during the action Moore kept an anxious eye out for wind. At 12:20 his puff of wind came. He put his rudder up, squared his yards just in time to catch the full effect, and skimmed between the *Guadaloupe* and the *Montezuma* with both broadsides thundering. The steamers staggered under the impact of the *Austin's* hits; their decks were littered with wounded and dying. One of the *Guadaloupe's*

[30] Undated fragment of New Orleans newspaper, Morgan Papers (Rosenberg Library).

[31] Edwin Ward Moore, *To the People of Texas*, p. 160.

[32] George F. Fuller, "Sketch of the Texas Navy," *The Quarterly of the Texas State Historical Association*, VII, 223.

[33] Morgan to Swartwout, 27 May 1843, Morgan Papers (Rosenberg Library).

paddles was put out of action.[34] Enveloped in her own steam,[35] she floundered off under the other, still firing her terrible guns. The *Montezuma* took a beating. The *Eagle* broke clear to the south and did not come into action again. Lothrop saw the change in wind too late, and missed his stays coming about. The *Wharton* fell behind as the *Austin* continued pursuit of the two big steamers fourteen miles south of Campeche. In twenty minutes, while closing the range, the *Austin* took nine heavy caliber hits from the *Guadaloupe,* including an airburst of a 68-pound Paixhans shell.

At No. 9 gun one hit injured Thomas Norris, who got patched up and returned to his battle station only to lose his left arm.[36] Midshipman George Fuller in his first action listened to salty Passed Midshipman Walke lisp, "That was devilish close."[37] Midshipman Andrew J. Bryant lay bleeding, with parts of his thigh and his right hand carried away. Lieutenant Snow was deafened.[38] Lieutenant Wilbur never fully recovered from his wounds. A two-inch splinter pierced the brain of Frederick Shepherd at No. 12 gun.[39] William Barrington was injured.

Still, for three hours the *Austin* pursued the two steamers as they fled clear of the battle area. The *Austin's* starboard rigging was badly shot up. Moore brought her about to the port tack to ease the strain. This caused her to heel over to starboard and submerged a hole in the starboard side until the magazine had three feet of water in it.[40] If Moore should come back to the starboard tack he would stand a good chance of losing a mast and so his ship. He brought the *Austin* back around toward Campeche, picked up the *Wharton,* and headed for his anchorage, cursing his luck. He sent for James Boylan, the acting commodore of the Yucatán squadron. Back in New Orleans Moore and Boylan had worked out tactics for co-ordination of the

[34] *El Siglo Diez y Nueve,* No. 292, 16 May 1843.

[35] Undated fragment of New Orleans newspaper, Morgan Papers (Rosenberg Library).

[36] E. W. Moore, *To the People of Texas,* p. 160.

[37] George Fuller, "Sketch of the Texas Navy," *The Quarterly of the Texas State Historical Association,* VII, 223.

[38] *Telegraph and Texas Register,* 25 September 1844, p. 1, col. 2.

[39] George Fuller, "Sketch of the Texas Navy," *The Quarterly of the Texas State Historical Association,* VII, 223.

[40] Morgan to Swartwout, 27 May 1843, Morgan Papers (Rosenberg Library).

two squadrons. When Boylan got aboard, looking frightened and deadly pale, Moore blazed out at him for his cowardice in failing to bring the Yucatán gunboats into action.[41]

In the battle of 16 May the *Austin* had three killed[42] and twenty-two wounded.[43] The *Wharton* had two killed when an over-eager gun captain fired while the gun was being loaded.[44] Reports of the Mexicans said that the *Guadaloupe* lost forty-seven killed and had thirty-two amputations and sixty-four wounded. The *Montezuma* lost about forty killed and wounded, including the captain.

Moore wrote: "Those 68-pound balls are tremendous missiles, and the way they did whistle or rather hum over our heads was a caution, I tell you. They fired a great many over the poop where I was standing, and several of them were disposed to be rather too intimate."[45]

The *Austin* had fired 530 rounds, almost all her ammunition. The *Wharton's* borrowed long-12 alone used sixty-five rounds. With less than two hours' ammunition still aboard Marín had to send the chartered U.S. schooner *Apalacheola* to Veracruz for more.[46] Some Mexican reports were that the *Austin* and the *Wharton* were taken. A special medal was awarded Marín's sailors for victory over the Texas squadron, and can be seen today in Chapultepec Castle.

While the two squadrons lay only seven miles apart Mexican and Texan carpenters and sailmakers were busy repairing damages and patching sails.[47] At no time in the past action had they been closer than a mile and three quarters. Moore had wanted to get close enough to use his 18-pound shell shot, but the range was so long that he could use but very few.[48] One did strike the *Guadaloupe* near the

[41] George Fuller, "Sketch of the Texas Navy," *The Quarterly of the Texas State Historical Association*, VII, 223.

[42] A. Walke, Log Book of Alfred Walke (Archives, Texas State Library).

[43] Enclosure with Elliot's letter to Aberdeen, 29 May 1843 (Public Record Office, London, ADM 1/5529).

[44] A. Walke, Log Book of Alfred Walke (Archives, Texas State Library).

[45] Enclosure with Elliot's letter to Aberdeen, 29 May 1843 (Public Record Office, London, ADM 1/5529).

[46] Marín to Secretary of War, 19 May 1843 (Archivo Militar, Mexico, D.F., XI/481.3/1973).

[47] Edwin Ward Moore, *To the People of Texas,* p. 160.

[48] Enclosure in Elliot's letter to Aberdeen, 19 May 1843 (Public Record Office, London, ADM 1/5529).

wheelhouse and did great damage. While the Texas ships were awaiting a strong breeze, Moore determined to harry the Mexican forces
retiring from Telchac. First, he sent two Yucatán gunboats under
commands of Lieutenant Gray and Lieutenant Lewis, who had recently re-entered the Navy. The Yucatecan crews had no heart for a
reckless, desperate adventure; so the expedition turned back.[49] Moore
then borrowed the *Independencia*, the largest gunboat, and manned
her with Texans.[50] Lieutenant Gray was in command. Colonel Cooke
went along, hoping to take some captives for exchange for Texans
still in Mexican prisons. The *Independencia* brought in the schooner
Glide on 26 May.[51] She had American papers for Laguna to supply
the Mexicans. Moore released her to the Yucatecos.

That same night Moore sent Gray and Cooke out again to capture
General Peña y Barragán, who was embarking in Telchac. The *Independencia* stopped by Sisal for the latest intelligence of Mexican
movements. Gray and Cooke heard that a ship had brought in a recent New Orleans newspaper, which they could not keep because it
had to be sent on to Mérida. But astounding news sent Gray and
Cooke hurriedly back to Campeche: President Houston had proclaimed Moore a pirate![52]

[49] A. Walke, Log Book of Alfred Walke (Archives, Texas State Library).
[50] Edwin Ward Moore, *To the People of Texas,* p. 162.
[51] *Ibid.,* p. 164.   [52] *Ibid.,* p. 165.

The Trap Is Sprung

When William Bryan left Texas in March 1843 with President Houston's instructions to the commissioners, Houston thought that at last the ships would be taken away from Commodore Moore, the crews disbanded, and the vessels sold. The commander of the Navy and the Navy commissioners were given no hint of a change in diplomatic tactics. The Navy commissioners received only a task, without background or reason for what they were to do. They knew only the well-publicized orders for the ships to resume action against Mexico if at all possible.

Houston, who had freed himself from the necessity of listening to advice from his Cabinet, wrote to Morgan:

The press of business has been so great since Colonel Bryan arrived, and in the absence of *all* my Cabinet, that I have not had time to write you only officially. You will see what I have done, and how I have done it. It seemed to me the only proper course. You will appreciate my situation, and I hope will bring those sinners to "taw" and to law. The case is new and unknown to any age or nation and must form a precedent. It is a most shameless transaction. By all means have the Commodore "yoked" and manacled, if possible. The law has appropriated the suitable punishment to mutiny, treason and piracy. All three offences are embraced in the conduct of Post Captain Moore. . . .[1]

Judge James Robinson, captured in Woll's September raid on San Antonio, bought freedom from Castle Perote by suggesting to Santa Anna that Texas might give up its struggle for recognition if Santa Anna would give it autonomy within the Mexican union.[2] Since Houston wanted to impress Captain Elliot with his opposition to annexation to the United States,[3] he arranged that Elliot be present as he received Robinson. Houston took Santa Anna's proposals from Robinson's hand, placed them in Elliot's, and asked Elliot to get Pakenham immediately on the job of arranging specific terms.[4] The rising sentiment in Texas for annexation to the United States was strongly opposed by Great Britain. If Texas could not remain independent, the Robinson proposals were exactly what Great Britain wanted. Elliot was excited at the progress he was making in carrying out his country's program, not knowing that Houston would be telling Joseph Eve what the United States wanted to hear: that the proposition was ridiculous.[5]

It fell in with Houston's design to assure both Elliot and Eve that Houston would not order any attack against Mexico while negotiations with Santa Anna were going on.

Yet an invasion of Galveston was imminent. Percy Doyle, the new British minister to Mexico, kept informed of events the chargé d'affaires in Texas, the British naval commanders in the Gulf, and the Foreign Office in London. On 17 April 1843 a steamer of war had brought erroneous news of the fall of Mérida, and there were public

---

[1] Amelia W. Williams and Eugene C. Barker (eds.), *Writings of Sam Houston*, IV, 175.

[2] U.S. consul at Veracruz, No. 172 to Secretary of State, 8 March 1843, Letters from U.S. consuls (National Archives, Washington).

[3] Enclosure in Elliot's letter to Aberdeen, 5 February 1843 (Public Record Office, London, F.O. 204/83).

[4] Elliot to Aberdeen, 14 April 1843 (Public Record Office, London, F.O. 204/83).

[5] Amelia W. Williams and Eugene C. Barker, *op. cit.*, IV, 183.

demonstrations of joy in Mexico.[6] Campeche, which still held out, was expected to fall under the force of the newest expedition being launched, and was said to be inclined to negotiate.[7] Santa Anna was "so elated with the successes his troops have met with in Yucatán that he had declared his intention of sending at once from thence an Expedition to Galveston, and of marching troops through the Interior to attack Texas on the other side."[8] The Mexican Foreign Minister, José Maria Bocanegra, warned British and French ministers to Mexico:

. . . [that whenever Mexican] troops enter Texas they will acknowledge no right whether of persons or property in individuals established in that country who may be taken prisoner, nor will they reply to any representation which may be addressed to them in favor of such Persons, whom they will treat as actual invaders and Enemies of the Republic, and punish them according to its laws. And that they will not acknowledge any Right in Foreign Consuls found in that Territory to be treated otherwise than as neutral foreigners, and as such only as long as they do not oppose directly or indirectly the right in its full extent whereby Mexico is endeavoring to recover possession of her territory.[9]

Doyle sent H.M.S. *Spartan* to Galveston[10] to warn Charles Elliot that "Mérida has just fallen and the new expedition will soon get started."[11] Juan Almonte, the Mexican minister to the United States, asked his government for instructions as to what to do when American troops entered Texas.[12]

[6] Percy Doyle to Foreign Office, 24 April 1843 (Public Record Office, London, F.O. 50/161, p. 280).

[7] Captain G. Elliot to Sir Charles Adam, 25 April 1843 (Public Record Office, London, ADM 1/5529).

[8] Doyle to Foreign Office, 24 April 1843 (Public Record Office, London, F.O. 50/161, p. 259).

[9] Doyle to Sir Charles Adam, 24 April 1843 (Public Record Office, London, ADM 1/5529).

[10] Doyle to Captain G. Elliot, 20 April 1843 (Public Record Office, London, F.O. 204/83).

[11] Doyle to Captain Charles Elliot, 20 April 1843 (Public Record Office, London, F.O. 75/23, p. 125).

[12] Almonte to Minister Relaciones Exteriores, 8 April 1843 (Secretaria de Relaciones Exteriores, Mexico, D.F., L-E-1069).

Houston was pretending to draw close to Great Britain, knowing that the United States would not tolerate a British satellite on the Gulf. Texas was weak. Mexico was organized to strike. If Houston wanted a weakened Texas in order to induce American intervention to save it, everything was ready.

Then, 15 April 1843, Commodore Moore's ships sailed.[13]

Instead of persuading the United States to come to the aid of Texas, instead of bringing Texas into the Union welcomed by North and South, Houston's negotiations became worthless. All he could rescue from the ruins was an armistice with Mexico.

Houston's chance for effecting a spectacular entry of Texas into the United States went with the sailing of the *Austin* and the *Wharton*.[14]

The Navy had insured Texas independence.

About 6 May, when Houston found out that Moore and Morgan had gone to Yucatán, he issued the piracy proclamation.[15]

PROCLAMATION,
BY THE PRESIDENT OF THE REPUBLIC OF TEXAS.

Whereas, E. W. Moore, a Post Captain commanding the Navy of Texas, was, on the 29th of October, 1842, by the acting Secretary of War and Marine, under the direction of the President, ordered to leave the port of New Orleans, in the United States, and sail with all the vessels under his command, to the port of Galveston, in Texas: and whereas, the said orders were reiterated on the 5th and 16th of November, 1842: and whereas, he, the said Post Captain, E. W. Moore, was ordered again, 2nd December, 1842, to "proceed immediately and report to the Department in person": and whereas, he was again, on the 2d January, 1843, ordered to act in conformity with previous orders, and, if practicable, report at Galveston: and whereas, he was again, on the 22d of the same month, peremptorily ordered to report in person to the Department, and to "leave the ship Austin and Brig Wharton under the command of the senior officer present": and whereas also, commissioners were appointed and duly commissioned, under a secret act of the Congress of the Republic, in relation to the future disposition of the Navy of Texas, who proceeded to New Orleans in discharge of the duties assigned them: and, whereas, the said

---

[13] Edwin Ward Moore, *To the People of Texas,* p. 170.
[14] Amelia W. Williams and Eugene C. Barker, *op. cit.,* VI, 84.
[15] Edwin Ward Moore, *op. cit.,* p. 170.

Post Captain, E. W. Moore, has disobeyed, and continues to disobey, all orders of this government, and has refused, and continues to refuse, to deliver over said vessels to the said commissioners in accordance with law; but, on the contrary, declares a disregard of the orders of this Government, and avows his intention to proceed to sea under the flag of Texas, and in direct violation of said orders, and cruize upon the high seas with armed vessels, contrary to the laws of this Republic and of nations: and, whereas, the President of the Republic is determined to enforce the laws and exonerate the nation from the imputations and sanction of such infamous conduct; and with a view to exercise the offices of friendship and good neighborhood towards those nations whose recognition has been obtained; and for the purpose of according due respect to the safety of commerce and the maintenance of those most essential rules of subordination which have not heretofore been so flagrantly violated by the subaltern officers of any organized Government, known to the present age, it has become necessary and proper to make public these various acts of disobedience, contumacy and mutiny, on the part of the said Post Captain E. W. Moore; Therefore: I, SAM HOUSTON, President, and Commander-in-Chief of the Army and Navy of the Republic of Texas, do, by these presents, declare and proclaim, that he, the aforesaid Post Captain, E. W. Moore, is suspended from all command in the Navy of the Republic, and that all orders "sealed" or otherwise, which were issued to the said Post Captain, E. W. Moore, previous to the 29th October, 1842, are hereby revoked and declared null and void, and he is hereby commanded to obey his subsequent orders, and report forthwith, in person to the Head of the Department of War and Marine of this Government.

And I do further declare and proclaim, on failure of obedience to this command, or on his having gone to sea, contrary to orders, that this Government will no longer hold itself responsible for his acts upon the high seas; but in such case, requests all the governments in treaty, or on terms of amity with this government, and all naval officers on the high seas, or in ports foreign to this country, to seize the said Post Captain, E. W. Moore, the ship Austin and the brig Wharton, with their crews, and bring them, or any of them, into the port of Galveston, that the vessels may be secured to the Republic, and the culprit or culprits arraigned and punished by the sentence of a legal tribunal.

The Naval Powers of Christendom will not permit such a flagrant and unexampled outrage, by a commander of public vessels of war, upon the right of his nation and upon his official oath and duty, to pass unrebuked; for such would be to destroy all civil rule and establish a precedent which would jeopardize the commerce on the ocean and render encouragement and sanction to piracy.

In testimony whereof, I have hereunto set my hand and caused the great seal of the Republic to be affixed.

Done at Washington, the 23d day of March, in the year of our Lord, one thousand eight hundred and forty-three, and of the Independence of the Republic the eighth.

Signed,

By the President.   SAM HOUSTON

JOHN HALL,
Acting Secretary of State.[16]

Even after they heard about the proclamation, Morgan and Moore hoped that the *Republicano* would bring them authority to continue the attacks on the Mexicans. But on 6 June Cox came in without a single official message from Houston.[17]

He had declared Moore a pirate, and that was that.

The proclamation had the effect Charles Elliot knew it would; Moore's hold over his crew was broken.[18] Whereas, a few days before, his men would gladly charge the overwhelming superiority of the Mexican Navy, and even helped man Campeche's walls on their free time, now they would fight only to save their own skins. They were not afraid to face death in battle, but none wanted to be hanged for piracy. There was no question but that Santa Anna would hang them; the President of Texas had tied the legal knot.

The United States and Great Britain did not take the piracy proclamation seriously. Vice Admiral Adam, RN, wrote to the Foreign Office that, since Moore had a Navy commissioner aboard, there would have to be a definite piratical act before he would order British ships to do anything.[19] The United States Navy took no official notice of the situation, although the *Vincennes*, under Commander F. P. Buchanan, was said to have intended to try to capture the Texas ships.[20]

---

[16] *Ibid.*, p. 168.   [17] *Ibid.*, p. 173.

[18] Elliot to Aberdeen, 25 April 1843 (Public Record Office, London, F.O. 204/83).

[19] Sir Charles Adam to Foreign Office, 30 June 1843 (Public Record Office, London, F.O. 50/109, p. 308).

[20] George Fuller, "Sketch of the Texas Navy," *The Quarterly of the Texas State Historical Association*, VII, 223.

Moore and Morgan decided that the only thing they could do was to return to Texas as soon as they could, and justify their actions.[21] The two ships remained at anchor in sight of the Mexican squadron for two weeks awaiting powder enough to risk sortie. Moore says that, except for the piracy proclamation, he would have launched a surprise night attack during this time. On 14 June the remaining British sailors and officers all left the Mexican ships, unpaid and disgusted at the Mexican failure to attack a weaker squadron.[22]

On 16 June the SS *Charlotte* arrived with powder, but still Moore did not leave, perhaps because of contrary winds, or perhaps because of contrary sailors.

On 25 June the *Austin's* foretopmast was splintered by lightning. Moore had the foreroyal mast cut off and a stump foretopgallant mast made. This took two days.

At last, when dawn broke on 27 June, the Mexican squadron had left. Though both sides claimed the victory, the advantage lay with the Texans. Marín was awarded a *Cruz de Honor* by his government,[23] and Moore was declared a pirate and mutineer by his; yet the more powerful Mexican force withdrew, and invasion plans against both Yucatán and Texas were completely frustrated.[24] It is possible that news of the Armistice of 14 June had arrived in Yucatán, though neither Ampudia nor Moore mentions it. The Texans shoved off for Sisal, where they picked up the last $1,700 due the Texas Navy from Yucatán. Moore paid this sum to his officers and men so they would not be penniless in Galveston. Acting Governor Miguel Barbachano wrote Moore his thanks, hoping his differences with President Houston would be settled amicably. Moore assured him that the people of Texas still sympathized with Yucatán. At Sisal Lieutenant Lansing died of congestive fever aboard the *Wharton,* but was carried back to Galveston for burial. The two ships went to the Arcas Islands, where they got fifty-six turtles in order to give the sailors much needed meat, and then headed for Galveston.

Commodore Moore brought the *Austin* and the *Wharton* into a

[21] Edwin Ward Moore, *op. cit.,* p. 168.   [22] *Ibid.,* p. 175.
[23] Document XI/Lii/3–1035 (Archivo de Cancelados, Mexico, D.F.).
[24] William R. Manning (ed.), *Diplomatic Correspondence of the United States, Inter-American Affairs, 1831–1860,* XII, 290.

Galveston Bay filled with small boats loaded with excited, cheering people. He anchored off Menard's Wharf at 1:30 P.M., 14 July 1843. Mayor John M. Allen and a committee came out to ask him not to leave the *Austin* until four o'clock so that the citizens and military could make proper preparations for the reception of Moore and his officers. Moore told the committee that not only would he not leave at four, he would not leave at all until he should have surrendered himself in accord with Houston's proclamation.

The committee went back and got Sheriff H. M. Smyth, who came out to the flagship. Not until Smyth had refused to arrest Moore, saying he had no warrant or other instructions, and agreed to confirm this in writing, would Moore accept the official greeting and leave for Menard's Wharf.[25]

Galveston regarded the Navy as its savior and Moore as its personal hero.[26] The ladies had held meetings and made handsome badges for the officers to wear.[27] Laudatory resolutions had been passed by various groups.[28] The people gave a testimonial dinner to Moore and his officers on 28 July. Moore was extravagantly admired for his headlong valor. Some people realized that his squadron's action had pushed Mexico into agreeing to an armistice.[29] Everyone knew he had saved Galveston from annihilation. Houston was burned in effigy on the streets. Texans were proud of their Navy's gallantry and skill.

Moore's victories over the Mexicans were made pointless; his sacrifice was made in vain; he was the hero of a cause which had disappeared while he was at sea. Now, instead of the patriotic hopes of 1839–1841, there were only personal attacks against the President by

[25] Edwin Ward Moore, *Doings of the Texas Navy*, p. 21.

[26] James Love to General Albert Sidney Johnston, 15 May, 22 May, 1 June 1843, Mrs. Mason Barret Collection of Johnston Papers (Howard-Tilton Memorial Library, Tulane University, New Orleans).

[27] A. Walke, Log Book of Alfred Walke, 4 June 1843 (Archives, Texas State Library, Austin).

[28] The Honorable James C. Jones, *Speech of Hon. James C. Jones of Tennessee, in Defense of Commodore Edwin W. Moore, of the Late Navy of Texas, in the United States Senate, August 3, 1854, In Reply to the Speech of General Sam Houston, of July 15, 1854.*

[29] James Love to General Albert Sidney Johnston, 21 June 1843, Mrs. Mason Barret Collection of Johnston Papers (Howard-Tilton Memorial Library, Tulane University).

a radical minority, while the rest of weakened and confused Texas wearily accepted loss of independence as the price of peace and prosperity. Texas had been maneuvered back to its 1836 position: awaiting acceptance to enter the United States.

Four years ago Moore had been an affable, friendly man, always ready to swap sea stories, or determinedly making plans for the permanent Navy of the Republic of Texas, Now, feeling cheated of the glory which should have been his, sick, tired, and embittered, he lost control of himself at a most critical time. Within a week of his return he insulted both Samuel M. Williams and James Love to the point of arrangements for duels.[30] These two men, with Morgan and Francis Moore, were the best friends Moore and the Navy had, and were men of influence. Mutual friends prevented the duels from taking place, but Moore lost support just when he needed it most.

Five days after the ships arrived, Houston had Secretary Hill issue dishonorable discharges to Moore, Lothrop, and Snow. Moore's was for disobedience of orders, fraud, desertion, piracy, and murder. Lothrop's was for failing to relieve Moore. Snow's was for leaving the *San Bernard* instead of starving to death aboard her. Moore and Lothrop were ordered to turn over their ships to the next senior officers. Shortly before the dismissals, Lieutenant William Brashear was appointed naval commissioner in place of Morgan.

The dismissals were received on 25 July. Moore and Lothrop obeyed at once. For the past week Moore had asked the commissioners for provisions, but received nothing, except those he bought with his own money. One day's supply of bread remained. Making this final report, Moore left his beloved flagship. Lieutenant Gray fired a thirteen-gun salute, and all hands joined in three cheers for their gallant Commodore. Nearby, Lothrop was yielding command of the *Wharton* to Lieutenant A. I. Lewis, and receiving eight guns and three cheers.

The next day Lieutenant Gray and all the commissioned officers of the *Austin* and the *Wharton* except Lieutenant Tennison resigned and left the vessels.[31] Brashear and Bryan offered command to officer after officer until First Boatswain John Rice, and, next day, Sailing Master Daniel Lloyd agreed to take command.[32] Lieutenant William Tennison took command of the *Wharton,* then moved over to the *Austin.*[33]

Brashear got rid of the sailors as soon as possible. He discharged over a hundred men from the *Austin.* They went about Galveston threatening to capture the *Austin* and open fire on the customhouse unless they were properly paid off.[34] This alarmed the commissioners so much that they held almost the entire crew of the *Wharton* aboard, discharging only twenty. Ten days later most of the midshipmen and sailors had been sent to New Orleans, forty by the brig *Sam Houston.* Among the forty were Midshipman Fuller, who sixty years later wrote his experiences; A. Walke, whose diary told about seagull eggnog on Arcas Island; Charles Arcambal, who drank out of a flower pot on the *Archer*; and William E. Glenn, who had joined late, at Campeche. Remaining behind in the *Austin* were E. F. Gray, a midshipman who later graduated in the Annapolis class of 1852–1853, and Seaman Thomas Norris, who had lost an arm. Dr. T. P. Anderson treated the Navy's sick and wounded ashore long after the Navy had disbanded.

This marked the end of the seagoing part of the Texas Navy, and also accounted for the existence of so few known descendants of Texas Navy sailors. The resignations of the officers were not accepted; it became obvious that Houston wanted to starve them into desertion and disgrace.

The *Wharton* lent Brashear her second cutter, and the *Austin*'s log shows this entry: "Delivered Commodore Moore 21 powder kegs empty" on 14 September—possibly for stowing his personal gear.

On 12 August 1843 the Houston *Citizen* published accounts of Houston's dismissal of Moore, Lothrop, and Snow. On the sixteenth Moore wrote to the editor, pointed out various misstatements, and

[31] A. Walke, Log Book of Alfred Walke, 27 July 1843 (Archives, Texas State Library).

[32] *Appendix to the Journals of the Ninth Congress of the Republic of Texas,* pp. 75–90.

[33] Log of the *Austin,* 27 July 1843, Navy Records (National Archives).

[34] Bryan and Brashear to G. W. Hill, 29 July 1843, *Journals of the House of Representatives of the Ninth Congress of the Republic of Texas.*

made clear that he expected to be tried by court-martial for the offenses alleged by Houston. Moore knew that an impartial trial would vindicate him. The law provided that no naval officer could be deprived of his commission without court-martial. Houston did not want public examination of his actions, and preferred to bury the issue; so neither the Secretary of War and Marine nor the President would order a court-martial.

On 21 September Moore issued a pamphlet *To the People of Texas*. This carefully written, 201-page booklet contains almost every important official document concerning the Texas Navy between September 1841 and July 1843. Moore made no pretense of being a writer. His strongest statements are pale when compared to the superb invective and clever wording of Houston. But one thing shines through his words: Moore is sincere, dedicated, narrow, perhaps, in his outlook, but always striving to give Texas a strong Navy and to win Mexican recognition. In contrast, Houston and his Cabinet subordinates are regularly lacking in candor, improvising reasons, and constantly avoiding the real issues and decisions. This pamphlet was widely read. Followed by a letter to the Congress,[35] it had the desired effect: the Eighth Texas Congress investigated the controversy. Even with a Houston majority in both houses, Congress determined that Moore had been illegally dismissed, and ordered a special general court-martial to try Snow, Lothrop, and Moore.

During the summer of 1843 the *Zavala's* parts had been sold at auction. Now, outhouses from the Navy Yard, medicine, lanterns, books, flagstaffs, lumber, charts, and so on went the same way. The total sales amounted to something less than $1,000.

In the fall of 1843 repeated efforts were made to sell the ships. On 14 October an auction was held. Judge Benjamin Franklin, whose wife Eliza had led the women's committee to make badges for the officers, bid $1,000 for the *San Bernard* in the name of the people of Galveston,[36] but Thomas F. McKinney won with a bid of $1,100 in the name of the people of Texas. The *Archer* was sold in a similar man-

[35] Edwin Ward Moore, "To the Honorable the Senate and House of Representatives of Texas in Congress Assembled," 11 January 1844, Texas Navy Papers (Archives, Texas State Library).

[36] *Telegraph and Texas Register,* 18 October 1843.

ner for $1,500. The auctioneer, G. B. James, received $100 as his fee. All this got Houston in a speech-making mood in Huntsville. He took opportunity to fling out some eloquent equivocations concerning Moore and the Navy. Once more word went out to the commissioners to sell the Navy. This time R. P. Jones admitted that he was authorized by a foreign government to buy the ships, but he did not know whether they would be used for war or merchant purposes. The people stopped this sale, too.[37]

Galveston was afraid of an invasion, now that Mexico had heard of the laying up of the Navy. Houston's coast defences and the parading militia offered only faint reassurance. The Eighth Congress repealed the secret act to dispose of the Navy, and placed all the ships in ordinary. This gave them at best emergency capabilities, and made the coastal folk feel only a little better.

Houston persuaded the new U.S. minister, William S. Murphy, to request a U.S. squadron to be placed at Murphy's disposal. President Tyler sent Commodore Conner's squadron;[38] the ships, when they arrived, more than filled the gap left by the Texas Navy. This shield was available, however, only as long as Texas annexation was pending. Texas had lost its sovereignty as soon as the United States took over its national defence. The *Montezuma* and the *Guadaloupe* went to New York for extensive repairs.[39] In the fall of 1844, while Moore was in New York, Arrangoiz said that Moore was trying to gain control of the steamers.[40] When the Mexican War began, the ships were caught in Cuba, still unpaid for.[41]

The same Congress appropriated $76,000 to be prorated among the naval officers to whom the government owed back pay. As Moore had not been paid once since he entered the Navy, Texas owed him

[37] James Love to General Albert Sidney Johnston, 6 November 1843, Mrs. Mason Barret Collection of Johnston Papers (Howard-Tilton Memorial Library, Tulane University).

[38] J. C. Calhoun to Van Zandt and Henderson, 11 April 1844 (typescript, Archives collection, University of Texas, Austin).

[39] Brower to Van Zandt, 27 July 1844, George P. Garrison (ed.), *Diplomatic Correspondence of the Republic of Texas*, II (1), Part II, 299–300.

[40] Ministerio de Relaciones Exteriores, letter of 6 December 1844 (Archivo Militar, Mexico, D.F., XI/481.3/1520).

[41] Mackenzie to Bancroft, 7 July 1846, Commanders Letters, July–December, 1846, Navy Records (National Archives).

$11,000. His portion of the pay would be quite large, but the act forbade payment of any of the money to an officer whose accounts had not been settled. Houston's administration would not settle Moore's.

Houston's authority and personal popularity were at their lowest in the spring of 1844. The country was almost in anarchy. The dispute with Moore was the most dramatic of his troubles. Until a few days before Moore's court-martial, many people believed Houston would never let it take place.

The court-martial met at Washington-on-the-Brazos on 20 May 1844, with the Republic's new major general, Sidney Sherman, as president. Sherman was appointed by the Congress, and was considered anti-Houston. The other members, all militia officers and appointed by Houston, were Brigadier General Alexander Somervell, Brigadier General Edwin Morehouse, Colonel Thomas Sypert, and Colonel James Reily, a lawyer who had been Houston's minister to the United States. Three judge advocates were appointed. Barry Gillespie became sick, and had to retire. Another man also acted, but Thomas "Ramrod" Johnson was the principal one. Ramrod Johnson received his nickname as Houston's faithful editor of the *Texian and Brazos Farmer*, and later, of the *National Vindicator*.

Lieutenant Snow was tried and exonerated for having deserted the *San Bernard* and having taken some of her gear to Moore in New Orleans.[42]

Lothrop left command of the *Neptune* in April 1844 and reported to Washington for his trial. Charges against Lothrop were dropped on 29 May by order of Secretary Hill, and Lothrop was restored to his former rank in the Navy.[43]

Yellow fever had been brought to Texas from Veracruz by the U.S. Steamer of War *Poinsett* under Lieutenant Raphael Semmes, USN, and an epidemic broke out all over that part of the country.[44] William Kennedy wrote that more than 10 per cent of the people of Galveston had it, and many died. Downing Crisp, who had returned from Eng-

[42] Joint Resolution for the relief of Charles B. Snow, *Journals of the Senate of the Ninth Congress of the Republic of Texas,* 24 January 1845.

[43] *Telegraph and Texas Register,* 12 June 1844, p. 3.

[44] Kennedy to Aberdeen, 29 July 1844, Ephraim D. Adams (ed.), *British Diplomatic Correspondence Concerning the Republic of Texas,* p. 350–352.

land and taken command of the *Austin* in January 1844, died of yellow fever in Galveston, 3 June 1844. Lothrop was struck down on 14 August. The court adjourned, and went to his funeral. Lothrop was buried with his sword at his chest.[45] He had served seven years in the Texas Navy, a competent, resourceful, admired officer. He was only thirty when he died, but he had been with the Texas Navy through its entire history. Moore was administrator of Lothrop's estate.

Moore was finally charged with and tried for:

Wilful neglect of duty	(6 specifications)
Misapplication of money—embezzlement of public property and fraud	(3 specifications)
Disobedience of orders	(6 specifications)
Contempt and defiance of the country	(5 specifications)
Treason	(1 specification)
Murder	(1 specification)

Piracy was not charged.

Moore's trial lasted seventy-two days in the muggy heat of Washington's summer. Time after time witnesses had to be summoned long distances. Morgan, Mason, Pursers Wells and Stephens, Brashear, and Hill, who tried to avoid testifying. Houston stayed in Washington to keep an eye on things, and said that Moore "slept with, ate with, drank with, and staid with the president of the court and a part of its members."[46] All during the trial Moore kept notes on the testimony, but they cannot be found.

As Moore stepped forward to surrender his sword to General Sherman, he said:

Mr. President—I appear before this court under the provisions of a joint resolution of the Congress of our country to answer to grave and serious charges preferred by the individual filling the office of Secretary of War and Marine, charges in which not only my reputation as an officer and standing in society are at stake, but if found guilty, my life itself is involved.

I place in your keeping, Mr. President, and gentlemen of this court, my

[45] D. F. Duerr, Diary (typescript, Archives Collection, University of Texas Library).

[46] Amelia W. Williams and Eugene C. Barker, *op. cit.*, VI, 30.

sword, which I have worn in this and my native country upwards of nineteen years, and in this country of my adoption for nearly five years, and which I can safely say I have always used to the utmost of my ability, with prudence, firmness, discretion and humanity. It is the first time, gentlemen, since it was put in my hands, while a mere boy, that its functions have been suspended or even an imputation has been cast upon it.

From the intelligence of this court I confidently believe that after a full investigation of the charges and specifications, I will receive at your hands an impartial verdict, which is all I ask.[47]

Moore's counsel was James S. Mayfield, who had so aggressively attacked Houston two years before in Congress. The fact that Houston, as well as Moore, was on trial did not escape Mayfield, but at the same time he conducted such a masterful defence that Reily wrote Anson Jones that he had rather have Mayfield defend him than any other lawyer in Texas.

One peculiarity of the trial was that prosecution and defence both used the same documents and, in general, the same witnesses, but drew different conclusions from them.

The first two charges dealt largely with Moore's handling of Navy funds. Moore and Mayfield tried to get Moore's accounts audited to show that the government owed Moore, not vice versa.

The auditors had refused to take up the Yucatán rental money on the books, as Houston had called the transaction illegal. Moore had got an act of Congress passed, requiring him to be charged with this money. Moore said that the reason he had been slow in making returns was that mail was irregular and insecure. These two charges were investigated very thoroughly. The facts were on Moore's side.

The charge of disobedience of orders concerned the letters Moore had received in the fall of 1842 and spring of 1843. He did not deny receiving the orders, but pointed out that they were either conditional (". . . proceed if practicable . . ." or ". . . you will therefore report in conformity (if practicable) with your previous orders . . .") or impossible ("If you cannot with the means at your command prepare the squadron for sea, you will immediately with all the vessels under your command sail . . .")

[47] New Orleans *Tropic*, 18 June 1844.

Contempt and defiance of the laws and authorities of the country were alleged in connection with Moore's initial replies to the commissioners, and in his ordering Snow to New Orleans.

The charges of treason and murder were not pressed by Johnson. As a matter of fact, Johnson praised Moore highly for his valor, patriotism, and skill.

Moore had to await the next session of Congress for the highly secret findings of the court to be announced. In the meantime he went to Houston and Galveston, where the citizens gave him testimonial dinners. There was wide speculation as to the outcome of his trial. The consensus, backed by Moore's appearing at parties in dress uniform, was that he had been found not guilty.[48]

Moore went to New York, where he and former President Lamar formally met Texas friends in the Governor's Room at the City Hall, and, as distinguished visitors, were entertained at the theatre and conducted through the arsenal by General Storms.[49] While Moore was in Washington, D.C., he once more fell ill with the fever for several weeks. He went on to Virginia to see relatives. His namesake, Edwin Ward Moore II, only son of the Commodore's elder brother, Albert Berkeley Moore, had recently died in infancy. Albert came back to Texas with the Commodore for a visit, and moved his family to Seguin in 1847, where he became county judge.

By the time Moore got back to Texas, Houston had pulled another of his high-handed tricks. Since Congress ordered the court, the findings should have been delivered and published by it. Houston had Secretary Hill order General Sherman to deliver the findings to the Department of War and Marine to be held until a new Speaker of the House was elected. The Speaker broke the seals, but instead of showing the findings to Congress, he gave them to President Houston.[50]

Houston found that the court had acquitted Moore of all charges and specifications except four specifications under "Disobedience of Orders." These were the conditional or impossible orders. No sentence was given.

[48] Kennedy to Aberdeen, 23 September 1844, Ephraim D. Adams, *op. cit.*, pp. 364–367.

[49] New York *Herald,* 8 and 13 January 1845.

[50] La Grange *Intelligencer,* 7 October 1845.

Houston endorsed the findings: "The President disapproves the proceedings of the court in toto, as he is assured by undoubted evidence of the guilt of the accused . . ."[51]

The net effect was that since Moore's dismissal was illegal and his trial had been disapproved he was legally entitled to his commission as post captain, Texas Navy.

All he had to do was to get it from the President who was still certain of his guilt!

[51] Edwin Ward Moore, *Doings of the Texas Navy,* p. 23.

Moore's Later Years

Moore had not been well enough to return to Texas for the opening of the Ninth Congress. His major of marines in the *Austin*, W. G. Cooke, who had been elected to Congress, called upon the Acting Secretary of War and Marine for the record of Moore's trial. Hamilton refused to deliver it. Cooke introduced a resolution asking that Hamilton be removed for using indecorous language to Congress.[1] This failed, but the new President, Anson Jones, appointed Cooke Secretary of War and Marine in the place of Hamilton. Moore then was finally able to be officially notified of the court-martial findings in his case.

Houston's Treasurer had refused Moore his prorata share of appropriations for back pay for naval officers. Initially, this was proper. One provision of the act was that no officer was to be paid until his accounts were settled. Moore had been exonerated by court-martial of all charges having to do with financial matters. Still, Houston's auditor would not audit the accounts, even after Moore offered to

[1] *Journals of the House of Representatives of the Ninth Congress of the Republic of Texas*, p. 244.

count those $18,812 exchequer bills as specie (four times their value).[2]

The House passed a bill in January 1845, requiring payment of Moore's prorata share, but the Senate did not act. In the special session to consider annexation, both houses passed resolutions for Moore's relief. These provided that Moore, Snow, and others should be restored to their ranks, positions, and emoluments.

President Jones vetoed the resolutions. He first wrote that Congress had no right to pardon anyone. Then he repeated some of the charges Moore had been acquitted of, shed tears for the hanged mutineers, and ignored the audits.[3] Moore's supporters lacked the strength to override the veto. The House voted thanks to Moore and his officers and men, and said that Moore was entitled to continue in his position as commander of the Navy.[4] The Senate passed a resolution that the court should be considered "final and conclusive."[5]

Morgan wrote of the veto:

Pres. Jones has kilt Commodore Moore dead with his veto—the Commodore's own fault. He would never listen to reason or take advice except from those who urged him on to his own vein. He is down, often, never to rise again—I tried my best to save him but his inordinate vanity and bad advisory has ruined him. Well might he exclaim, "Save me from my friends."[6]

Meanwhile, J. G. Tod had been busy acting as a courier to Washington, D.C. Jones appointed him the post captain of the Texas Navy in August 1845, backdating his commission to 1841. The Annexation Convention was then meeting, and the Texas Senate never approved the appointment.

In the spring of 1846, while negotiations were underway for the annexation of Texas, it was agreed that the Texas Navy would be ab-

[2] Edwin Ward Moore, "Memorial to the Convention," La Grange *Intelligencer,* 1 February 1844.

[3] Executive Record Book 47, 27 June 1845 (Archives, Texas State Library).

[4] *Journals of the House of Representatives of the Ninth Congress of the Republic of Texas, Special Session,* p. 86.

[5] *Journals of the Senate of the Ninth Congress of the Republic of Texas, Special Session,* p. 75.

[6] Morgan to Swartwout, 16 August 1845, Morgan Papers (Rosenberg Library, Galveston).

sorbed by the U.S. Navy. Nothing was written about the officers and men, but the U.S. representative, Andrew Jackson Donelson, assured Anson Jones that they would be taken care of.[7]

Brashear, now a commander, Tennison, Lewis, Bunner, and Hurd stayed with the ships under Commander V. M. Randolph, USN, until August 1846, for three months' service under the U.S. flag.[8] After annexation the *Wharton,* the *Archer,* and the *San Bernard* were sold at auction in Galveston on 30 November 1846 for a total of $935.[9] The *Austin* was towed to Pensacola and there made a station ship for several years. Texas Navy sailors finished their enlistments as U.S. Navy men. The Texas naval officers wished to enter the U.S. Navy, and at their Texas Navy ranks. U.S. naval officers objected. They opposed in particular Moore, whose contemporaries were still lieutenants. As promotion was strictly by seniority, and there was no retirement, the entry of even one captain would effectively slow down the entire promotion system.

Senator Rusk, Congressman Kaufman, and even Senator Houston introduced and spoke for measures to get the Texas officers into the U.S. Navy. Houston's efforts carried either the spoken or unspoken reservation that Moore was not the post captain he was talking about. Commanders S. F. Du Pont, Franklin Buchanan, and G. A. Magruder helped stall efforts for action, and many officers, including Matthew Fontaine Maury, petitioned Congress not to admit the Texans. They published several pamphlets, to which Moore replied. The pamphlets were largely restatements or reprints of old arguments but Moore's *Doings of the Texas Navy,* published in 1847, included a few items not in his *To the People of Texas.*

Legislature after legislature prodded the Texas senators, and Moore continued lobbying.[10] In 1853 and 1854 bitter debates between Houston and James Alfred Pearce of Maryland on one side and James

[7] *Congressional Globe,* 1171, 31 July 1846.

[8] Brashear to Secretary of the Navy, 8 November 1846, Commanders Letters, July–December 1846, Navy Records (National Archives, Washington).

[9] Randolph to Mason, 1 December 1846, Commanders Letters, January–July 1847, Navy Records (National Archives).

[10] Memorial of the Officers of the late Texas Navy, Texas Folder, Navy Records (National Archives).

C. Jones of Tennessee on the other took place.[11] With Moore sitting in the balcony (and undoubtedly feeding Jones information), Jones finally got Houston's goat, and the Senate got a fine exhibition of Houston's temper. But the best Moore and the Texas officers could do was to receive five years' pay of officers on leave, providing they would give up their claims to rank in the U.S. Navy.[12]

In addition to Moore, officers receiving pay were Alfred G. Gray, Cyrus Cummings, William Tennison (now a third lieutenant in the Revenue Service), Charles B. Snow (now of the U.S. Coast Survey), William Oliver, Pursers James F. Stephens, James Moore, and Norman Hurd. In addition, the estate of John G. Tod received in 1883 payment for the debt owed him, and P. W. Humphries received in 1858 pay for having been a commander. Humphries was really a clerk in the Navy Department, but Lamar had appointed him a commander, without confirmation, in 1840.[13] The midshipmen received nothing.

Wilbur, Brashear, and Bunner had died. Armstrong I. Lewis had been captain of the *Creole* with Fayssoux as his First Mate in a Lopez expedition to Cuba. Fayssoux went on to become commander of William Walker's navy in Nicaragua.

In Mexico, Tomás Marín had retired from the Navy, but was later to side with Maximilian as an active Rear Admiral and Brigadier General.[14] In 1847 Sebastian Holsinger, under fire, leaped over the parapet, recovered a fallen Mexican flag, and nailed it to a mast while defending Veracruz against the United States.

Moore continued to dicker for just a little more; he said that as the only Texas captain he ranked as senior captain, which position drew $1,000 more a year in the U.S. Navy than a plain captain. Houston

[11] Amelia W. Williams and Eugene C. Barker (eds.), *Writings of Sam Houston*, VI, 29, 30, 84, 97; speech of James C. Jones to the U.S. Senate, 3 August 1854, Navy Records (National Archives).

[12] *The United States Statutes at Large*, Vol. 11, 34th–35th Congress, 1855–1859, p. 248.

[13] Humphries to Toucey and endorsement, 8 July 1857, Folder VU, Navy Records (National Archives).

[14] Service Record of General Brigadier Tomás Marín, Departamento de Archivo (Archivo de Cancelado, Mexico, D.F.), XI/LII/3–1035.

wrote the Secretary of the Navy that to pay Moore anything at all was a personal insult to the Senator.[15] President Buchanan himself made final decision to pay Moore, but as a captain only.[16] Moore's back pay amounted to some $12,500.

Moore had to wait almost as long for money from Texas, as reimbursement for funds of his own which he had spent for Texas and as payment of back salary, as he had to wait for his adjusted retirement pay from the U.S. On 24 February 1848 he received $11,398 for money he had advanced the Navy, and $15,202.06 for supplies he had bought for the Navy, and $3,575.39 as part of his back pay.[17] Over a year later, 17 April 1849, he received another $9,190.17 in back pay through 1 January 1844. At last, on 4 February 1856, he received $5,290 as final settlement of his accounts as naval agent in 1841.[18] Thus Moore, rather than being a defaulter to the government, or even an officer guilty of fraud, was found, after many careful audits, to be the creditor of Texas to the amount of $44,655. As further remuneration he received in 1852[19] a grant of 320 acres of land in Burnet County.

The U.S. Navy sent an additional squadron of ships to the Gulf in 1845 to prevent Mexican invasion while the annexation question was being considered by Texas. In command was Commodore Robert Field Stockton of the great New Jersey Stockton family. Commodore Moore was a member of the committee for a ball for Stockton and his officers in Galveston on 21 May 1845.

The following unsigned, undated letter among the papers of Callender Fayssoux in the Howard-Tilton Library of Tulane seems to report an incident which occurred on that occasion:

By request of Comod. E W Moore was present at a meeting of Commodore Moore, T.N., & Sam Houston, President of Texas and Comm.

[15] Houston to Toucey, 13 March 1857, Texas Folder, Navy Records (National Archives).

[16] Copy of letter, Buchanan to H. L. Stevens, 13 October 1857, Texas Papers, Navy Records (National Archives).

[17] H. P. N. Gammel (comp.), *Laws of the Republic of Texas*, III, 351.

[18] Public Debt Papers, 4 February 1856, Archives (Texas State Library, Austin).

[19] Certificate 2453/2554 (Federal Land Office, Austin).

Stockton U.S. Navy, a Friend of Moore, Moore denounced in the most bitter terms S Houston—said Commodore Stockton, are you aware that you are walking with the damnedest scoundrel on the face of the earth, the damnedest villian unhung. Comd. Stockton said to Moore, take my arm Com. Moore, they walked off together. S. Houston turned and walked off alone—it was dropped by Houston. . . .[20]

There is no telling whether this incident actually did take place. Moore had written to Houston on 5 May 1845 a letter intended to bring about a duel. Houston ignored this, too, even after it had been published in the Galveston *Civilian.*

The Houston-Moore feud furnishes evidence that personal animosities may bring unexpected results. In 1855 Houston, trying to generate a presidential boom for himself, decided to visit Texas to get a favorite-son movement going. Arriving in Austin, he dropped in on the Senate, then stepped over to the House. One of his supporters, Isaac Parker, moved that Houston be invited to enter the bar of the House. Before this resolution could be voted on, Mathew D. Ector moved to amend the invitation to include Commodore Moore, who also happened to be in town. This brought about some parliamentary bickering, which lasted three hours while Houston waited out on the porch.[21] This may have stopped a whirlwind campaign for Houston.

Perhaps it was through Commodore Stockton that Moore met Stockton's distant cousin, the beautiful and wealthy Emma Matilda Stockton Cox, widow of a U.S. Navy contemporary of Moore's, Lieutenant John Wentworth Cox, who had died in 1842, just after serving aboard the *Ohio* with Stockton. Emma, the daughter of the late William Tennant and Anna Williamson Stockton, lived on Sansom Street in Philadelphia. In April 1848 Moore made out his will in favor of his beloved Emma M. Cox.[22] They were married in St. Luke's Church, Philadelphia, on 16 August 1849.[23]

Apparently the Moores spent most of their time in Washington,

[20] Callender I. Fayssoux Collection of William Walker Papers, Middle American Research Institute (Tulane University Library, New Orleans), Folder 131.

[21] Austin *State Gazette,* 22 December 1855.

[22] Federal District Court Record of Wills, A W No. 13, Folio 131 new, 132 old (Washington, D.C.).

[23] Clarksville *Northern Standard,* 22 December 1849, p. 3, col. 3.

D.C., New York, and Charlottesville. The Commodore became a partner with C. B. Cluskey of Washington, D.C., in a construction firm. They were the low bidders on a new, Parthenon-type custom-house in Galveston, the first federal building to be erected in the new state. They received the contract in December, 1846.

For three years there were delays. Some thought the proposed customhouse was too small, that the plans should be enlarged before construction started. Some wanted the originally planned building immediately. Some thought the location poor. A rival builder claimed Moore was himself stirring up all the dissension because he could not possibly fulfil the contract at his unfair low bid. Moore's builders, Blaisdell and Emerson, grew impatient.

Moore had to interrupt business to testify as a government witness in a piracy case, one of a series arising from the defiant reopening of the slave trade by Charles A. L. Lamar with his speedy sloop the *Wanderer*.[24] Lamar was a cousin of former Texas President Mirabeau B. Lamar. Moore had interviewed J. Egbert Farnham, Captain of the *Wanderer*, at Washington and in the jail at Savannah. Moore's testimony so implicated Lamar that he insulted Moore, who challenged him to a duel, which was fought with pistols at Screven's Ferry, near Savannah, on 24 May 1860.[25] Both missed, and Lamar apologized. The affair was settled, and the prominent Lamar kept it from the Savannah papers, though it was widely reported throughout the country. Moore's second in this duel was Hamilton Couper, the U.S. district attorney for Georgia during the trial. Couper resigned his position in December 1860 to promote secession.

Interest in the *Wanderer* was wide. Lamar had challenged the United States to stop him from importing the Negroes, and as all the suits had ended in mistrials, it looked as if his claim that a court would never convict him was true. The former Texas Navy lieutenant, William Ross Postell, had been supercargo on another of Lamar's slave ships. During the Civil War he was First Mate of the brig *Jefferson Davis*, a successful Confederate privateer.

Back in Washington, D.C., Cluskey backed out. Then a new con-

[24] C. A. L. Lamar, "A Slave Trader's Letterbook," *North American Review*, CXLIII (No. 5), November 1886, pp. 451–457.
[25] Augusta (Georgia) *Daily Constitutionalist*, 25 May 1860.

tract for the larger building was negotiated, with James Willcox of New York City and Moore's brothers, A. B. Moore and James W. Moore, serving as Moore's securities.

All the talk of secession worried the builder, A. Blaisdell, who had much of his own money tied up in this U.S. government building in a Southern state. So he was anxious to get started in order that he could get his money free before trouble came. Moore was in New Orleans, but had no travel money to come to Texas. Blaisdell, frantic, offered to pay Moore's travel costs from his own pocket so that Moore would come to Galveston and get the work started. He wrote that it would be worth $500 to him to get Moore here. He had the workmen lined up; they had actually started work, but had been stopped, being unable to show proper authority. Moore had to come. Moore came. The thirty-five workmen started a feverish rush to get the building done before the state might secede. On March 23 the Secession Convention ratified the constitution of the Confederacy and adjourned three days later. Texas was in the Confederacy. The next day Blaisdell reported the work on the U.S. customhouse finished.

Moore's stand in the Civil War is unknown, but it appears he remained in the North. In 1863 Emma was in Philadelphia, trying to get permission to cross into the South to Charlottesville, where her mother and her sister, Mrs. Thomas Farish, lived with a large family at "The Farm," the house where General George A. Custer spent the night when Charlottesville surrendered.

The days were long gone when Moore's glory could have rested on his being victor of the world's first battle between steamships. The rusted, sunken *Zavala* precluded that chance. History has generally given to the Russians, at Sinop in 1853, the credit for the first use of explosive shells in a sea engagement. Ten years earlier the Mexican and Texan vessels had faced each other with explosive shell, but because the Mexicans had fled so fast before Moore, only once did he get within close enough range to hit them with explosive shells. Thus, at a time when the sea traditions of a thousand years were being shattered, Moore's small fame incongruously rests on his victory of wooden vessels, sail, and solid shot over iron, steam, and Paixhans. His is the only recorded victory of sail over steam in battle.

Fate struck Edwin Ward Moore his last disappointment.

Moore had passed several years working upon mechanical inventions. The latest was a revolutionary type of steam engine which Moore expected would cast all other inventions of the last century into the shade and create an undreamed-of saving of coal. Radiant with success and filled with plans for the future, he passed a pleasant evening with his wife and friends on Tuesday, 3 October 1865.[26] As he left his wife the next morning he said, "Next week we expect to astonish the world."

Success was within reach. That afternoon, Wednesday, he was struck down with apoplexy, and brought home speechless. He died on Thursday, 5 October 1865.

He was first buried in the grounds of the First Presbyterian Church, Germantown, Pennsylvania. Later his body was moved to the Ivy Hill Cemetery, near the graves of his father-in-law and his sister-in-law. The stone reads:

> ERECTED / BY HIS WIDOW / IN MEM-
> ORY / EDWIN W. MOORE / FORMERLY
> LIEUTENANT / NAVY OF U.S.A. / COM-
> MODORE OF / TEXIAN NAVY / BORN
> JULY 15, 1810 / DIED OCTOBER 5, 1865

Mrs. Moore lived in Charlottesville in a quaint little house on Maiden Lane. Until her death in the 1880's she was said to be receiving one pension as the widow of Cox and another as the widow of Moore, a veteran of the Florida War. Her property, including a nearby farm, was left to a nephew, Richard S. Farish.

In 1876 a portion of Bexar County, Texas, was designated Moore County in honor of Commodore Edwin Ward Moore, Texas Navy.

[26] Department of Health, Bureau of Records and Statistics, Borough of Manhattan, New York City.

Appendixes

A.

Commanding Officers of Texas Navy Vessels

(Principal Assignments)

Austin

1840	Captain E. W. Moore	April–December
1841	Captain E. W. Moore	January–June
	Lieutenant Alfred G. Gray	
		July–December (in ordinary)
	Captain E. W. Moore	December
1842	Captain E. W. Moore	January–December
1843	Captain E. W. Moore	January–July

Zavala

1839	Commander A. C. Hinton	April–December
1840	Commander A. C. Hinton	January–February
	Commander John T. K. Lothrop	February–December
1841	Commander John T. K. Lothrop	January–October
	Lieutenant William C. Brashear	
		October–December (in ordinary)
1842	Lieutenant William C. Brashear	
		December–March (in ordinary)

Archer (in ordinary)
Wharton

1839	Captain E. W. Moore	November–December
1840	Captain E. W. Moore	January–February
	Lieutenant James E. Gibbons	April–June (in ordinary)
	Commander George W. Wheelwright	June (in ordinary)
1841	Lieutenant Appleton	February (in ordinary)
	Lieutenant E. P. Kennedy	February–June (in ordinary)
	Commander John Clark	
		July–December (in ordinary)
1842	Commander John T. K. Lothrop	January–December
1843	Commander John T. K. Lothrop	January–July

San Antonio

1839	Lieutenant Francis B. Wright	November–December
1840	Lieutenant Francis B. Wright	January
	Lieutenant J. O'Shaunessy	February
	Lieutenant Alexander Moore	May–December
1841	Lieutenant Alexander Moore	January–June
	Lieutenant William Seegar	July–December
1842	Lieutenant William Seegar	January–September

San Bernard

1839	Commander A. C. Hinton	September–November
	Lieutenant William R. Postell	November–December
1840	Lieutenant William R. Postell	January–May
	Lieutenant William S. Williamson	May–November
	Lieutenant Thurston W. Taylor	November–December
1841	Lieutenant Thurston W. Taylor	January
	Lieutenant James O'Shaunessy	January–March
	Lieutenant Armstrong I. Lewis	March
	Lieutenant Downing Crisp	March–December
1842	Lieutenant Downing Crisp	January–February

San Jacinto

1839	Commander John T. K. Lothrop	June–November
1840	Lieutenant James E. Gibbons	February–April
	Lieutenant Alexander Moore	April–May
	Lieutenant William R. Postell	May–September
	Lieutenant James O'Shaunessy	September–November

B.

Officers of the *Austin*, 1843

Post Captain Edwin Ward Moore, Commanding
Alfred Gray, First Lieutenant
Cyrus Cummings, Second Lieutenant
Charles B. Snow, Third Lieutenant
Daniel C. Wilbur, Fourth Lieutenant
Lieutenant William Oliver
William Glenn, Acting Master
William G. Cooke, Captain of Marines
Norman Hurd, Purser
Thomas Anderson, Surgeon
James Peacock, Assistant Surgeon
James Moore, Commander's Secretary
William Gordon, Professor of Mathematics
Midshipmen: Robert Clements, Alfred Walke, George Fuller, E. Fairfax
 Gray, Andrew J. Bryant, G. W. Ripley, F. C. Masson. (Midshipman
 James Litch joined off Campeche 2 May. Midshipman Goodall came to
 Campeche from Galveston to join 4 June from the *Archer*. William
 Haveslin and William Cochrane, Acting Midshipmen, joined after 1
 June. Midshipmen Edward Mason and Robert Bradford apparently came
 aboard late, probably in May 1843.)
Seldon Hubbard, Captain's Clerk
John Salter, Gunner
John Rice, Boatswain
Peter Ryerson, Sailmaker
Robert Kell, Carpenter
Colonel James Morgan, Navy Commissioner
Mr. Stephens, Secretary to Morgan

C.

The Vessels of the Texas Navy

Name	Type	Origin	Date Commissioned	Design		
				Tonnage	Length	Beam
Austin (*Texas*)	Sloop-of-War	Baltimore	5 January 1840	600	125′	31′
Zavala (*Charleston*)	Steamship-of-War	Charleston	23 March 1839	569		
Wharton (*Colorado*)	Brig	Baltimore	18 October 1839 (delivered)	405	110′	28′
Archer (*Galveston*) (*Brazos*)	Brig	Baltimore	25 April 1840	400	110′	28′
San Jacinto (*Viper*)	Schooner	Baltimore	27 June 1839	170	66′	21′6″
San Antonio (*Asp*)	Schooner	Baltimore	7 August 1839	170	66′	21′6″
San Bernard (*Scorpion*)	Schooner	Baltimore	31 August 1839	170	66′	21′6″
Louisville (*Striped Pig*)	Schooner (tender)		25 September 1839 (bought)	95		

Characteristics			Final Disposition
Draft[1]	Crew, if fully manned	Guns (actual)	
12'6"	23 Officers and Warrant Officers 151 Sailors and Marines	16 24-lb Medium 2 18-lb Medium 2 18-lb Long (16 May 1843)	Transferred to U.S. Navy, 11 May 1846; towed to Pensacola; run aground and broken up, 1848.
	24 Officers 102 Sailors and Marines	4 12-lb Medium 1 9-lb Long (12 January 1842)	Run ashore, June 1842; broken up, sold for scrap, about 18 June 1843.
11'	17 Officers 123 Sailors and Marines	15 18-lb Medium 1 12-lb Long (16 May 1843)	Transferred to U.S. Navy, 11 May 1846; sold to Galveston for $55, 30 November 1846.
11'	17 Officers 123 Sailors and Marines	14 18-lb Medium (12 January 1842)	Transferred to U.S. Navy, 11 May 1846; sold for $450, 30 November 1846.
8'	13 Officers 69 Sailors and Marines	4 12-lb Medium 1 9-lb Long (brass) (pivot)	Wrecked in storm at Arcas Island, 31 October 1840.
8'	13 Officers 69 Sailors and Marines	4 12-lb Medium[2] 1 12-lb Long (pivot) (12 January 1842)	Lost at sea, September 1842.
8'	13 Officers 69 Sailors and Marines	4 12-lb Medium 1 12-lb Long (pivot) (12 January 1842)	Beached at Galveston September, 1842; repaired and transferred to U.S. Navy, 11 May 1846; sold for $150, 30 November 1846.

[1] Or depth of hold.
[2] Described in letter of Moore to Lamar, 12 November 1843.

D.

NAVAL GENERAL ORDER.

Navy Department,
13th March, 1839.

Hereafter, the Uniform Dress of the Officers of the Navy of the Republic of Texas shall be as hereinafter described, and to which all Officers are directed to conform.

NAVY UNIFORM.

CAPTAINS.

FULL DRESS. COAT of dark blue cloth, lined with white, double breasted, with long lapels, the width of which is to be in proportion to the size of the coat, and cut with a swell; the lapels are to be buttoned back with nine buttons on each lapel. *Collar* to be lined with white, and embroidered in gold round the upper edges and sides with a rope and a broad pennant worked in gold, as long as the collar will admit, with a star of the same in the centre thereof, as per pattern. The *Cuffs* to have four buttons, and buttonholes worked in twist, and embroidered with live oak leaf and acorn, with a rope on the upper part, above the button, as per pattern. The *Pocket-flaps* to be embroidered the same as cuffs, the lower part and sides to have a rope and four buttons underneath. The *front* of the coat, on both sides, to be embroidered in gold with live oak leaves and acorns interspersed, commencing at the collar and running down the breast and skirts to the tail, the lower part of the breast rounded off to the skirt; one button on each hip, two under the middle of the folds and one at the bottom of each skirt; the pockets to be in the fold. Two gold epaulets, one on each shoulder.

VEST, white, single breasted, with as many small navy buttons as are worn on the breast of the coat. *Collar,* standing, coming to the edge of the breast and sloping in a line with it. *Breast,* straight, with pocket-flaps, under each of which there shall be four small buttons.

BREECHES, white, with small navy buttons and gold or gilt kneebuckles—or plain white pantaloons over short boots, or with shoes and buckles.

UNDRESS. COAT, in all respects the same as full dress, except the embroidery of live oak leaf and acorn from the collar along the breast and skirt to the tail, none of which shall be upon the undress. Or, a *double breasted Frock Coat,* lined with white, standing collar, and epaulets as in full dress.

VEST, either white or blue, same as in full dress.

PANTALOONS, plain blue, or, in warm weather, white; to be worn over half-boots, or shoes and stockings.

COMMANDERS.

FULL DRESS. Same as Captain, with the following exceptions: COAT to be without the embroidery of live oak leaf and acorn from the collar along the breast and skirts to the tail; and a long pennant embroidered upon the collar instead of the broad, and longer and less than half the width of that for Captain. Three buttons on the wrists and under the pocket-flaps, instead of four; one on the folds of the skirts, instead of two.

UNDRESS. COAT of dark blue cloth, frock, double breasted, standing collar, lined with white; buttons the same as in full dress. A stripe of gold lace and one epaulet on each shoulder, or stripes without epaulets; in other respects same as Captain.

LIEUTENANTS.

FULL DRESS. Same as Commander, with the following exceptions: No embroidery upon the cuffs. One epaulet, instead of two, and that to be worn upon the right shoulder. A speaking-trumpet embroidered upon the collar, instead of the long pennant, as per pattern.

UNDRESS. Same as Commander, except one epaulet instead of two.

PASSED MIDSHIPMEN.

FULL DRESS. Same as Lieutenant, with the following exceptions: *Collar* to be embroidered with a foul anchor and star of five points, (as all the embroidered stars in the naval uniform must be,) arranged as per pattern; no epaulets.

UNDRESS. Same as Lieutenant, except the epaulet.

MIDSHIPMEN.

FULL DRESS. COAT, dark blue cloth, lined with white, standing collar, single breasted; nine buttons on the right breast and short button holes on the left. Embroidery, a star upon the collar, and none on the pocket-flaps.

UNDRESS. Same as Passed Midshipman, except the star on the collar. They will also be entitled to wear a round jacket, single breasted, standing collar, and an anchor inserted thereon: buttons the same.

SURGEONS.

FULL DRESS. Same as Lieutenant, with the following exceptions: no epaulet; collar embroidered with the club of Æsculapius, and two stripes of gold lace upon the wrists of coat, one half inch wide each.

UNDRESS. Same as Lieutenant, except the epaulet; collar plain; stripes on the wrists same as full dress.

ASSISTANT SURGEONS.

FULL DRESS. Same as Surgeon, except one stripe of gold lace on the wrists, instead of two.

UNDRESS. Same as Surgeon, except one stripe of gold lace on the wrists, instead of two.

PURSERS.

FULL DRESS. Same as Surgeon, except to substitute the cornucopia instead of the club of Æsculapius, and no stripes of lace upon the wrists.

UNDRESS. Same as Surgeon, except the stripes of lace upon the wrists.

GUNNERS.

FULL DRESS. Same as Passed Midshipman, with the following exceptions: a great gun upon the collar, as per pattern, instead of the anchor and star, and no embroidery upon the pocket-flaps.

UNDRESS. A round jacket, rolling collar, one small button upon each side of the collar, double breasted, nine buttons on each breast, and three upon each pocket-flap.

BOATSWAINS, CARPENTERS AND SAILMAKERS.

FULL DRESS. Same as Gunner, except the Boatswain to have a call embroidered upon the collar; Carpenter a broad-axe; Sailmaker a jib.

UNDRESS. Same as Gunner.

CHAPLAINS.

Plain black coat, vest and pantaloons, to be worn over boots or shoes; or, black breeches and silk stockings with shoes. COAT to have three black covered buttons under the pocket-flaps and on the cuffs.

SCHOOLMASTERS AND CLERKS.

Plain blue cloth coat, single breasted, rolling collar, and made according to the fashion prevailing among the citizens at the time, with six navy buttons on each breast, one on each hip, and one at the bottom of the skirts.

CHIEF ENGINEER.

Same as Pursers, except the embroidery on the collar, which will be the lever-beam of the engine.

EPAULETS.

All officers entitled to wear epaulets are to wear gold lace straps on their shoulders three-quarters of an inch wide, to distinguish their rank when without epaulets. Epaulets are not to be worn, in foreign ports, with round hats, but with cocked hats or caps.

Captains are to wear two epaulets of gold, each with two rows of bullion; on each strap of the epaulet, an anchor and star in gold. Captains in command of squadrons, by order of the Secretary of the Navy, to have the star above the anchor of silver, during the time they are in actual command. The Senior Officer of the Navy, at all times, entitled to wear the silver star.

Commanders to wear two epaulets of gold, the same as Captains, except the ornaments on the straps.

Lieutenants to wear one epaulet of gold, plain, like the Commanders, on the right shoulder.

SWORDS

Are to be basket hilted cut and thrust; the blade not to exceed thirty inches in length, nor to be less than twenty-six, and to be slightly curved; in breadth not to exceed one inch and three tenths, nor less than one inch and two tenths; the gripe of those for Captains, Commanders, Lieutenants and other commissioned officers and Midshipmen to be white; of other officers entitled to wear swords, black; all to be yellow mounted, and basket hilts, with heads like the navy-buttons, and black leather scabbards. All Officers in full dress, or when wearing their epaulets on shore, are to wear swords, except Chaplains, Schoolmasters and Clerks.

Belts. Blue webbing for undress, white webbing for full dress; the clasp to bear the coat of arms of the republic.

Sword-knots. Blue and gold rope, with twelve gold bullions.

All Officers, when in undress, will be allowed to wear dirks, yellow mounted, except in foreign ports.

HATS.

All the Officers, except the Chaplains, Schoolmasters, Clerks, Boatswains, Gunners, Carpenters and Sailmakers, are to wear, in full dress, cocked hats, bound with black silk riband, to show one inch and a half on each side, with gold tassels formed with five gold and five blue bullions, and a black silk cockade with a plain gold or gilt star one inch in diameter in the centre.

Captains and Masters Commandants to wear, when in full dress, gold laced cocked hats, with a solid gold star one inch and a half in diameter on the cockade.

Officers, in undress, may wear blue cloth caps, with or without epaulets. Captains, Commanders and Lieutenants to wear a band of gold lace, one inch and a half wide, around their caps; the caps of all other officers to be plain.

STOCKS.

All officers are to wear stocks or cravats of black, the white of the shirt collar to be shewn above it, both in full and undress.

GENERAL LICENSE.

All Officers, when on board ship, may wear short blue jackets, with the number of buttons as designated for their respective coats; grey cloth, brown drilling, yellow or blue nankeen trowsers; also black or figured vests, of any colour except red.

All Officers will be permitted to wear, as undress, a citizen's blue cloth dress coat, cut after the fashion prevailing at the day, with the requisite number of buttons as in full dress, and the straps on the shoulders for those who are entitled to wear epaulets.

All Officers commanding by order from the Navy department to have a binding of gold cord around the bottom of the collar, the breasts and the skirts to the tail.

Bibliography

Bibliography

Manuscripts

UNOFFICIAL

Austin, Log of. Collection of Mr. Harry Pennington, San Antonio, Texas.

Butler, Jonas. Document acknowledged 15 March 1848 by E. W. Moore. Collection of the Daughters of the Republic of Texas. The Alamo.

Clark, Margaret. "Certain Facts Relative to the Surrender of Charlottesville, March 3, 1865." Alderman Library, University of Virginia.

Dienst, Alex. Papers. Archives Collection, University of Texas Library, Austin.

Duerr, Christian Friedrich. Diary, 1834–1844. Typescript. Archives Collection, University of Texas Library, Austin.

Franklin, Benjamin C. Papers. Folder for 1849. Archives Collection, University of Texas Library, Austin.

Gomez-Farias, Valentin. Letters. Latin-American Collection, University of Texas Library, Austin.

Grayson, Jennie T. Letter to Commander Tom Wells, July 5, 1954. Collection of Commander Tom H. Wells, Norfolk, Virginia.

Hinton, A. C. Papers. Archives Collection, University of Texas Library, Austin.

Houston, Sam. Unpublished correspondence in typescript, III. Archives Collection, University of Texas Library, Austin.

Houston, Sam. Letter to Mrs. A. C. Hinton, 12 May 1850. Archives, Dallas Historical Society.

Johns, Edward. Papers. Archives Collection, University of Texas Library, Austin.

Johns, Edward. Journal. Archives Collection, University of Texas Library, Austin.

Johnston, General Albert Sidney. Mrs. Mason Barret Collection of Johnston Papers. Howard-Tilton Memorial Library, Tulane University, New Orleans.

Miller, Washington D. Papers. Archives, Texas State Library, Austin.

Morgan, James. Papers. Rosenberg Library, Galveston.

Sawyer, Commander H. B., U.S.N. Memorandum Book. Library of Congress, Washington, D.C.

Semmes, Raphael. Letter Book, 1848–1858. Library of Congress, Washington, D.C.

Sink, Julia. Memoirs. Typescript. Archives, University of Texas Library, Austin.

Smith, Justin H. Notes. Latin-American Collection, University of Texas Library, Austin.

Starr, James Harper. Papers. Archives Collection, University of Texas Library, Austin.

Tod, John G. Papers. Archives Collection, University of Texas Library, Austin.

Tucker, Philip C. A History of Galveston, 1543–1869. Archives Collection, University of Texas Library, Austin.

Walke, A. Log Book of Alfred Walke. Archives, Texas State Library, Austin.

Walker, William. Callender I. Fayssoux Collection of William Walker Papers, Folder No. 131. Middle American Research Institute Library, Tulane University, New Orleans.

Williams, Samuel M. Papers. Rosenberg Library, Galveston.

PUBLIC DOCUMENTS

Great Britain
   Admiralty: 1/5529, 1/9260-1, 1/1829, 50/224.
   Foreign Office: 5/383, 50/109, 50/152, 50/155, 50/160, 50/161, 50/162, 50/167, 50/169, 50/157, 50/158, 50/159D, 75/6, 75/8, 75/18, 75/23, 204/77, 204/79 Part 1, 204/79 Part 2, 204/80, 204/83.
   Index 12192.
Mexico
   Archivos General de la Nacion. Historia: Tomo 573 No. 9.
   Departamento de Archivo Correspondencia y Historia (Archivo de Cancelado):
      XI/481.3/1569, XI/481.3/1573, XI/481.3/1754, XI/481.3/1977, XI/111/3-1035, 1117.D/111.6/1923.

Secretaria de la Defensa Nacional (Archivo Militar): XI/481.3/1520, IX/481.3/1741, IX/481.3/1745, IX/481.3/1747, IX/481.3/1750, XI/481.3/1919, XI/481.3/1928, XI/481.3/1971, XI/481.3/1972, XI/481.3/1973, XI/481.3/1974, XI/481.3/1975, XI/481.3/1986, XI/481.3/1987.

Secretaria de Relaciones Exteriores. Sucesos entre Mexico y Los EE UU de A.

Relaciones con Texas y otros Estados Limitrofes:
L-E-1065, L-E-1066 (1842), L-E-1067 (1842), L-E-1068 (1842), L-E-1069.

The State of Texas

Texas State Archives, Texas State Library, Austin.
Civil Service File.
Consular Papers, 1838–1875.
Domestic Correspondence.
Executive Record Book Nos. 40, 47.
General Land Office Records.
Memorials and Petitions.
Moore, E. W., Miscellaneous File.
Navy Papers.
Public Debt Letters and Papers.
State Department Navy Papers.
Treasury Papers.

The United States of America

Library of Congress, Washington:
Microfilm, P.R.O., F.O. No. 75, V 1–4, 5–8, Manuscript Division.
Wanderer Papers, Manuscript Division.

National Archives, Washington:
Area 8 File, 1775–1910. Navy Records.
Austin, Log of. Navy Records.
Boston, Log of. Navy Records.
Captains' Letters, March 1839–June 1839. Navy Records.
Census Records.
Commanders' Letters, July–December 1846. Navy Records.
Commanders' Letters, January–July 1847. Navy Records.
Dawson, Schott, and Whitney. Petition for the U.S. To Pay for Texas Navy. Miscellaneous Document No. 27, 20th Congress, 1st Session, 1848.
Galveston, Texas, Post Office and Customhouse Letters, 1855–1881. Public Building Service.
General Letter Book XXXVI. Navy Records.
Group 60. Justice Department Records. Letter Book B 3.
Information Relating to Service of Navy and Marine Corps in Florida War.

Letters from Officers of Rank below that of Commander (Officers' Letters), 1834–1840. Navy Records.

Letters received from U.S. Consuls, Mexico and Texas, 1839–1846.

Letters Sent Conveying Appointments and Orders and Accepting Resignations. Navy Records.

Letters to Officers, Ships of War, XXVI, XXVII.

Master Commandants' Letters. Navy Records.

Miscellaneous Letters, February, 1846. Navy Records.

Officers Letters, 1844–1845. Navy Records.

Record Group 15 A. General Services Administration.

Record Group 59. General Records of the Department of State.

Report of the Secretary of the U.S. Navy, 1842.

Resignations of Officers of the U.S. Navy, 1834–1840.

San Bernard, Log of. Navy Records.

Senate Journal, 1858.

Texas Papers. Navy Records.

Texas, Galveston, Courthouse. Title Vault. Public Building Service.

Vandalia, U.S.S., Log of. Navy Records.

VU folder, Texas Navy. Navy Records.

Wharton, Log of. Navy Records.

Will Book No. 30, No. 31. Charlottesville, Virginia.

Will Book, Federal District Court, A. W. No. 13, Folio 131 new, 132 old, Washington, D.C.

Newspapers and Periodicals

(many available in only scattered issues)

Alexandria Gazette
American (New York)
American Beacon and Virginia and North Carolina Gazette (Norfolk)
Army-Navy Chronicle
Charleston Daily Courier
City Gazette (Austin)
Civilian and Galveston Gazette (Galveston)
Commercial Advertiser (New York)
Congressional Globe (Washington, D.C.)
Daily Constitutionalist (Augusta, Georgia)
Daily Globe (Washington, D.C.)
Daily Ledger and Texan (San Antonio)
Daily National Intelligencer (Washington, D.C.)
Daily News (Galveston)

Daily Picayune (New Orleans)
Daily Tropic (New Orleans)
El Censor de Vera Cruz
El Siglo Diez y Nueve (Mérida)
Galvestonian (Galveston)
Herald (Dallas)
Herald (New York)
Intelligencer (La Grange)
Los Pueblos, Periodico Oficial del Gobierno del Estado Libre de Yucatan (Mérida)
Morning Herald (New York)
National Intelligencer (Washington, D.C.)
New York Daily Tribune
New York Herald
Northern Standard (Clarksville, Texas)
Niles National Register (Baltimore)
Niles Weekly Register (Baltimore)
Planter (Columbia, Texas)
Register and Journal (Mobile)
Southern Argus (Norfolk)
Southern Intelligencer (Austin)
State Gazette (Austin)
Telegraph and Texas Register (Houston)
Texas Times (Galveston)
Texian Democrat (Houston)
Tri-weekly Telegraph (Houston)

Books and Pamphlets

Ancona, Eligio. *Historia de Yucatan desde la epoca mas remota hasta nuestra dias*. Mérida: Universidad del Suroeste. 1917.

Adams, Ephraim Douglass (ed.). *British Diplomatic Correspondence Concerning the Republic of Texas, 1838–1846*. Austin: Texas State Historical Association. 1918.

———. *British Interests and Activities in Texas, 1838–1846*. Baltimore: Johns Hopkins Press. 1910.

Aznar, Tomás y Carbó. *El estado de Campeche*. Campeche: Ediciones de "El espiritu publico." 1955.

Baqueiro, Serapio. *Ensayo historico sobre las revoluciones de Yucatan desde 1840–1864*. Mérida: Universidad del Suroeste.

Baxter, James Phinney, III. *Introduction of the Ironclad Warship*. Cambridge: Harvard University Press. 1933.

Bonilla, Captain Juan de Dios. *Apuntes para la historia de la Marina Nacional.* México, D.F.: 1946.

Brockett, F. L. *The Lodge of Washington.* Alexandria: G. H. Ramey and Son. 1899.

Brown, John Henry. *History of Texas,* II. St. Louis: L. E. Daniell. 1893.

———. *Life and Times of Henry Smith, the First American Governor of Texas.* Dallas: A. D. Aldridge and Company. 1887.

Buchanan, F., S. F. Du Pont, and G. A. Magruder, Commanders, U.S.N. *In Relation to the Claims of the Officers of the Late Texas Navy.* New York: [n.pub. n.d.].

Burr, Henry L. *Education in the Early Navy.* Philadelphia: Temple University. 1939.

Callahan, Edward W. *General Navy Register, List of Officers of the U.S. Navy, 1775–1900.* Washington, D.C.: Government Printing Office. 1901.

Carroll, H. Bailey. *The Texan Santa Fe Trail.* Canyon: Panhandle-Plains Historical Society. 1951.

Christian, Asa Kyrus. *Mirabeau Buonaparte Lamar.* Austin: Von Boeckmann-Jones Company. 1922.

Conner, Seymour V. and others (eds.). *Texas Treasury Papers; letters received in the Treasury Department of the Republic of Texas, 1836–1846,* IV. Austin: Texas State Library. 1955–1956.

Dahlgren, J. A. *Shells and Shell Guns.* Philadelphia: King and Baird. 1856.

Documents Relative to the dismissal of Post-Captain Edwin Ward Moore from the Texian Navy consisting of E. W. Moore in 1843; the Argument of the Hon. Thos. Johnson, Judge-Advocate; Proclamation of President Sam Houston; Veto of President Anson Jones. Washington: T. Barnard. 1847.

Emmons, Lieutenant George F., U.S.N. *The Navy of the U.S. from the Commencement, 1775 to 1853.* Washington: Cideon Company. 1853.

Falconer, Thomas. *Expidition to Santa Fe.* New York: Dauber and Pine. 1930.

Flournoy, H. W. (ed.). *Calendar of Virginia State Papers and Other Manuscripts from January 1, 1799 to December 31, 1807; Preserved in the Capitol, at Richmond,* IX. Richmond: James E. Goode, Printer. 1890.

Folsom, Charles J. *Mexico: A Description of the Country, Its Natural and Political Features.* New York: Wiley and Putnam, Robinson, Pratt and Company. 1842.

Friend, Llerena. *Sam Houston: The Great Designer.* Austin: University of Texas Press. 1954.

Gambrell, Herbert. *Anson Jones, the Last President of Texas.* Garden City: Doubleday and Company. 1948.

Gammel, H. P. N. (comp.). *Laws of the Republic of Texas*, II. Austin: Gammel Book Company. 1898.

Garrison, George P. (ed.). *Diplomatic Correspondence of the Republic of Texas*. 3 vols. Washington: Government Printing Office. 1908–1911.

Gouge, William M. *The Fiscal History of Texas*. Philadelphia: Lippincott. 1852.

Griffin, S. C. *History of Galveston, Texas*. Galveston: Cawston. 1931.

Gulick, Charles A., Jr., and others (eds.). *The Papers of Mirabeau Buonaparte Lamar*. 6 vols. Austin: Von Boeckmann-Jones. 1921–1927.

Hill, Jim Dan. *The Texas Navy in Forgotten Battles and Shirtsleeve Diplomacy*. Chicago: University of Chicago Press. 1937.

Houstoun, Mrs. Matilda Charlotte Fraser. *Texas and the Gulf of Mexico*, II. London: J. Murray and Company. 1844.

Ikin, Arthur. *Texas: Its History, Geography, Agriculture, Commerce and General Statistics*. London: Sherwood, Gilbert, and Piper. 1841.

James, Marquis. *The Life of Andrew Jackson*. Indianapolis, New York: The Bobbs-Merrill Company. 1938.

———. *The Raven: A Biography of Sam Houston*. Indianapolis: The Bobbs-Merrill Company. 1938.

Johnston, William Preston. *The Life of General Albert Sidney Johnston*. New York: D. Appleton and Company. 1879.

Jones, Anson. *Memoranda and Official Correspondence Relating to the Republic of Texas, Its History and Annexation—Including a Brief Autobiography of the Author*. New York: D. Appleton and Company. 1859.

Jones, The Honorable James C. *Speech of Hon. James C. Jones, of Tennessee, in Defense of Commodore Edwin W. Moore, of the Late Navy of Texas, in the United States Senate, August 3, 1854, In Reply to the Speech of General Sam Houston, of July 15, 1854*. Washington, D.C.: Congressional Globe Office. n.d.

Lerdo de Tejada, Miguel M. *Apuntes historicos de la heroica ciudad de Veracruz*. Tomo II. Mexico: Imp. De Vicente Garcia Torres. 1857. Reeditados por la Oficina de Máquinas de la Secretaría de Educación Pública. México. 1940.

Lester, C. E. *The Life of Sam Houston*. New York: Derby. 1855.

Lewis, Charles Lee. *Admiral Franklin Buchanan*. Baltimore: Norman Remington. 1929.

Lull, Edward P., Commander, U.S.N. *History of the U.S. Navy Yard at Gosport, Virginia*. Washington: Government Printing Office. 1874.

Maclay, Edgar Stanton. *A History of the United States Navy from 1775 to 1902*. New York: D. Appleton. 1901.

Manning, William R. (ed.). *Diplomatic Correspondence of the United States, Inter-American Affairs, 1831–1860*, VIII (Mexico), XII (Texas and Venezuela). Washington, D.C.: Carnegie Endowment for International Peace. 1939.

McRae, Sherwin (ed.). *Calendar of Virginia State Papers*, VI. Richmond: A. R. Micou, Superintendent of Public Printing. 1886.

Meade, Bishop William. *Old Churches, Ministers and Families in Virginia*, II. Philadelphia: Lippincott. 1889.

Menendez, Carlos R. *Noventa años de historia de Yucatan (1821–1910)*. Mérida: Compañía Tipográfica Yucateca, S.A. 1937.

Miller, Edmund T. *A Financial History of Texas*. Austin: A. C. Baldwin and Sons. 1916.

Memorial of the Officers of the Late Texas Navy to the Congress of the United States. Washington: [n. pub.]. 1850.

Molina Solis, Juan Francisco. *Historia de Yucatan desde la independencia de espana hasta la epoca actual, 1921*, I. Mérida: Universidad del Suroeste. 1921.

Moore, Sir Allen, Bt. *Sailing Ships of War, 1800–1860*. London: Halton and Truscott Smith, Ltd. 1926.

Moore, Edwin Ward. *A Brief Synopsis of the Doings of the Texas Navy Under the Command of Com. E. W. Moore; Together with His Controversy with Gen. Sam Houston, President of the Republic of Texas; in which he was sustained by the Congress of that Country Three Different Sessions; by the Convention to Form a State Constitution; and by the State Legislature; Unanimously*. Washington: T. Barnard. 1847.

——. *To the People of Texas*. Galveston: [n. pub.]. 1843.

——. *E. W. Moore to Sam Houston, U.S. Senator*, July 10, 1854 [n.pl. pub.: n.pub. n.d.].

——. *Reply to the Pamphlet by Commanders Buchanan, du Pont and Magruder in Relation to the Late Texas Navy*. Washington: [n. pub.]. 1850.

—— and others. *Memorial of the Officers of the Late Texas Navy to the Congress of the United States* [n. pl. pub.: n. pub.]. January 1850.

Morgan, James. *To the Public*. Houston: Telegraph Office. 1843.

Morison, Samuel Eliot, and Henry Steele Commager. *Growth of the American Republic*, I. New York: Oxford University Press. 1937.

Morrison, A. G. *The Beginnings of Public Education in Virginia, 1776–1860*. Richmond: Davis Bottom, Superintendent of Public Printing. 1917.

Norman, Benjamin Moore. *Rambles in Yucatan; or Notes of Travel Through the Peninsula, including a visit to the remarkable ruins of Chi-chen, Kabah, Zayi, and Uxmal*. 2nd edition. New York: J. & H. G. Langley. 1843.

Palmer, William P., M.D. (ed.). *Calendar of Virginia State Papers*, III. Richmond: James E. Goode, Printer. 1883.

Potter, E. B. (ed.). *The United States and World Sea Power*. Englewood Cliffs: Prentice-Hall, Inc. 1955.

Pratt, Willis (ed.). *Galveston Island: The Journal of Francis C. Sheridan, 1839–1840.* Austin: University of Texas Press. 1954.

Quaife, M. M. (ed.). *The Diary of James K. Polk during His Presidency, 1845 to 1849.* Chicago: A. C. McClurg and Company. 1910.

Rawlings, Mary. *Ante-Bellum Albemarle.* Charlottesville: The Michie Company. 1935.

——. *The Albemarle of Other Days.* Charlottesville: The Michie Company. 1925.

Register of Officers of the Confederate States Navy, 1861–1865. Washington, D.C.: U.S. Navy Department. 1931.

Ripley, Mrs. Eliza. *Social Life in Old New Orleans.* New York: D. Appleton and Company. 1912.

Roche, James Jeffrey. *The Story of the Filibusters.* London: T. F. Unwin. 1891.

Sailing Directions for East Coasts of Central America and Mexico, 4th Edition. Washington, D.C.: U.S. Government Printing Office. 1939.

Sanchez Anaya, General Brigadier Ignacio (comp.). *Guia del Archivo Historico Militar de Mexico.* Mexico, D.F.: Archivo Historico Militar Mexicano. 1948.

Semmes, Raphael. *Memoirs of Service Afloat during the War Between the States.* Baltimore: Kelly, Piet and Company. 1869.

——. *Service Afloat and Ashore during the Mexican War.* Cincinnati: W. H. Moore and Company. 1851.

Siegel, Stanley. *A Political History of the Texas Republic, 1836–1845.* Austin: University of Texas Press. 1956.

Smither, Harriet (ed.). *Journals of the Fourth Congress of the Republic of Texas.* 3 vols. Austin: Von Boeckmann-Jones. 1929.

——. *Journals of the Sixth Congress of the Republic of Texas.* 3 vols. Austin: Von Boeckmann-Jones. 1940.

Stewart, Robert Armistead. *Index to Printed Genealogies Including Key and Bibliography.* Richmond: Old Dominion Press. 1930.

Stockton, John Wharton. *A History of the Stockton Family.* Philadelphia: Press of Patterson and White. 1881.

Stockton, Thomas Coates, M.D. *The Stockton Family of New Jersey, and other Stocktons.* Washington, D.C. The Carnahan Press. 1911.

Texas, Republic of. *Journals of the House of Representatives of the Republic of Texas: Fifth Congress—First Session. 1840–1841.* Austin: Cruger and Wing. 1841.

——. *Journals of the Senate of the Republic of Texas. Fifth Congress—First Session. By order of the Secretary of State.* Houston: The Telegraph Office. 1841.

——. *Journals of the House of Representatives of the Seventh Congress of the Republic of Texas. Convened at Washington, on the 14th Nov., 1842. Published by Authority.* Washington: Thomas Johnson. 1843.

——. *Journals of the Senate of the Seventh Congress of the Republic of Texas, Convened at Washington on the 14th Nov., 1842. Published by Authority.* Washington: Thomas Johnson. 1843.

——. *Journals of the House of Representatives of the Eighth Congress of the Republic of Texas. Published by Authority.* Houston: Cruger and Moore. 1844.

——. *Journals of the Senate. Eighth Congress of the Republic of Texas. Published by Authority.* Houston: Cruger and Moore. 1844.

——. *Journals of the House of Representatives of the Ninth Congress of the Republic of Texas. Published by Authority.* Washington: Miller and Cushney. 1845.

——. *Journals of the Senate of the Ninth Congress of the Republic of Texas. Printed by Authority.* Washington: Miller and Cushney. 1845.

——. *Appendix to the Journals of the Ninth Congress of the Republic of Texas. By authority.* Washington: Miller and Cushney, Public Printers. 1845.

Thrall, Homer. *A Pictorial History of Texas.* St. Louis: N. D. Thompson and Company. 1879.

The United States Statutes at Large. Vol. 11. Boston: Little, Brown and Company. 1859.

The War of the Rebellion. Series I, Vol. 33; Series II, Vol. 5. Washington, D.C.: United States War Department; Government Printing Office. 1900.

Woods, The Reverend Edgar. *Albemarle County in Virginia.* Charlottesville: Michie Company. 1901.

Yoakum, Henderson. *History of Texas, from Its First Settlement in 1685 to Its Annexation to the United States in 1846.* New York: J. S. Redfield. 1855.

Wharton, Clarence R. *El Presidente: A Sketch of the Life of General Santa Anna.* Houston: C. C. Young Printing Company. 1924.

Williams, Amelia W. and Eugene C. Barker (eds.). *The Writings of Sam Houston.* II, III, IV, V, VI, VII, VIII. Austin: University of Texas Press. 1938–1943.

Winkler, E. W. (ed.). *Secret Journals of the Senate. Republic of Texas.* First Biennial Report of the Texas Library and Historical Commission. Austin: [n. pub.]. 1911.

Articles from Journals and Other Periodicals

Anonymous. "The Dismasted Brig; or Naval Life in Texas," *Colburn's United Services Magazine.* October 1845 and later.

Boucher, Chauncey S. "In Re That Aggressive Slavocracy," *Mississippi Valley Historical Review*. VIII No. S: 1 and 2, 13.

Carter, Robert Foster. "The Texas Navy," *United States Naval Institute Proceedings*. Vol. 59 (July 1933), No. 7.

Cox, C. C. "Recollections," *The Quarterly of the Texas State Historical Association*. October 1902.

Dienst, Alex. "The Navy of the Republic of Texas," *The Quarterly of the Texas State Historical Association*. XIII (No. 1, July 1909), 1–43; XIII (No. 2, October 1909), 85–127.

Du Bois, William E. B. "The Enforcement of the Slave Trade Laws," *American Historical Association Annual Report*. 1891. Pp. 163–174.

Fuller, George F. "Sketch of the Texas Navy," *The Quarterly of the Texas State Historical Association*. VII, 223.

Lamar, Charles Augustus Lafayette. "A Slave Trader's Note Book," *North American Review*. CXLIII (No. 5. November 1886) 447–461.

Mabry, Midshipman James. "Journal," *Galveston Daily News*. 9 January 1893.

Moore, Edwin Ward. "Memorial to Convention," *La Grange Intelligencer*. 7 October 1845.

Robison, Rear Admiral S. S., U.S.N. (Ret.). "The Texas Navy," *United States Naval Institute Proceedings*. LXII, No. 9, Whole No. 403, September 1936), 1305–1310.

Charts

Moore, Edwin Ward, and others. *The Coast of Texas*. London: Hydrographic Office, the Admiralty. 20 August 1844. (photostat) Archives Collection of the Eugene C. Barker Texas History Center, University of Texas Library, Austin.

Index

Index